Student Evaluation in Higher Education

Stephen Darwin

Student Evaluation in Higher Education

Reconceptualising the Student Voice

 Springer

Stephen Darwin
Universidad Alberto Hurtado
Santiago
Chile

and

University of Canberra
Canberra
Australia

ISBN 978-3-319-82457-4   ISBN 978-3-319-41893-3   (eBook)
DOI 10.1007/978-3-319-41893-3

This Springer imprint is published by Springer Nature
The registered company is Springer International Publishing AG Switzerland

For my father, who always passionately believed in the liberating power of education, and in my potential where others did not.

Preface

This book considers the foundations, function and potential of student evaluation in higher education. It is particularly focused on the work of formal methods of deriving student feedback, primarily in the form of end-of-semester, quantitative surveys.

Conventionally such surveys pose a range of closed answer questions about teaching, teachers, curriculum, assessment and support issues and offer students a Likert-type rating scale ranging from the strong agreement to strong disagreement. They sometimes also include the opportunity for a limited number of open-ended comments by students.

Student evaluation is now a ubiquitous and formidable presence in many universities and higher education systems. For instance, it is increasingly critical to the internal and external quality assurance strategies of universities in the USA, the UK and Australia.

Student opinion is an increasingly important arbiter of teaching quality in higher education environments, gradually being institutionalised as a valid comparative performance measure on such things as the quality of teachers and teaching, programmes and assessment, and levels of institutional support.

As a result, student evaluation also acts a powerful proxy for assuring the quality of teaching, courses and programmes across diverse discipline and qualification frameworks across higher education. This centrality represents a meteoric rise for student evaluation, which was originally designed as a largely unexceptional tool to improve local teaching (albeit in response to student unrest and rising attrition rates).

However, despite being firmly entrenched in a privileged role in contemporary institutional life, how influential or useful are student evaluation data? Is it straightforward to equate positive student evaluation outcomes with effective teaching (or learning), or even as a proxy for teaching quality? Similarly, can it be simply assumed that negative student evaluation outcomes reflect poor teaching (or that positive results equate to good teaching)?

Moreover, there are other significant assumptions about student evaluation that demand critical analysis. For instance, can students be reasonably expected to objectively rate their teaching and can these ratings than simply be compared to other teaching and discipline outcomes? Is the increasingly visible presence of student evaluation benign in influencing or distorting academic decision-making? And perhaps most significantly given the origins of student evaluation, is the extensive data being generated by student evaluation actually meaningful in guiding or inspiring pedagogical improvement?

Yet despite these important questions naturally arising in considering student evaluation, much of the research in higher education environments in the USA, Europe and Australia over the last three decades has remained largely centred on the assurance (or incremental refinement) of quantitative survey tools, primarily focused on the design, validity or utility of student rating instruments. In addition, there has also been other research interest into effective strategies to ensure the outcomes of such student surveys influence teaching practices and improve student learning.

However, it is conspicuous that there has been far less scholarly discussion about the foundational assumptions on which student evaluation rests. This gap is rendered all the more problematic by the rapidly emerging role of student evaluation as a key pillar of quality assurance of teaching in contemporary higher education. It is difficult to explain exactly why the foundational epistemologies of student evaluation has not attracted the attention of educational researchers and has remained largely confined to the more technical domains of statistical analysis or of localised field practitioners. Perhaps the answer lies with the 'everydayness' of student surveys, which often relegates it to an administrative sphere of practice. This has perhaps meant the student voice has been largely understood as of peripheral value to educational practice and therefore less important than fundamental questions of curriculum, pedagogy and assessment.

Yet the use of student feedback has arguably been a reality of higher education since its very conception. It was reputedly the basis for the death of Socrates at the behest of an Athenian jury, which affirmed the negative assessment of his dialectic teaching approaches by students (Centra 1993).

However, as Brookfield (1995) notes, until relatively recent times the quality of teaching in higher education tended to be primarily determined on demonstrations of goal attainment by students. This was either in the form of achievement of defined behavioural objectives, or in acquisition of specified cognitive constructs. This inevitably meant the quality of teaching was largely related to positive or negative outcomes of student assessment, and this was primarily considered in deliberations about academic appointment or promotion.

Having said this, the concept of quantitative student surveys itself is not a recently developed model. The core of the quantitative approach was pioneered in behaviourist experimentation in the USA in the 1920s. Yet it has only been in the last three decades in response to rising social and institutional pressures that student evaluation has been widely adopted in US, European and Australian universities as a legitimate and respected form of evaluation of teaching effectiveness (Chalmers 2007; Harvey 2003; Johnson 2000; Kulik 2001).

In its broadest sense, any form of student evaluation involves an assessment of the value of an experience, an idea or a process, based on presupposed standards or criteria. Its interpretation necessarily involves the 'collection and interpretation, through systematic and formal means, of relevant information which serves as the basis for rational judgments in decision situations' (Dressel 1976, p. 9).

At its essence, student evaluation necessitates a judgment being exercised from a particular viewpoint (*the subject*) on an identified and bounded entity (*the object*). Conventional quantitative forms of student evaluation invite the judgment of individual students to be exercised on the value of teachers, teaching approaches and courses at the end of the semesters. The criteria for such judgments are inherently subjective, but its outcomes are objectively framed in numeric rating scales that form the basis of student feedback reports. The explicit intention of these student feedback reports is to inform future academic decision-making.

However, the relationship between these reports and the broader evaluative processes around the effectiveness of academic teaching and course design remains largely ambiguous. Given the tangible nature of student feedback data, it represents an explicit representation of teaching and course effectiveness. Yet other often less visible forms of evaluative assessment, such as assessment outcomes, student reactions and peer interaction also mediate academic judgment. It is therefore unsurprising that student feedback creates some tensions in teaching environments, particularly if the explicit nature of these data challenges other forms of evaluative assessment of an academic.

Moreover, as institutional motives for student feedback have moved from quality improvement to quality assurance, these tensions have tended to be aggravated. At its essence therefore, student feedback inevitably negotiates the complex intersection between individual and collective interests in institutions (Guba and Lincoln 1989).

There can be little doubt that student evaluation is now educationally powerful in the contemporary institution. As such, it has the distinct capacity to influence, disrupt constrain and distort pedagogies. Therefore, the core foundational assumptions of student evaluation do matter and deserve and demand much greater critical scrutiny than they have encountered, particularly as its status as a proxy for teaching quality flourishes within institutions and in the metrics of burgeoning global league tables.

Hence, this book seeks to move beyond these well-researched debates around the design of questionnaires and the deployment of evaluation data. It will also not debate the optimal use of quantitative student feedback or seek individual perspectives on experiences working with it. Instead, it seeks to explore the less researched foundational paradigms on which student evaluation rests.

A fundamental element of this analysis will be the consideration of the forces that have shaped (and continue to reshape) the form and function of student evaluation in higher education. These forces include the following:

- the desire to use student feedback to improve the quality of teaching approaches and student learning outcomes;
- the need to demonstrate and assure teaching quality, principally by identifying where requisite standards are not met;
- providing evidence for individual and collective forms of academic performance management; and
- fuelling institutional marketing and rankings in an increasingly competitive higher education environment.

Specifically, the book explores the mounting tension between the first two of these imperatives: the competing discourses of quality improvement and quality assurance that largely shapes the contemporary form, acceptance and perceived value of student evaluation in higher education. Critical to this has been the rising imperatives of neo-liberalism over the last three decades, which has necessitated the creation of market mechanisms to allocate resources in higher education. This has led to rising demands for transparent measurement tools to guide student-consumer choice. Student evaluation has progressively become such a measure, despite its distinctive origin and uncertain suitability for such a purpose.

Finally, the book also considers the rich potentiality of the student voice to tangibly influence the professional dialogue and pedagogical work of teaching academics. Using case study research conducted in a university environment, empirical evidence is presented as to the prospective value of student evaluation as a stimulus for pedagogical improvement when used in more sophisticated forms to harness more complex understandings of student learning (and learning practices).

Specifically the expansive potential of the student voice is explored—beyond these quality assurance paradigms—to discover what methods may enhance the provocative power of student evaluation and how this could be harnessed to actually spark pedagogical improvement.

Origins of This Book

The origins of this book are manifold. Firstly, it stems from quite practical beginnings in my own unsettling experiences of teaching in a postgraduate teacher education programme for university teachers. Over several years, I taught a subject on evaluative practices in education, which included an element on student evaluation. In this subject, it was consistently apparent that student feedback provoked unexpectedly frequently powerful and emotional reactions amongst teachers, eliciting responses that were as divergent as they were determined.

These teachers—who taught both in vocational and higher education environments—expressed a range of differing anxieties in response to their experiences with student evaluation. Such anxieties ranged from how to most effectively address student dissatisfaction, through to an outright rejection of the validity and/or value of the student voice in influencing pedagogical labour. Amongst teachers, there was variously empathy, scepticism and hostility and cynicism about student evaluation.

It was also evident that teachers' personal experiences with the student evaluation were highly influential in shaping their relative perspectives on the value or otherwise of the student voice. These sharp reactions tended to defy the conventional notion of student evaluation as merely an objective and largely benign measure of student opinion. Instead, these experiences suggested that teacher encounters with student evaluation had actually been volatile and laden with considerable (inter)subjectivity.

More surprising, the majority of teachers found it difficult to see the relevance of critically reflecting on the nature or pedagogical potential of the student voice. Despite the influential role student evaluation increasingly has in shaping local institutional perceptions about the value of their pedagogical work, it was generally greeted with either defensive reactions or resigned indifference.

So instead of contemplating the potential student evaluation may actually hold to enhance the quality of pedagogical work, much of this discussion primarily centred on its ritualistic inevitability and/or its increasingly influential quality assurance function that largely shaped institutional perceptions of teaching quality. Indeed, despite determined teaching interventions, most often any actual function student feedback may have in contributing to the improvement of teaching itself was largely overwhelmed by these various anxieties surrounding its institutional use. This sentiment proved remarkably difficult to disrupt.

A second driver for thinking about writing a book like this was the difficult and confounding experience of attempting to reform an existing student evaluation system in a leading international university. Although the university quantitative student evaluation system was well established—being one of the first founded in the nation in the early 1980s—its usefulness was being increasingly contested amongst academics, students and university management. However, it was evident that these various stakeholders held quite divergent concerns.

Although participation in student evaluation remained voluntary for teaching academics, the system was being increasingly perceived by academics as the imposition of a perfunctory quality assurance mechanism on their work. Underlying this was the intensifying use of student evaluation data as usefully reductive evidence for promotional processes, performance management and teaching grants. Paradoxically, this made student evaluation a high stakes game even though regard for it was clearly in decline. Unsurprisingly, this dissonance around the work of student evaluation often produced intense academic reactions where it proved a negative in these important deliberations.

Alternatively, student representatives frequently let it be known that they believed that their evaluation work was doing nothing to actually improve teaching quality. They argued that there was little real evidence that their feedback was being seriously considered—let alone actually being acted on. As the costs of study increased over time, so had the associated expectations of what student evaluation was meant to do as a device for consumer (dis)satisfaction.

Despite student evaluation data providing some form of empirical ground for decision-making about teaching quality, university management asserted that more comparable statistics was needed to ensure deficits that could endanger institutional reputation were rapidly identified and acted on. This would allow the establishment of benchmark averages by which adequate and inadequate teaching quality could be determined. Although this was explicitly framed as a response to student concerns about inaction on their feedback, the implicit reality was the rising competitive and marketing pressures around perceptions of teaching quality in the contemporary university. These were seemingly more persuasive in engineering this sentiment.

Leading this system as change was debated meant encountering frequent bouts of end-of-semester anger, defensiveness or despair from academics seeking answers to negative student feedback outcomes or student demands for action. Conversely, the outcomes for those not aggrieved tended to remain largely abstract, anonymous and seemingly unproblematic.

These divergent conceptions as to the value of student feedback were broadly similar and equally as diverse as those that emerged in the earlier teaching environment. However, here more tangible and potent issues of academic identity, professional autonomy and regard for the student voice were all in immediate play, intensifying varying responses.

Moreover, attempts to generate a critical debate within the university academic community in response about the possible prospective role and function of student evaluation generated far more heat than light amongst academics and students. Again, the possibility of the student voice performing as a tool of pedagogical improvement was largely abstract within these alternative narratives.

A specific proposal to significantly disrupt the entrenched teacher-centred axiom of the existing quantitative student evaluation model created unexpectedly intense anxiety within university management. This proposition—to redesign the student evaluation system to draw more qualitative student perceptions of their learning experience—seemed to be an affront to institutional quality assurance strategies which stressed measureable outcomes.

Evidence was quickly discounted that illustrated that academics were most influenced by the limited qualitative data they derived from the current system. Put simply, unacceptable risk was perceived in moving from measurable student feedback surveys (centred on teachers, teaching and courses), to a more open formulation focused on student opinion of their learning (and embodying a broader understanding of quality improvement).

The eventual outcome of this attempted reform largely preserved these seemingly immutable teacher-centred characteristics, rendering the system redesign more incidental than paradigmatic. This episode demonstrated the surprisingly strongly held shared values amongst university management about the importance of retaining quantitative student evaluation focused squarely on teachers and teaching.

There was powerful importance attributed to retaining a simple and accessible quantitative measure of comparative teaching performance. This seemingly sprung from a strongly held managerialist desire to sanction perceived teaching deficits and reward success. Significantly, the overwhelming majority of teaching academics greeted this debate about the reformation of student evaluation with largely resigned indifference.

This proximity to the reality of student evaluation in a large institution, particularly where it was disrupted, proved a further revelation about the increasingly fraught role the student voice has in the contemporary higher education. Whilst academics more and more questioned its value as an accountability tool, students expected further from it as a consumer-response mechanism to their opinions. Meanwhile, university managements possess a seemingly irresistible attraction to the comparable metrics of teaching performativity it offers.

These complex experiences in working with student evaluation provide the catalyst for this book. Student evaluation was originally introduced to universities as a localised means of improving student retention and assessment results through the improvement of teaching strategies to engage students. Over the three or so decades, student evaluation systems have become a stubbornly entrenched landform in the terrain of higher education.

However, the *purpose* of student evaluation has undergone significant transformation (despite the model maintaining a remarkably similar form). This transformation has left unresolved core questions around what role the student voice should have in teaching improvement, in quality assurance of academic practices and in assessments of institutional quality.

As student evaluation has progressively become more institutionally and socially prominent, so arguably has its power to potentially shape pedagogies and other educational practices. Therefore, student evaluation is a matter of major consequence in higher education. It deserves dedicated scrutiny of its origins and evolution if its contemporary purpose is to be understood and its potential realised.

Structure of the Book

Although—as noted earlier—there has been considerable research interest in the quantitative instruments of student feedback and the effective use of their outcomes, research around its contemporary function is much more limited. This book attempts to address this gap, by exploring the forces that have shaped the progressive emergence student evaluation in higher education and the influence it exerts on contemporary approaches to academic teaching.

This analysis is developed through a series of interpretive lenses. The book firstly analyses the historicity of student evaluation—both at a general level and in its specific evolution in higher education. This encounters the forces that have shaped its design and use, as well as the tensions that have been fundamental to this evolved form and function.

Secondly, by analysing the current institutional framing of student evaluation, the book considers the complex demands that shape its contemporary state. This adopts a particular focus on the increasingly ambiguous relationship of student feedback with pedagogical and academic development that results from elevating tensions between various drives for quality improvement, quality assurance, performance management and institutional marketing.

Thirdly, several qualitative case studies involving cohorts of postgraduate teachers in a contemporary university setting are considered. The research used the explanatory potential of cultural historical activity theory (CHAT) with the objective of generating a critical understanding of the development, function and potential of student evaluation.

These situated cases provide a critical insight into the current state and the developmental potential of student evaluation in higher education environments. These outcomes are analysed to further understand the increasingly complex relationship between student evaluation and institutional demands, professional discourses and pedagogical change. It also provides a means of considering the broader developmental potential that arises from collective forms of academic engagement derived from the elevated use of qualitative forms of student feedback.

Based on this analysis, the latter part of the book confronts the practical challenges of student evaluation practices and strategies to effectively harness the potential of the student voice. Particular focus is given to critically reflecting on what student evaluation practices can afford and what it hinders in pedagogical analysis and innovation. Finally, the prospects of more complex engagement with the student voice is considered, to assess its ability to incite more substantial forms of pedagogical and academic development in higher education environments.

Santiago, Chile   Stephen Darwin

References

Brookfield, S. (1995). *Becoming a critically reflective teacher*. San Francisco: Jossey-Bass.

Centra, J. A. (1993). *Refelctive faculty evaluation: Enhancing teaching and determining faculty effectiveness*. San Francisco: Jossey-Bass.

Chalmers, D. (2007). *A review of Australian and international quality systems and indicators of learning and teaching*. Retrieved from Strawberry Hills: http://www.olt.gov.au/system/files/resources/T%26L_Quality_Systems_and_Indicators.pdf

Dressel, P. L. (1976). *Handbook of academic evaluation*. San Francisco: Jossey-Bass.

Guba, E. G., & Lincoln, Y. S. (1989). *Fourth generation evaluation*. Newbury Park: SAGE Publications.

Harvey, L. (2003). Student feedback. *Quality in Higher Education, 9*(1), 3–20.

Johnson, R. (2000). The authority of the student evaluation questionnaire. *Teaching in Higher Education, 5*(4), 419–434.

Kulik, J. (2001). Student ratings: Validity, utility and controversy. *New Directions for Institutional Research, 109* (Spring 2001).

Acknowledgements

It should be noted that several chapters of this book are developed from earlier published work. These articles were as follows:

- Darwin, S. (2012) Moving beyond face value: re-envisioning higher education evaluation as a generator of professional knowledge. *Assessment and Evaluation in Higher Education.* Vol. 37, No. 6.
- Darwin, S. (2011) Learning in Activity: Exploring the methodological potential of Action Research in Activity Theorising of Social Practice. *Educational Action Research.* Vol. 19, No. 2.
- Darwin, S. (2010) Can you teach an old dog new tricks? Re-envisioning evaluation practice in higher education. Proceedings of the 2010 Australasian Evaluation Society Conference, Wellington NZ.

Finally, this book would never have been possible without the wisdom and invaluable advice of Dr. Linda Hort and other colleagues including Professor Gerlese Akerlind, Dr. Nick Hopwood and Dr. Lynn McAlpine. I also acknowledge the importance of the love, wisdom and support of my wife, Dr. Malba Barahona Duran, and the wise optimism of my son, Jesse.

Contents

Chapter 1
The Emergence of Student Evaluation in Higher Education

Abstract In this introductory chapter, the broad social and epistemological origins of student evaluation in higher education are systematically considered. This includes discussion of the formative development of student evaluation, which was shaped in its earliest form by behaviourist experimentation around the nature of student responsiveness. From these foundational influences, the chapter will then considers the emergence of more developed systems of student evaluation in the United States (and later elsewhere) in the late 1960s under the pressure of rising student unrest and broader social dissatisfaction around educational quality. It is argued that this developing student militancy—in tandem with the mounting challenges of student retention in growing and diversifying higher education systems—provided initial credibility to the student voice and the subsequent broadened adoption of early forms of student evaluation. Significantly, what was characteristic of these earliest forms of student evaluation was the use of student feedback to directly influence and improve teaching quality. The chapter uses examples of the growth in the use of student feedback in the United States and Australia to illustrate the nature of these initial formations.

Keywords Origins of student evaluation · Higher education teaching · Teaching improvement · Student evaluation in the US · Student evaluation in Australia

Introduction

Student-driven forms of evaluation of teaching and programs—based on quantitative student opinion surveys—is now an accepted and largely unquestioned orthodoxy in major higher education systems across the globe, including North America, the United Kingdom and Australia (Chalmers 2007; Harvey 2003; Knapper and Alan Wright 2001). Indeed, it can be argued that student evaluation is so normalised is that is now axiomatic in the contemporary higher education

© Springer International Publishing Switzerland 2016
S. Darwin, *Student Evaluation in Higher Education*,
DOI 10.1007/978-3-319-41893-3_1

environment. It performs distinctive and powerful work as a seemingly ever more reliable proxy for teaching quality at an individual, institutional and sectoral level.

Institutions continue to expand the range and sophistication of student evaluation systems. It is now common for teaching academics to be compelled to participate in student evaluation, through either explicit direction or the implicit risks of failing to do so. Considerable resources are being expended on capturing student opinion course-by-course and program-by-program, with outcomes comparatively (and often forensically) assessed against institutional benchmarks. This data is then disseminated—normally privately, though increasingly publicly—with the intent of teaching academics having to account for shortfalls in student satisfaction. Often where data is shared beyond the individual teaching academic, there are related and most often abstracted demands for 'improvement' or the risk of sanction should the results continue to be beneath averaged or historically benchmark figures.

Moreover, it is also increasing characteristic that student evaluation data has an active function in various internal assessments of academic performance, as well as in related judgments about the quality of such things as curriculum design, learning and support activities and assessment. Therefore, in essence student evaluation has become increasingly recognised as a valid empirical foundation for the institutional assessment of all matters related to teaching: teachers, teaching and academic programs.

The data generated by student evaluation is also becoming a foundational metric for various university ranking scales and popular guides for students that rate comparative institutional quality. This is meaning it is gradually becoming more prominent in the institutional and international marketing of institutions. Most recently in the reforming of higher education policy in the United Kingdom and Australia, student evaluation has even been speculated on as a prospective as a metric for the assessment and prospective funding of higher education institutions.

Yet, at the same time, student evaluation also remains largely a frequently unwelcome fringe dweller in contemporary academic teaching life, often responded to with suspicion and unease (Edstrom 2008). A key reason for this response no doubt lies in the focus of student evaluation. The primary object of student feedback is firmly established in the mind of the institution, the student and even the teacher themselves as *the teacher and their teaching*. This is even when other issues relating to learning activities, assessment and institutional support are rated.

Moreover, it has been argued that despite its considerable and influential institutional power, student evaluation is widely perceived by academics to be inherently narrow and superficial (Edstrom 2008; Kulik 2001; Schuck et al. 2008). Some academics are unconvinced about the capacity of student feedback to effectively mediate the increasingly complex environments of higher education teaching and learning. It has been suggested that orthodox forms of student feedback are inadequate to analyse and respond to these demanding contemporary expectations on academics to generate high quality learning for growing, heterogeneous and increasing remote student populations (Arthur 2009; Johnson 2000; Kember et al. 2002).

This raises the legitimate question as to whether student evaluation is a suitable mechanism for institutions to negotiate understandings of teaching performativity in this complex ecology. As student feedback is now central data feeding institutional quality assurance assessments and performance management discourses around teaching effectiveness, it is a matter that deserves a greater level of scrutiny than it has received.

Similarly, with increased competition for students and the escalating private costs of higher education, student feedback is also now increasingly performing a further and perhaps more troubling role: as a measure of consumer satisfaction or 'product' effectiveness. In many higher systems across the world, the seductive attraction of neo-liberalist market mechanisms over the last two decades have had the cumulative effect of sharply reducing the levels of social contributions to higher education institutions. In tandem, the individual responsibility for funding education costs has been elevated, heralding the emergence of the discriminating *student-as-consumer* (Coledrake and Stedman 1998; Marginson 2009). This has also created an environment where teaching academics are working under mounting pressure to systematically demonstrate efficiency and effectiveness to—and for—students. Therefore, it has been argued that student feedback has been appropriated as a key means of assuring prescribed educational outcomes are defined, measured and evaluated in abstraction from mediating professional discourses (Chalmers 2007).

Yet the early adoption and use of student evaluation was toward a fundamentally different role. It emerged under the pressure of student dissent and student retention, performing as a tool for situated pedagogical analysis and teaching development. This residual motive remains inherent in the design of student evaluation tools, despite their adaptation to a foregrounded role in institutional quality assurance strategies. This rising conflict reflects an important dimension of student evaluation in the contemporary institution: that is, the contested *motive* for undertaking it.

Essentially, student evaluation has been gradually been torn between the conflicting discourses of consumerist quality assurance (*what students want to receive*) and academic quality enhancement (*what students need to effectively learn*) (Bowden and Marton 1998; Walker 2001). In order to fully understand this contemporary state of student evaluation in higher education, it is firstly important to consider how its evolution has shaped its form and function.

Origins of Student Feedback

Informal forms of student evaluation are likely to have origins as ancient as the university itself, though this is difficult to establish definitively. However, its earliest formal forms were most likely to be identified in the early medieval European universities. Here committees of students were appointed by rectors to assure teachers adhered to defined orthodoxies and met prescribed time commitments, with penalties in place for miscreant teachers (Centra 1993).

In addition, students were afforded a further and quite tangible form of evaluation with their feet. This was manifested quite literally as a direct form of in-class disapproval or by simply not attending class—as teacher salaries were formed by student attendance fees (Knapper 2001). Perhaps fortuitously, such forms did not sustain themselves (at least in this harsh form) into the current age of universities.

The modern appearance of student evaluation is generally linked to two closely related activities. The first was the introduction of a student ratings form at the University of Washington in 1924 and several other US universities in the following years. The second was the release of a study on the design of student ratings by researchers at Purdue University in 1925 (Flood Page 1974; Kulik 2001; Marsh 1987).

The outcomes of the experimental Washington student ratings are unclear, however the work of Remmers (1927) and his colleagues at Purdue did continue to resonate in isolated parts of the American higher education system. The instrument developed by Remmers (the *Purdue Rating Scale for Instructors*) focused on establishing whether judgments about teaching by students coincided with that of their peers and alumni (Berk 2006). For instance, in the early 1950s it was estimated that about 40 % of US colleges and universities were using this type of instrument for student evaluation (McKeachie 1957). However, an actual study in 1961 suggested only 24 % of a broad sample of US colleges and universities were regularly using quantitative student evaluation drawn from the Remmers model (Flood Page 1974).

Emergence of Student Evaluation in the United States Higher Education

However, Centra (1993) contends student evaluation was largely in decline until a pressing need emerged for its re-invigoration as a result of the broad student protest movement that swept US universities in the late 1960s. Rising levels of student dissatisfaction with US intervention in the Vietnam War and support for gender and race-based liberation movements generated militant and well-organised student movements. The development of these student organisations, predicated on a range of democratic struggles, inevitably also turned their attention to the form and quality of education university students were experiencing during this period. As Centra (1993) observes:

> ...the student protest movements that rocked so many campuses ...were in reaction not only to the Vietnam War and related national policies but also to policies in effect on their campuses. An irrelevant curriculum and uninspired teachers were among frequently heard student complaints. Increasingly student saw themselves as consumers. They demanded a voice in governance; they want to improve the education they were receiving. (p. 50)

Student evaluation was not the only demand by protesting students—for instance, there was a strong push for a voice in university governance. However, student feedback carried an iconic status, as it represented a potent symbol of a democratising university campus. To this end, increasingly in this period students began to develop their own ratings systems in the form of alternative handbooks. These offered unreliable yet influential insights into the quality of university teachers and teaching for intending students.

It was within this increasingly volatile context the American universities rapidly moved to introduce formal student evaluation systems. Given the intensity of the student movement and the consequent need to respond rapidly to rising student discord, the original student ratings model pioneered by Remmers three decades before became the overwhelming choice of approach (Flood Page 1974). However, as Chisholm (1977) observed, this form of student evaluation was:

> spawned under the least favourable circumstances – pressure…in many instances a result of a gesture by harassed administrators in response to the demands of militant students in an ugly frame of mind. (p. 22)

So rapid was the introduction of student evaluation systems that they had virtually reached all US universities by the end of the 1960s (Centra 1993; McKeachie et al. 1971). It is difficult to overestimate the scale of this transformation, which over just the period of a few years dramatically reframed the traditional and largely distant relationship between institution, teacher and student.

Reflecting the scale of this change, the influential text, *Evaluation in Higher Education* (Dressel 1961)—published less than a decade before—dedicated just five of its 455 pages to student evaluation. It cautioned against the limitations on the validity and reliability of the instruments of student feedback and their inherent capacity to incite faculty discord. Although this prominent compendium grudging recognised the potential ancillary value of student opinion, it stressed an essential ingredient was the reciprocity of students in rating their own efforts and application. The primary relationship between students and evaluation was seen here was as means of students learning 'something of the making of wise judgments by being both an observer and a participant in the (teaching) process' (Dressel 1961, p. 26).

Therefore, the development of student-feedback based evaluation in US universities was a clear response to the broad social forces for change that was manifested in widespread student militancy in the late 1960s and early 1970s. The introduction of student feedback was to provide a safety valve to rising discontent about the quality of teaching and what was seen by students as the an ingrained disregard of student opinion.

However, this drive was in almost immediate tension with the very structures it sought to influence. As Chisholm (1977) observes, university administrators imposed these student feedback systems on academic teaching without a clear motive beyond addressing rising dissent (and perhaps these alternative handbooks). This was the origin of a seminal tension around student feedback that has become more significant over time. This was between the competing motives of student feedback as a means of improving the quality of teaching by informing academic judgment, as opposed to a quality assurance mechanism of teaching quality responding to student (and institutional) demands.

This core tension was to become highly significant as the student evaluation model was taken up more broadly. Having said this, in its early forms in the US, student feedback models remained voluntary and localised for academic use. Nevertheless, elevating pressures to accede to the student voice put considerable pressure on academics to participate in student feedback systems, particularly if they were to seek promotion or tenure (Centra 1993).

However, those academics choosing to participate quickly discovered that although student opinion may prove illuminating, it was often difficult to find academic or resource support to facilitate the changes demanded (Chisholm 1977). Here a second related tension appears in early student feedback models around the notion of the student-as-consumer. This is demonstrated in core tension between what students want to receive (as expressed in student feedback outcomes) and what an academic can reasonably (or be reasonably expected to) provide in response.

The haste with which feedback was introduced in US institutions meant little institutional support had been established for academics to either interpret or effective respond to this often-confusing data. Nor was there until much later a more critical research-led debate on the validity and reliability of student rating systems. This was despite the fact that these had rapidly evolved during this period from the temporally distant Purdue instrument. Meanwhile, some of those not engaged in feedback systems darkly warned of the imminent arrival of 'intellectual hedonism'.

Student evaluation was elevating the anxiety of academics unconvinced by the move to this form of student judgment, particularly given the broader democratising of governance that were emerging as a result of student protest movement (Bryant 1967). This was seen to foretell academic reluctance to challenge, disrupt or unsettled the student, all of which was seen as an essential dimension of teaching and learning. In this assessment we again we see a critical early tension manifested between academic judgment and the potentially powerful influence of student ratings in the assessment of teaching quality.

This is the ontogeny of later debates around its potentially positive and negative implications of student feedback for the understanding and development of pedagogical practices.

This formation, as well as the tensions it created in its preliminary adoption, provides an important insight into the later evolution of a much broader system of student evaluation. Most significantly, student feedback became a legitimate form of exchange between the university and the student. In essence, the student voice was credited for the first time as a capable evaluator of academic teaching practices and courses. This was also firmly founded on a deficit conception of academic work: that is, problems were to be discovered through student feedback and action taken to correct them.

The mediating sense of what was the 'desirable' model of academic practice remained ambiguous in this evaluative construction. It appeared to vacillate between the Purdue/Remmers questionnaire-driven conceptions of 'good' teaching and curricula, and the idealised visions of democratised learning environments pursued by student activists (Chisholm 1977).

Hence, in this earliest formation the teaching academic was held to account via this uncertain formation. In essence, the origin of this formation in student dissent effectively diminished the significance of professional judgment around the nature of productive pedagogical labour and effective curriculum design. This introduced student voice became a valid means of producing the desired outcome of this object-orientated activity: assuring the quality of teaching and curriculum. This embodied an explicit acknowledgement that students were legitimate evaluators of teaching activity.

Yet some of the real limitations on teaching practices—such as allocated resources, broader program structures and educational facilities—were rendered largely moot in this new focus on the perceived quality of teaching and curriculum in the instruments adopted. This also had the effect of redefining the position of the student from their conventional position as a participant in higher education to one more akin to student-as-consumer. Now instead of being a mere recipient of academic labour, the student was recast as a potentially discriminating actor. As the student fees subsequently grew, this ontogenesis would prove highly significant in defining the later relationship between student opinion (as defined in the emergent higher education 'marketplace') and academic teaching practices.

The consequences of this simple reform on the academy were profound. The relationships in university communities were progressively redefined, the rules of how teaching quality was understood were rewritten and the roles of teacher and student effectively blurred. Unsurprisingly this redefined relationship generated considerable tension in US universities, as the traditional division of labour between the academic and the student was disrupted with such legitimacy being engendered in the inherently heterogeneous and arguably unpredictable student voice.

Moreover, the orientation of university administrators was toward a deficit conception of academic teaching, which represented a significant historic concession on the quality of such practices. Yet the conception of what constituted the 'ideal' form (and the related deficiencies) of academic practice that student evaluation sought to identify remained uncertain. Although this was mediated both by the historical framing of the dominant Purdue instrument and the demands of student activists for new formations of university learning, its form remained implied, ambiguous and arguably therefore unattainable.

Here we see the emergence of another clear tension formed around student feedback: students were to rate to an indeterminate standard, for which remedial action was implied should it not be achieved. Hence, this raised the critical question: who was to define (and enforce) quality academic practices: the teaching academic, the institution or was this to be shaped by the very student dissent that initiated the evaluative activity itself?

Further, although the traditional teacher and student division of labour was preserved at one level (by things such as pedagogy and assessment), it was fundamentally disturbed at another level. As the student voice became an arbiter (in at least in some form) of academic teaching performance, it blurred the distinction between the relative positions of teacher and student. As the activity of student evaluation emerged in the years immediately following, this tension was to become a more significant issue as academic tenure and promotion were later to further intersect with this activity.

Early Adopter: Student Evaluation in Australian Higher Education

The Australian higher education system was another early adopter of student evaluation. The reasons that several Australian universities initially embraced this model to some extent mirrored the same circumstances that prompted its rapid embracing in the United States: rising student unrest over teaching quality in the late 1960s. However, other situational factors were influential over time in its more widespread adoption. Such factors included increasing rates of student attrition (with growing enrolments) motivated greater attention to teaching quality and was another prompt for the trialing of quantitative student evaluation instruments from the United States in several Australian universities.

One of key observations of a major report into Australian higher education in 1964 was that the teaching methods then in use in Australian higher education had not kept pace with advances in pedagogical knowledge. It therefore urged reform, arguing this represented a 'challenge to universities to take active steps to consider the nature and improve the quality of their teaching' (Committee on the Future of Tertiary Education in Martin 1964). The report recognised some recent localised attempts to improve the quality of teaching, including the opening of a small teaching development and research units at several universities. It also anticipated an issue that would grow in significance in coming years. This was to prove prophetic, though perhaps not for the reasons anticipated by this Inquiry.

As was the case in the United States, rising levels of student activism were to be a powerful catalyst for attempts to improve the quality of undergraduate teaching. In 1969, the National Union of Australian University Students demanded a range of improvements to university teaching including the establishment of teaching and learning units in all universities, compulsory teaching qualifications for new academics and an assessment of teaching ability in decisions about tenure and promotion (Johnson 1982).

These sentiments were quickly reflected in the rising protests against university administrations around teaching quality, particularly in newly established universities (such as Monash, La Trobe and Flinders). This increasing dissent was harnessed by national student leaders to influence the upcoming triennial negotiations between the Australian Universities Commission and government to highlight the need for improved teaching quality (Marginson 1997). The evolving student movement in Australia was beginning for the first time to operate in the mold of trade unions, advocating for improved conditions for tertiary students through active research, representation and debate.

This level of focused student activity inevitably created interest from Australian universities and teaching academics about the responses being devised to respond to similar student unrest in the American higher education system (Marsh and Roche 1994). This included the initial discussion of student evaluation as means of responding to rising student dissatisfaction and by implication, to differing levels of quality in Australian university teaching.

However, the introduction of student evaluation in Australian higher education can be most directly traced to the progressive establishment of academic develop-ment units in universities during the late 1970s and early 1980s. The emergence of academic development was a result of two key drivers. Firstly, this rising stu-dent discord over teaching quality from more articulate and active student bodies provided an initial imperative. Much of this student concern was directed toward what was perceived to be the unchallenged authority in academic disciplines and the sense of teaching as being merely an 'impersonal pontification or expounding' (AVCC 1981, p. 1).

Iconic of this movement was the rapid development of 'alternative handbooks' that were produced by student associations or activist groups. These provided intending students with an informal and often scandalous interpretation of the quality of various academics and their approaches to teaching.

However, these units were also an explicit and largely necessary response to rising government demands for improved institutional performance and real fund-ing reductions, as the strains of market liberalism took hold. Academic devel-opment units developed from smaller and disparate research units focused on academic teaching that formed during the preceding decades in several universi-ties. Johnson (1982) observed these research units were created:

> quite pragmatically to find out information about their students in order to reduce wastage (including failure in courses); and they appointed staff to advise on teaching methods for the same reason. (p. 9)

Most of these research units were based in faculties of education and sought to work in formative educational development activities around teaching and learning to improve student retention and performance. Much of the work of these early research units was motivated towards the identification of primary arenas of stu-dent failure and the design of specific interventions to encourage more effective teaching strategies to enhance student retention (AVCC 1981).

With the growing number of academics and opportunities for promotion, there was also increasing anxiety in university administrations, amongst academics and, to a lesser extent, in government about the continuing abstract link between teach-ing capability and academic tenure and promotion. However, growing student demands and increased competition for tenure and promotion caused by funding declines over the previous decade meant this issue was gaining considerable trac-tion in university discourses of the early 1980s.

This imperative, combined with increasing public debate on the quality of academic teaching as the numbers of students (and therefore families) exercised judgments on university education, created a strong pressure for the more systematic judgments on the quality of teaching being offered across institutions. These range of social forces were identified as a key driver in the emergence and rapid expansion in the creation of academic development units (Johnson 1982). Indeed, by the late 1970s, most universities had such units, albeit in various configurations, though with often-unclear roles and uncertain purpose (AVCC 1981; Johnson 1982).

Nevertheless, a common responsibility of these emerging academic development formations was to provide courses and advice on effective teaching and assessment practices. An experimental tool used in some established universities were quantitative student feedback questionnaires. These were offered as one means (amongst a menu of options) to inform academic thinking about teaching improvement.

Unlike the early forms of student evaluation in universities in the United States (which primarily centred on academic accountability), in Australian institutions this initial adoption of student feedback was framed as a voluntary model for individual academics to improve their teaching. In some of these institutions, it also became a form of early data to support claims for tenure and promotion (Miller 1988; Smith 1980).

Reflecting this, much of the early discourse around models of student evaluation was framed by higher education researchers and isolated academic developers. This early focus was on the potential of student feedback as a means of sparking interest in professional development offerings designed to improve the quality of lecture-based teaching and assessment—and consequently individual prospects for tenure and promotion (Johnson 1982).

This was also considered as a necessary response to the danger of the potential complacency that could emerge as universities moved into a more 'steady state' following the relatively tumultuous period of strong student activism and university expansion over the preceding decade (Smith 1980). This reality meant that the early design of student evaluation models were institutionally driven. This meant such models remained eclectic and idiosyncratic in form and both voluntary and inconsistent in its use across universities and in teaching environments (Moses 1986).

However, significantly reflecting the historical construction of student feedback in the US, these models were almost exclusively based on adaptations of quantitative, ratings-based student feedback questionnaires. They also embodied in their design the core quantitative logic of student rating scales as a valid means of assessing teachers and teaching approaches.

Student evaluation progressively redefined the division of labour in the design of university teaching in Australian higher education. Teaching effectiveness was now subject to the potential challenge of the student voice and university management. Both entities would subsequently contribute more significantly to the framing of teaching expectations and conceptions of quality over time, as student evaluation systems were more broadly adopted across Australian universities under much stronger demands from government for the assessment of teaching quality.

Conclusion

The foundations of student evaluation—particular in its originating quantitative form that was based on the *Purdue Rating Scale for Instructors* pioneered in the United States—provide an important context for its later evolution in higher education settings. The urgency for strategies to assuage student unrest was a catalyst for the relatively rapid assimilation of student surveys as a direct means of affording student opinion on teachers and their teaching.

In the United States, student evaluation progressively became an accepted diagnostic tool to provide teachers metric-based feedback on the effectiveness of their teaching. In a relatively short period of time, student evaluation became an expected element of institutional administration. The new data it generated also began to be used in by some universities as a method of assessing teaching effectiveness for such things as tenure appointment or promotion or to provide guidance for students in selecting courses or teachers (Marsh and Roche 1994).

Situational reasons saw the these experiences of student evaluation become popularised in Australian universities as they also struggled to respond to rising student militancy and anxieties around rates of student attrition. The early focus of the Australian approach was more idiosyncratic according to the local histories of institutions, but was driven by new academic development units who were charged with driving teaching improvement. However, unlike in the United States, the focus of student evaluation remained firmly on providing individualised data for teachers seeking to improve the quality of their teaching. However, as the attraction of indicators of higher education effectiveness grew, so did the sense that student feedback data could perform a broader function as a potential institutional quality assurance indicator.

It is notable that another major higher education system—the United Kingdom—did not see any real adoption of quantitative forms of student evaluation until the 1990s, and then only in isolated instances. Indeed, it was only decades later that quantitative student evaluation would become seen as a legitimate mechanism. However, this was in quite a different form as it had emerged in the United States and Australia, being embraced as a primarily global quality assurance measure, rather than one centred on localised teaching improvement. Yet, as we will see in the next chapter, this was something that was also to become a more critical focus for student evaluation more generally as the effects of neoliberal reform of higher education began to take hold of educational policy.

Chapter 2
Research on the Design and Function of Student Evaluation

Abstract The exploration of the primary research focus of student evaluation—particularly the processes and integration of quantitative forms of survey-based student feedback—is foregrounded in this chapter. The critical foundations of this research have been largely framed around the validity and reliability of ratings-based metrics for teaching and course effectiveness. More contemporary research on student feedback has continued to focus on the improved survey design methods, as well as the development of frameworks for enhancing the capacity for comparative analysis of student evaluation data (such as against faculty, institutional or sectoral benchmarks). Other research has sought to investigate how the outcomes of student evaluation could be more effectively disseminated and integrated into the pedagogical actions of teachers. However, less research interest has been directed toward the foundational epistemological assumptions that underpin the use of quantitative student evaluation data for pedagogical and administrative decision-making in higher education. In this chapter, the broad range of research directed toward student evaluation is assessed, along with some of the issues that have received less scholarly interest. What this demonstrates is that student evaluation has attracted much stronger research interest from statisticians and academic developers than educational researchers.

Keywords Student evaluation research · Quantitative student evaluation · Epistemologies of student feedback · Limitations of student evaluation research

Introduction

In higher education environments, student evaluation is being increasingly employed to respond to multiple imperatives around quality improvement, quality assurance and performance management. In the complex teaching and learning environments of contemporary institutions, it is performing significant work as a usefully reductive and comparable signifier of teaching quality. Aside from student

© Springer International Publishing Switzerland 2016
S. Darwin, *Student Evaluation in Higher Education*,
DOI 10.1007/978-3-319-41893-3_2

evaluation being normalised within institutional life, over the last two decades student evaluation data has also moved beyond the academic and faculty level. Progressively it has become a highly regarded comparator for institutional assessment and a critical input in various university ranking scales.

As a consequence, it is also significantly shaping prospective student (and broader social) perceptions as to the value of higher education institutions and the programs they offer. For instance, the *Course Experience Questionnaire* has been used in Australia since 1993 to collect data from graduates about their experiences of university study. Similarly, since 2005 the *National Student Survey* has been offered to last year undergraduates in all universities and some colleges in the United Kingdom. In both instances, this institutional survey data is made publicly available via government-endorsed websites orientated to facilitating student choice.

In the case of the United States, where the higher education system is less centralized in its structure, institutional comparisons are more driven by the internal student survey data made public by individual institutions. In addition, a more sophisticated measure, the *National Survey of Student Engagement* is also offered to inform student decision making.

Therefore, there is clear evidence that student opinion data is continuing to evolve as an ever more powerful internal and external metric in higher education. Importantly, as will be detailed further in this chapter, extensive research over the last three decades has clearly demonstrated the robust validity and reliability of well designed quantitative instruments characteristically used in student rating systems (Benton and Cashin 2014; Marsh 2007). Increasingly, such research has tended to stress the need for multidimensionality in understanding the complex work of teachers in the interpretation of such outcomes.

Similarly, as the stakes surrounding improved student opinion continues to elevate, so research interest in how to more effectively address student expectations as reflected in such ratings data grows. This has characteristically centred on how student evaluation data can be most effectively assimilated into pedagogical practices of teachers, often based on situated case studies of practice investigating improved connections with professional development, mentoring or faculty engagement strategies.

However, what is notable is where the primary interest in student evaluation research has emanated: being dominated by statistical researchers (in the case of quantitative method of valid and reliable methods of student rating) and practitioners such as in-situ academic developers (in the case of enhancing responses to student opinion data). Interestingly, far less critical interest is apparent in the issue of student evaluation amongst higher education scholars, when compared to the weight of research energy dedicated to other dimensions of the higher education teaching and learning practices (such as curriculum design, pedagogical methods, learning technologies and student assessment).

Indeed—as will be argued in this chapter—although some significant reservations have been identified around the epistemic foundations of quantitative student feedback, it is polemists rather than researchers have primarily mounted these arguments. Research on student evaluation has tended to leave undisturbed the foundational epistemologies of quantitative ratings-based design of student feedback in its focus on statistical validity and strategies to enhance engagement with ratings data.

This lack of emphasis is somewhat more perplexing given the rising institutional and social weight of student opinion data. Specifically, contemporary student evaluation increasingly labours under the weight of several competing (and arguably conflicting) discourses. In broad terms, these discourses can be framed around two distinct and divergent motives for seeking student feedback, which themselves reflect the complex sociocultural formation of student evaluation in higher education. These distinct motives can be broadly characterised as:

- *quality enhancement of pedagogical and other practices:* reflecting the foundational professional and scholarly imperatives around student feedback to enhance the quality of higher education teaching. In this discourse, the inherent value of student feedback is toward pedagogical development (and related academic development), or other practices associated with enhancing student learning.
- *institutional quality assurance of teachers and teaching standards*: based on a largely deficit conception of teachers and teaching, student feedback is used to benchmark individual or collective teaching performance based, on internal and/or external comparators. This is primarily directed towards demonstrable shortfalls in performance requiring intervention or sanction. It also provides a metric for assessment of comparative academic performance for such things as appointment, promotion and awards.

As Walker (2001) observes, such motives are not only in inevitable tension, but also central to the formation of professional identities in the contemporary academy. The orthodox student feedback model has become normalised as a legitimate and 'common sense' arbiter of teaching quality. The consequence of this has been to challenge autonomous academic judgment on teaching effectiveness.

The originating quality improvement motive for student evaluation has become effectively subordinated to the more powerful demands of institutional quality assurance systems and individual performance management discourses. This has resulted in an ever more fragile settlement between these competing discourses (Kenway in Walker 2001).

Primary Research on Student Evaluation

This increasingly demanding context in which student ratings data is being used in contemporary institutional life would appear to provide fertile ground for more expansive educational research interest. Yet a review of research literature in this subject area reveals a continuing predominance of critical statistical investigations of the validity and reliability of the primary instruments employed for student rating systems internationally (Spencer and Pedhazur Schmelkin 2002).

Such research—which boasts an impressive three-decade history mirroring the rise of student evaluation systems—has most frequently centred on the confirmation or enhancement of the reliability and validity of the primary student ratings methods (Benton and Cashin 2014). This research stream has deep roots in significant formative research around student ratings and their utility. Examples of these seminal contributions include:

- Biggs and Collis' *Evaluating the Quality of Learning* (Biggs and Collis 1982) which introduced the SOLO evaluative taxonomy which introduced a measurement logic for assessing levels of student learning (and therefore teacher performativity).
- Marsh (1982a, 1987) whose research situated work pioneered the socialising of US quantitative student evaluation into Australian higher education settings.
- Ramsden (1991, 1992) who, building on the SOLO taxonomy, developed a quantitative student feedback model centred on levels of learning (which was later adapted to form the foundations for the iconic CEQ discussed earlier in this chapter).
- Centra (1993) who highlighted the significance of reflective evaluative enquiry based of quantitative student feedback.

Further, the considerations of quantitative student feedback strategies within broader academic development discourses are also relevant. Here the work of higher education researchers such as Prosser and Trigwell (1999), Toohey (1999), Laurillard (2002), Biggs and Tang (2007) are prominent.

Considerable research can be identified which is drawn from these foundational epistemologies of quantitative student feedback. Research with a focus on the usefulness or adaptation of prominent student feedback instruments (such as the widely regarded *CEQ*) is conspicuous in this research domain. Examples of that represent this research genre include Marsh (1982a), Cashin (1988), Miller (1988), Marsh and Roche (1994), Johnson (2000), Griffin et al. (2003), Dommeyer et al. (2004), Davies et al. (2009), Richardson (2005), Marsh (2007), Tucker et al. (2008), Nulty (2008) and Huxham et al. (2008). As this impressive range of research reflects, this orientation provides a substantial epistemological foundation for much of the contemporary research into approaches to deriving student feedback. A key focus of much of this research effort remains orientated toward assuring the multidimensionality of ratings scales—so as to generate a representative characterization of the broad teaching effort and to limit of the potential distorting effect of variables on outcomes (so as to limit the prospects of respondent bias). Inevitably, a matter of persistent interest is construct validity in questionnaire design (i.e. how to evaluate most effectively, instrument design and methodological adjustment). Without doubt this focus remains by far the most prominent and influential scholarship around issues related to student evaluation.

Hence, it is indisputable that extensive research has been undertaken since the originating work of important developers of the valid and reliable student rating scales (most notably Ramsden and Marsh). Indeed, it has been argued that this research interest in the technical design of student ratings—be it related to instrument reliability or validity of ratings as a measure—has been the most researched dimension of higher education in recent history (Willits and Brennan 2015).

This strong empirical foundation has achieved much in the development of effective designs, enhanced technical precision and strategies to enhance the trust-worthiness of quantitative, ratings-based forms of student evaluation. As a result, as noted in the first chapter, this research has provided the foundation for contem-porary institutional (and increasingly social) confidence in the metrics generated by student ratings. This research work has been significant in securing widely held beliefs in the usefulness of student ratings as a valid form of evidence in assess-ing the effectiveness of teachers and their approaches to teaching. It has also been successful in both identifying and responding to some of the possible fragilities in the validity and reliability of student feedback (Richardson 2005). Such fragilities have largely centred on limiting the effects of potential subjectivities in student ratings, most notably through the introduction of elements of multi-dimensionality in ratings assessment. For instance, a variety of studies have sought to investigate and respond to potential subjectivities in student ratings outcomes where students:

- are participating in a relatively smaller class (as opposed to those in larger subjects)
- have been able to opt to participate, such as in an elective subject (as opposed to core or mandatory courses)
- are studying in relatively more accessible content areas (over those more diffi-cult to apprehend)
- are engaged in more discussion-based subjects (compared to those involving primarily lectures or laboratory sessions)
- have a appealing academic figure, such as the experience of a favoured 'type' of individual (including gender, age or ethnicity) as their teacher.

Other research has sought to consider the sensitivity of student ratings to the timing of survey completion (i.e. pre/post final assessment), the context used to introduce surveys, student expectations of the eventual use of ratings data, stu-dent grade satisfaction and the level of student confidence the relevance of the instrument (Richardson 2005). The broad consensus developed from extensive field-based research is that the effect of such subjectivities in student ratings is frequently overstated, with less evidence of specific biases and more of variables necessitating specific responses to be effectively controlled (Benton and Cashin 2014; Gravestock and Gregor-Greenleaf 2008). Equally, there are a number of areas, particularly related to the effects of disciplines, teacher performativity and levels of subject difficult where some more equivocal outcomes have emerged in research (Aleamoni 1999; Wachtel 1998). Further outcomes have suggested that such variables can be successfully mitigated, either through improved question-naire design or enhanced methods of survey administration (Marsh 2007).

Unsurprisingly, an important emerging area of intensifying research interest within this domain is the transformation of student rating instruments from their traditional paper-based form to online completion. One critical consequence of the move from the paper has been the spatial move from the relative control of the classroom to the more open domain of online completion. The effect of this has been to lower student response rates and potentially negatively affect the reliability of ratings outcomes (Avery et al. 2006).

Some recent research has begun to more systematically explore this issue, investigating the impact of higher levels of non-response on he validity of student ratings derived online and its potential to accentuate the influence of specific variables. For instance, research by Adams and Umbach (2012) explored the implications of these lower response rates across 22,000 undergraduates, discovering that online administration of student ratings tended to aggravate the potential for bias as poorer performing students were more likely not to participate. This is likely to be an area of intensified interest as concerns continue to mount about the potential implications of lower student response rates on the reliability—and consequently validity—of online student ratings systems.

A second important research focus in recent research around student ratings can be broadly cast as functional investigations into how to more effectively integrate or capitalise on the outcomes of ratings data. In particular, such research has tended to be situated within institutional contexts and explores strategies around how to more productively assimilate these student ratings outcomes into improved teaching practices.

Hence this research has most commonly investigated and reported on localised, experimental strategies and methods to more effectively respond to student rating outcomes. This often centres on how to strengthen student evaluation systems to ensure identified deficits are more effectively responded to, primarily through more tangible links to such things as academic or professional development strategies, provision of mentored support or via the use of specific pedagogical interventions. Another current of this research has developed around the vexed question of methods to strengthen the relationship between student feedback and faculty or institutional quality assurance mechanisms. More specifically, characteristic forms of this research has tended to broadly cluster around:

- extending the functional usefulness of student ratings by improving student evaluation systems, exemplified by the work of Martens (1999), Harvey (2003), Watson (2003), Fisher and Miller (2007), Kember and Leung (2008), Stein et al. (2012);
- better understanding of how students perceive ratings systems, evidenced in the work of Spencer and Pedhazur Schmelkin (2002);
- understanding how student rating outcomes are being used by teaching academics, such as Schmelkin et al. (1997), Moore and Koul (2005);
- strategies to more effectively link student ratings to improved teaching-teacher performance, for example Powney and Hall (1998), Ballantyne et al. (2000);
- how to harmonise student ratings outcomes with quality assurance strategies, such as Barrie et al. (2005); and
- enhancing links between student ratings outcomes and academic development, for example Arreola (2000), Smith (2008).

Hence, as this analysis demonstrates—as well as those also offered by researchers such as Richardson (2005)—the primary focus of student feedback research has remained firmly centred either on the instruments for deriving valid and reliable ratings (and particularly strategies to enhance quantitative validity) or on the effective use of the outcomes of student feedback to prospectively influence teaching practices. It remains conspicuous that there remains a relative paucity of research on the legitimacy of quantitative student feedback as a means of understanding and improving teaching pedagogies: that is *of itself*. Indeed, there appears to be almost an assumed inherent legitimacy in the student ratings method.

Similarly, there is also seemingly limited scholarly interest in how quantitative student feedback had evolved into a valid means of understanding and developing teaching. Reflecting this, it is difficult to identify significant research that analyses the sociocultural foundations of the quite specific form in which conventional student evaluation has evolved in higher education environments. Equally, there is little substantial work that critically reflects on how student ratings may actually work in practice to afford or constrain the enhancement of academic teaching. There is less interest still in the mediating effect of the student feedback on collective forms of pedagogical work in the changing realities of the contemporary university. This results in the unavoidable conclusion that the fundamental epistemological assumptions that underpin the design of quantitative student feedback models remain largely unchallenged.

This also suggests that student feedback is a matter of lesser critical interest when compared to other dimensions of the higher education teaching and learning process. It is apparent from this analysis that student feedback as a scholarly area of inquiry remains less disturbed by educational researchers than by the primarily technical drives of statisticians, institutional managers and occasional sectoral polemicists. Given the complex and multi-faceted character of the student voice in institutional life, it is difficult to understand why student evaluation has remained relatively anonymous in research when compared to other areas of scholarly inquiry in higher education such as curriculum design, pedagogical strategies, research supervision and assessment. This is all the more puzzling given its increasingly significant function in the professional assessment of academic teaching.

The Limits of Student Ratings-Based Models

So it can be reasonably asserted that the primary scholarship around student evaluation has been firmly focused on the design of student rating instruments and the more effective integration of quantitative outcomes in situated practice. Moreover, there is no doubt that considerable and impressive development work has occurred around the design and deployment of student ratings as a result. More recently, this research on student feedback has become accepted as the backbone for the comparative analysis of teaching quality within and between other related courses, and increasingly against faculty or institutional averages.

Similarly, it is certainly the case that demonstrable teaching improvements have occurred as a consequence of this determined research focus, which has improved the reliability and validity of student ratings and thereby the influence of the student voice on academic deliberations and the work of individual teachers. As this research focus continues to grow, so it will concern itself more with the troublesome issues of moving online and how to assure the continuing validity and reliability of ratings-based metrics in the face of declining levels of student response.

However, despite these realities, there remains a core unresolved epistemic question around quantitative forms of student ratings. It is a question that continues to limit its acceptance amongst many within higher education and even creates hostility toward the value and usefulness of the student voice. This question is whether the inherently reductive nature of student ratings—regardless of their demonstrable validity and reliability—can provide the critical insights necessary to drive improved teaching and student learning in the increasingly complex and multi-layered learning environments of contemporary tertiary-level learning.

As it frequently cautioned by student ratings researchers themselves, ratings can be only considered as one means of assessing the quality of teaching. As noted earlier in this book, in their emboldened contemporary manifestation student ratings are performing *of themselves* ever more powerful forms of work as a tool of individual and collective performance assessment, as well as a key indicator for institutional quality assurance. Put simply, increasingly student ratings are becoming a proxy for teaching quality.

Yet contemporary teaching—with its fragmenting certainties, heightening demands and, in most cases, diminishing resources—is less reducible than ever to inevitably one-dimensional rating scales and statistical reporting. As Barrie et al. (2008, p. 7) observe, the nature of how we chose to evaluate student learning inevitably reflects specific beliefs about '*what* is important to be measured, beliefs about *who* should do the measurement and what measurement might *mean*' (original emphasis). Further, the form we adopt to understand the nature of student opinion and how it is then absorbed into the life of the academy inherently embodies a specific theory of learning and a conception of what is required (and what is not) of a teacher to afford student learning.

Therefore, it is increasingly necessary to transcend narrowing conceptions of student evaluation that are increasingly the centre of institutional conceptions of quality assurance, if we are to be serious about genuinely encouraging (and engaging with) the student voice to improve the quality to teaching, of curricula, of pedagogies, of assessment and of online technologies. As will be demonstrated through the prism of a series of case studies featured in this book, it is increasingly unlikely that conventional systems centred on student ratings will be able to achieve such an outcome. Instead, more sophisticated understandings of the student voice are necessary to both legitimately represent the depth of student opinion and to engage teaching academics in the professional dialogue necessary to genuinely lead to sustainable teaching improvement.

So this book proposes reconceptualising how we understand the student voice and the methods we use to undertake what is broadly characterized as student evaluation. It asks us to reconsider student evaluation as a complex social activity that does considerable work in shaping teachers, teaching and courses, as well as the institutional and student sense of quality teachers and teaching. This suggests that perspectives on student evaluation must elevate beyond well-trodden debates about the nature of survey tools, statistical analysis or dissemination processes.

Moreover, as student evaluation performs ever more significant and influential functions at multiple levels in the contemporary university (and increasingly beyond), it is also time to reconsider the conflation of the discourses of quality improvement and quality enhancement within this spatial domain. The multiple purposes for which student feedback is now used mean it performs complex and heterogeneous work in the contemporary university. Some of these multiple dimensions of student feedback, and how they are manifested in contemporary higher education environments are outlined in Table 2.1.

Table 2.1 Dimensions and manifestations of student feedback in contemporary higher education

Dimensions	Manifestations
Multi-leveled	Student feedback is derived in both informal and formal means, as well as in formative and summative forms. This produces potential tensions between the quantified responses of students and the implicit intuitive sense of the teacher developed in the teaching environment. This creates potential tension between the relative validity and legitimacy of one form over the other
Multi-charactered	Student feedback is a somewhat unwelcome fringe dweller in teaching areas, being often poorly regarded, conceived of as largely ritualistic and of limited 'real' value (Anderson 2006; Edstrom 2008). Whilst at the same time, student feedback lives a regarded institutional life as a broadly reliable, robust and accountable indicator of comparative teacher quality and, by inference, student learning outcomes (Barrie et al. 2008)
Multi-voiced	Responses to student feedback are necessarily shaped by the differing experiences, expectations and anxieties of academics, faculties, disciplines and institutions. This means responses to student feedback cannot be considered homogenous in form and are necessarily multi-voiced. Responses are therefore a construction of differing meanings that are not necessarily shared at different levels of the institution
Multi-focused	The range of potential issues student feedback encounters includes such diverse objects as the teacher, pedagogical practices, student experiences, student engagement and curriculum suitability. In addition, its outcomes are also subject increasingly to broader inter and intra-comparability benchmarks of student opinion and courses. It therefore is also a measure of the relative value of individual and collective academic work
Methodologically eclectic	Approaches to deriving student feedback range along a continuum from highly subjective and interpretivist forms of situated judgment, to highly rationalist and abstracted quantitative surveys that rate teachers, teaching and courses.
Locally mediated	Forms of student feedback in higher education are locally mediated; being sociocultural constructions idiosyncratically shaped by the specific histories of student feedback models within institutions. Although this localism is in decline under the weight of standardised sectoral surveys, clear evidence of it remains (Barrie et al. 2008)

The Need to Broaden the Conventional Assumptions of Student Evaluation

Despite this burgeoning complexity, there is a relative paucity of research on alternative perspectives on the formation, use and contemporary functions of conventional quantitative student ratings. This tends to suggest that, despite its increasingly contested and disparate work in the contemporary university, student evaluation systems are generally regarded as a technical and benign (or even benevolent) in form. Schuck et al. (2008) contend this reflects the successful assimilation—and consequent heightened legitimacy—of standardised quantitative student ratings-based evaluation in contemporary higher education environments.

However, regardless of its origins, this limited breadth of research dialogue increasingly tends to limit the necessary scope of debate on this important area of higher education scholarship. Indeed, as argued earlier in this chapter, it could be reasonably asserted that student feedback (and its effect on pedagogical change) remains the least investigated element of higher education scholarship. Perhaps this is a consequence of its perceived peripheral assurance function or its low parity of esteem with other dimensions of the teaching and learning process (being consigned largely to being a 'student' issue). Perhaps it is the reality that the research space around evaluation has been largely and successfully occupied by statisticians and systems administrators investigating opportunities for ever-greater quantitative precision in the measurement and deployment of student opinion.

This reality is despite the rising challenges of increasingly complex environments of teaching and learning in the knowledge-technology era, where student feedback may usefully contribute greater insights to inform pedagogical decision-making. University teaching is under pressure as never before to respond effectively to the demands of more complex forms of knowledge, to abandon traditional pedagogies, to engage via multi-modal learning environments and to design relevant assessment to drive learning. All of these demands suggest an ever-greater need to understand more fully and completely the nature of student responses.

These imperatives also suggest the need to explore methods that go beyond refining traditional quantitative student feedback models to more sophisticated forms of engagement with the student voice. It is also all the more curious when considering that the outcomes of student feedback have recently become more contested within institutions, as its original quality improvement motive is challenged by the rising discourses of quality assurance, performance management and even institutional marketing. As a result, student evaluation is increasingly being called upon to do more complex work: some pedagogical, some individual, some institutional and some for the emerging student-consumer.

Moreover, in recent years, the outcomes of student evaluation are increasingly being made a public commodity, moving outside the individual professional domain of the teaching academic. This would seem to create both an imperative and a fertile space for critical research dialogue about the legitimacy of student feedback as a measure of teacher performativity. Yet critical questions remain elusive in scholarly research, including how student feedback actually *functions* to:

- inform or debase academic judgment
- afford or hinder pedagogic change
- incite or dissuade professional development
- encourage or dissuade the development of curricula enhancement, learning activities or assessment.

Moreover, the role and function of student feedback also brings into sharper relief important tensions around teaching and learning practices. For instance, it necessarily encounters important contemporary tensions around:

- what constitutes valid knowledge about teaching and learning to frame prospective pedagogical development? (i.e. the relative rights and responsibilities of academics and/or institutions around student feedback outcomes)
- the rising uncertainties around the professional identity of teaching academics (i.e. what rights do teaching academics have to determine the suitability of 'unpopular' pedagogies, assessment and other practices, compared to institutions and students?)
- relative levels of autonomy of teaching academics (i.e. who interprets and initiates action on student feedback: the academic, the faculty or the institution?)
- the expected capability of the contemporary academic (i.e. how much can be reasonably expected of the teaching/research academic in response to student feedback at a time of reducing resources and elevating expectations?)

Therefore, this identified gap also became the critical foundation for framing the case study-based research reported later in this book. It motivated the specific focus on how the student voice could be further harnessed to more effectively influence and develop pedagogical practices and student learning in the ever more complex pedagogical environments of higher education.

Potential Limitations of Quantitative Student Evaluation

To consider these broader questions, it is useful to explore the arguments of those who have deviated from the dominant research discourses around student evaluation. These perspectives provide a preliminary context for the analysis that is undertaken later in this book.

There are a small but increasing number of higher education researchers and polemists that are challenging the foundational assumptions of quantitative student feedback. This is particularly focused on whether students are able to reasonably discriminate what constitutes 'good' teaching, effective curriculum and approach assessment. That is, are students reasonably able to rate teachers, teaching and courses, and on what criteria is this based.

Similarly, can teaching be assumed to be 'good' if it is rated positively be students, or 'poor' if it is not rated highly? A related question is whether the 'object' perceived to be subject to evaluation (i.e. teachers and teaching approaches) is sufficiently distinct: are students evaluating the object they are assumed to be, or is it something else altogether (such as traits, environment or assessment outcomes)?

Researchers such as Schuck et al. (2008) argue that student evaluation is increasingly sustained on powerful mythologies that offer it considerable institutional credibility as a powerful demarcator of pedagogical quality. Some researchers have also raised questions about the inherently reductive nature of metric-based student feedback that is abstracted its social and individual contexts of meaning. Others have mounted research polemics to respond is perceived as the scepticism and disengagement by academics around quantitative student feedback. Such scepticism and disengagement is seen as arising from the inherently subjective, often inconsistent and retrospective nature of the data generated by quantitative student feedback (Edstrom 2008).

Researchers such as Johnson (2000), Kulik (2001), Kember et al. (2002), Zabaleta (2007), Schuck et al. (2008), Edstrom (2008) have identified and explored a series of other potential limitations in quantitative student evaluation models in higher education. Drawing from this collective research, a series of contestable assumptions around student evaluation can be quantified.

(a) *Higher satisfaction with teachers correlates with improved student learning:* It is axiomatic of conventional student evaluation that positive student feedback on teaching will correlate with improved student learning outcomes, yet the significance of this link is not clearly quantified in research outcomes. Although it has been more convincingly demonstrated that student- based evaluation may influence teachers to align self-perceptions with those of their students, it cannot be assumed this will actually lead to changed teaching behaviours or enhanced student learning outcomes (Richardson 2005).

Moreover, the relationship between higher evaluation ratings and higher student attainment remains contentious, with researchers such as Zabaleta (2007) failing to establish this in situated practice. Similarly precarious is the presumption that positive student feedback outcomes can be seen to equate to high quality teaching, and conversely that poor student satisfaction reflects low quality teaching. This is because the social practices of teaching are complex and often involve pedagogical or learning challenges that disrupt student certainties or confront misconceptions. Here the critical tension between the popular or charismatic teacher versus the effective or challenging educator can be complicated by student feedback. Students may understandably positively responding to the former or negatively responding to the latter. However, neither may actually provide a useful insight into pedagogical effectiveness.

(b) *Quantitatively measuring teaching quality improves student learning outcomes:* There is an implicit assumption in student evaluation models that in conducting student evaluations the quality of teaching (and therefore student learning outcomes) will demonstrably improve. This is based on the implicit belief that individualised forms of metrics-based, deficit-focused student feedback are the most productive means of generating pedagogical engagement by teaching academics.

However, as Kember et al. (2002), Schuck et al. (2008) have demonstrated, the correlation between evaluation and improved student learning is highly dependent on the active intervention of academic development or supplementary evaluative strategies (both of which are increasingly novel in academic environments).

Although it can be reasonably argued that the assumed relationship between quality and outcomes is predicated on expectations of ancillary support–such as timely academic development support or the intrinsic motivation for promotion or other recognition—this is a difficult generalisation to sustain in the resourcing reality of the contemporary academy where evaluation data emerges largely of itself and undisturbed. Conversely, given socialised student expectations of teaching approaches, evaluation may also paradoxically act as a conservatising brake on pedagogical change for academics cautious to avoid 'disrupted' (and therefore dissatisfied) students evaluating teaching (Gibbs n.d.).

(c) Quantitative student feedback *is essentially an objective, benign and valid measure of teaching effectiveness:* It is anticipated in the design of evaluation systems that students can clearly and consistently rate their experiences of teaching and learning and that this in turn can provide useful and legitimate insights towards pedagogical improvement. Moreover, it is conventionally assumed that students are able to adopt a consistent and comparable rating schema in assessing things like teaching quality in their range of evaluative response. Yet these assumptions are fragile at best. A range of subjective influences have been demonstrated to manifest themselves in student ratings, which may render student evaluation in particular contexts less a barometer pedagogical quality and more an essentially environmental barometer (Schuck et al. 2008).

Moreover, Likert-type scales inherently remain essentially interpretive and intersubjective, based on students' own definition of 'good' teaching, curricula and the further abstracted relationship to this imposed rating scale (Knapper 2001). There is the related assumption that no viable alternative methods of harnessing the student voice are able to improve the quality of teaching and learning as do metric-based evaluations. This is not to suggest that such ratings are simply dispensable or that they may not provide some forms of insight into sound or poor student approaches to learning. However the question is how much diagnostic value can be assumed from ratings-based, quantitative data and can this then be legitimately used to justify their literal use as a form of teaching performance indicator?

(d) *Institutional accountability improves professionalism:* Although it is inferred that accountability driven by student evaluation enhances teacher professionalism, such professional knowledge is predicated on autonomy, independence and expertise rather than compliance to an aligned to a prescribed notion of student arbitrated 'good teaching' (Eraut 1994).

Hence, the discourses of professionalism and accountability would appear to be in conflict where enhanced professional practice is automatically correlated with student accountability (Schuck et al. 2008).

(e) *Student feedback encourages teacher performativity:* There is a belief in the student evaluation model that correlates evaluative outcomes to improved teacher performance. Yet student feedback simultaneously responds to various institutional demands, such as those centred on quality improvement, quality assurance, performance management and institutional marketing.

When student evaluation goes beyond this first quality improvement drive, rather than achieving improved teacher performance, it may instead cultivate fear and self doubt, especially when aligned to punitive performance management or performance processes (Johnson 2000). Moreover, given the reality that university learning cannot be defined as a 'product', this approach may actually incite a perspective that the institution should provide students what they *want* as opposed to what they may actually educationally *need* (Furedi 2006).

(f) *Professionalism can be effectively codified:* Although it is generally assumed that 'good' teachers get 'good' ratings, this is based on the foundational conception that such 'good' knowledge, standards, behaviours and practices can be clearly defined, agreed and understood by respondents and readily compared. Given the contested nature of this conception, this represents a complex faith-based construction that may not be realistic, appropriate or dynamic in its form (Kulik 2001; Schuck et al. 2008).

These range of collective understandings serve to legitimise and sustain student feedback models that are now so predominant in contemporary higher education contexts. Given the extent of contestable logic, it is highly desirable that these actual foundational paradigms of student evaluation are subject to further critical scholarly enquiry. This task is all the more pressing in the transforming teaching environments, where potentially fragile and reductive data may not best serve the elevating needs for pedagogical development. This is all the more essential as student feedback is increasingly employed to inform academic performance management and frame institutional reputation.

Conclusion

This chapter provided an exploration of the dominant research literature around student evaluation, suggesting this was both substantial and at the same time clustered primarily around statistical, technical and dissemination issues. It demonstrated that the foundational epistemological assumptions that guide the conventional quantitative form of student feedback lie largely undisturbed in this research landscape. Yet there are a definable range of contestable assumptions around quantitative student feedback that deserve greater attention beyond the limited number of researchers and polemists who are engaged in this questioning.

This imperative has grown as student feedback is increasingly used for differing (and arguably contesting) functions in the contemporary university. Student evaluation has been increasingly called upon to perform more extensive functions within and beyond institutions. As a result the actual role and function role it should performs has been subject to contestation within higher education institutions.

These rising tensions around student evaluation suggest the need for a heightened research focus on the validity of the core assumptions that sustain this orthodox quantitative approach, as well as the potential of other more expansive forms of harnessing the student voice to restore its function as an important influence in pedagogical deliberation. As the evidence in this chapter has illustrated, the contemporary work of student evaluation (and the key assumptions that underpin) can only be fully understood in the context of how it has been historically and culturally shaped. This provides a means of more effectively understanding how student feedback has contributed (or otherwise) to the formation of contemporary teaching practices. This allows the consideration of possible alternative conceptions of the use of the student voice that may resonate with the elevating pedagogical demands of increasingly complex contexts of university teaching.

Chapter 3
What Higher Education Teachers Think About Quantitative Student Evaluation

Abstract There has been considerable research interest in both the technical dimensions and situated use of quantitative forms of student evaluation. However, the epistemological assumptions of student evaluation have remained largely undisturbed by this research effort. Similarly, limited attention has been directed to what academics actually think about student evaluation and—closely related to this—what pedagogical or other work it actually does in practice. Despite this, in the drive for the continued expansion of student evaluation systems, crucial assumptions are made by management in higher education about the levels of academic support for student evaluation and the willingness to adopt its outcomes. So what do academics actually think about quantitative student evaluation? Moreover, how willing are they or otherwise to analyse and/or accept its outcomes to modify their pedagogical approaches or other learning strategies? In this chapter, data collected from a broad range of academics working in a major, internationally recognised Australian university is detailed and its implications for the assumed roles and functions of orthodox student evaluation is analysed. This research provides insights into the complex realities that surround the contemporary work of student evaluation in higher education. The outcomes suggest that tensions are being increasingly formed around rising accountability and quality assurance discourses, which are challenging the seminal intent of student evaluation to guide pedagogical decision-making.

Keywords Teacher opinion on student evaluation · Student surveys · Qualitative research on student evaluation

Introduction

It is notable that in educational research in higher education settings, limited substantial research has been undertaken on the actual pedagogical implications of quantitative student evaluation on situated pedagogical practices. This is in stark

© Springer International Publishing Switzerland 2016
S. Darwin, *Student Evaluation in Higher Education*,
DOI 10.1007/978-3-319-41893-3_3

contrast to the considerable interest that has been directed toward the statistical robustness of the tools of student evaluation and the optimum methods of dissemination student evaluation data to influence academics. As a result, the perceptions held by teachers toward student ratings, as well as the consequent influence they have on the pedagogical decisions made by teachers in higher education remains largely a matter of inference and speculation (Arthur 2009). Given the considerable resources dedicated to sustaining student evaluation systems in many higher education institutions, this lack of attention to the real impact of student feedback seems somewhat puzzling. Moreover, the research that has been undertaken has generally pointed to paradoxical academic responses to student ratings, with simultaneous states of ambivalence toward student evaluation models in use and broadly positive sentiment toward the value of the student voice (Anderson 2006; Chan et al. 2014). Other studies have identified similar paradoxes. For instance, Surgenor (2013) found teachers understanding of student evaluation as both an opportunity and an obstacle, with value identified broadly in student feedback but considerable reticence in regard to the validity and use of student ratings data within institutions. In exploring academic perceptions of student ratings, Arthur (2009) generated a typology for the divergent responses revealed that included (academic) shame, (student) blame, tame (appeasement of students) and reframe (pedagogical change).

Given this somewhat curious conflation of ambivalence, optimism and deeper scepticism demonstrated in regard to student evaluation, there is a strong imperative to further investigate these perceptions (and therefore the impact) of its functioning in everyday practice. In order to explore these questions around perception and influence, a research project was undertaken involving university-based teaching academics centred on their experiences with the use of quantitative student feedback. In addition, this data was then used to form a foundation a broader case study-based research on the potential expansive use of the student voice.

This research provides unique and valuable insights into academic experiences and perceptions of orthodox student feedback, as well as the effect it has on approaches to teaching and learning. In this chapter, the outcomes of these data is reported and the implications of these outcomes analysed in the context of both research on student evaluation and prospective alternative forms of use of the student voice as a generator of improved pedagogical practice in higher education settings.

Setting the Context

In this research, 32 teachers from two teaching programs (who were participating in a broader case study research project) in a major, internationally recognised Australian university agreed to individual interviews and to participate in a broader forum about their experiences with quantitative student feedback and how influential it been in changing their pedagogical practices. All participating teachers had been identified as having used the university student evaluation system in semesters immediately preceding the research.

Fortuitously, the research involved two distinct cohorts of teachers that reflect the increasingly dichotomous reality of contemporary higher education environments. Teachers participating from one of the programs were engaged in a relatively recently established program. Reflecting this, most of these teachers were engaged under employment structures that are more characteristic of recent and market-exposed programs: having a relatively small core academic workforce, supplemented by a large peripheral teaching workforce of practitioners.

Conversely, teachers drawn from the second program worked in a longer established and more core program of the university. As a result, it had a large tenured teaching workforce and a relatively small group of adjuncts and tutors. These differences were clearly reflected in the relative divisions of labour in the two program cohorts examined in this research, with the employment status and institutional and professional experiences of academics producing divergent roles, often amplifying tensions around the role and functions of student feedback in shaping perceptions of relative teaching effectiveness.

The university where this research was undertaken was an early adopter of student evaluation. A range of quantitative student surveys were first made available for use by academics as a voluntary teaching improvement tool in the early 1980s, coinciding with the introduction of a dedicated academic development unit.

As student evaluation evolved within the university, it was used both for this form of academic development work, as well as gradually being assimilated as a potential source of evidence in regard to teaching capability to support (or deny) appointment, tenure and promotion. Although this system had broadened in use, its basic form had remained largely undisturbed.

However, coincidently as this research commenced, the university embarked on a major reformation of the university's student evaluation system. This reform introduced elements increasingly familiar in contemporary student evaluation systems in higher education. These changes included:

- compulsion on teaching academics to participate in the student feedback system and to demonstrably be seen to respond to its outcomes
- semi-public release of data to afford comparative analysis of outcomes
- explicit links between the data generated by student evaluation and the broader quality assurance strategies of the university
- integration of the outcomes of student evaluation into internal performance management processes, including regularised performance reviews and promotion assessments

Hence, the issues around the both the role and the expanding functions of quantitative student evaluation were being vigorously debated as the case studies commenced. This was heightened as the proposed reform of the system moved it being from being primarily framed within localised academic development discourse to one that had an explicit focus on the broader quality assurance and accountability ambitions of the university.

Usefully, this development tended to amplify perspectives on student evaluation during the research period. It unsurprisingly ignited some unusually focused debate about the desirable role and function of the student voice amongst academics. This catalyst was to provide fertile ground to investigate perceptions of student evaluation amongst teachers in the university.

Significantly, academics interviewed as part of this research generally had a substantial engagement with the existing student evaluation system. This was for several reasons. Academics in the two programs from which respondents were drawn from had an ongoing expectation placed on them they undertake regularised student feedback. This was driven by the desire of program leaders to consolidate its curriculum and pedagogical practices. Hence, program leaders did expects student evaluation outcomes to be a central component of teacher reporting on course outcomes. This tended to mean most teachers opted to participate in formal student evaluation system of the university, with most also (somewhat unusually) opting to share the outcomes of these surveys with their supervisors.

In the individual interview stage of the research, teachers and educational leaders of the programs were asked to reflect broadly on their experiences with formal student evaluation. The interviews were semi-structured around three key questions:

1. *What have been your experiences—both positive and negative—with student evaluation?*
2. *How useful have you found the quantitative outcomes of the surveys in better understanding student learning?*
3. *How much influence has the outcomes of student evaluation had on your approaches to teaching?*

The second collective dialogue was built around the two forums for the teachers and educational leaders within their respective program-based teams. Here the thematic outcomes of the individual interviews were presented for further discussion, clarification and debate. This data was also to become an important catalyst in subsequently formulating what specific action research approaches programs were to adopt to more effectively harness the expansive potential of the student voice (reported later in this book).

Exploring Tensions Around Student Evaluation

As noted earlier, in the period immediately prior to the commencement of this research, the university student evaluation system was being further elevated as an internal quality assurance tool and as a more powerful demarcator in promotional and performance management discourses. This effect had been further elevated by introduction of compulsion and the linking of student evaluation outcomes to academic performance through the reporting of outcomes to students, supervisors and even the university academic forums.

The potential implications of these changes were widely discussed and understood by most of the academics interviewed, albeit with differing levels of anxiety as to its likely prospective impact. Nevertheless, clear evidence emerged that there was a broad understanding that student feedback was to work increasingly as an effective proxy for the assessment of teaching quality (and therefore implicitly, individual academic performance).

This was often without any real clarity to the nature of the problem itself (given the general nature of rating scales) and tended to focus on individual teacher or course responses in isolation from the broader program context. This suggested the strength of the layers of history, formed artefacts, rules and assumptions drawn from the well-institutionalised student evaluation system.

A significant minority of tenured staff (and a handful of non-tenured staff) had recently completed subjects in a postgraduate higher education program offered by the university. This had included several of the leaders in each program. The effect of this was to raise their consciousness about the value of reflective engagement of student learning, including better using student evaluation to improve pedagogical practices.

As a result, there was an imperative to treat student feedback with greater regard than merely a quality assurance process and to further mine it for useful insights into the successes and failures of pedagogical practices. Although this drive was generating a strong conflicting sense around the value of quantitative student feedback amongst teaching academics, it also was clearly useful in gaining eventual support for exploring the potential value of the student voice.

At a general level, the broad consensus amongst teachers and educational leaders about the role of the student voice was unequivocal. Teachers overwhelmingly agreed that student feedback was a valuable (though inherently fragile) source of intelligence about the effectiveness of program design, teaching practices and assessment strategies.

It was apparent in the tone of responses that student evaluation was a normalised element of the semester's activities and a core dimension of identifying (and acting on) perceived deficits in teaching activities. Having said this, levels of affection for student opinion were highly variable amongst participants. On an initial analysis, this seemed to stem largely from two primary drivers.

The first was individual experiences—both positive and negative responses—encountered in student feedback. It was particularly apparent from the individual interviews that there was a clear correlation between their own personal experiences with student evaluation and their formed perceptions about the relative value of the student voice in shaping teaching approaches.

Significantly, this was not only at the obvious level of good or bad outcomes, but also where teachers felt they had not achieved what they were seeking to do, yet received positive student ratings (or vice versa).

The second driver was the related to the form and extent of the employment relationship the teacher had with the program. From the initial entry stages of this research, it was apparent that the various orientations towards student evaluation were strongly contextualised by these histories and workplace structures within the two programs.

How teachers were actually employed by the university tended had an effect in shaping impressions of student evaluation. For tenured teachers, there was generally a more abstracted relationship with student feedback (as one such teacher evocatively described it, an 'occasionally useful irritant'). Amongst this cohort, there was a general level of confidence that any problematic student evaluation outcomes could be balanced against other indicators of teaching effectiveness (such as completion rates, peer regard or alumnus successes). Having said this, some pointed to this being somewhat different in times of heightened attention by the university (such as promotional rounds or performance management) when student evaluation data became more pronounced.

However, for the significant numbers of teachers without ongoing employment contracts, the stakes of student evaluation outcomes were clearly much higher and its significance felt much more acutely. Given that a negative student evaluation result could easily result in subsequent non-engagement for the following semester, these teachers were highly conscious of the fragile realities of student opinion in potentially determining their fate as future teachers.

However, this effect tended to vary according to the levels of desire such temporary teachers had to sustain a long-term career as an academic. Those motivated to securing an academic appointment expressed the deepest anxieties about the potential effects of student evaluation data in shaping perceptions of their value as a teacher. Much of this related to the reality that such teachers also worked part-time, meaning student evaluation data provided a comparatively disproportionate influence on these perceptions (which for other tenured teachers was mediated by broader contact with program leaders, peers and greater engagement in internal pedagogical dialogue).

Alternatively, those working as part-time teachers whilst maintaining a professional career outside the university were less concerned about academic teaching reputation (though this remained generally of concern) and more uneasy about negative student evaluation outcomes reflecting on their levels of perceived professional competence.

Nevertheless, at a broader level the majority of these more precariously engaged teachers equally felt that student evaluation data was potentially helpful in further developing their teaching approaches. As most were relatively new to teaching, there was a clear consensus that the student voice was a critical source of intelligence in helping to shape their emergent pedagogical methods. Indeed, several non-tenured teachers reflected on the reality that—as a result of their temporary or part-time employment status—student evaluation tended to represent a much more tangible form of guidance than most other forms of insights they were offered by the university.

At times, they were however frustrated by the ambiguity of the metrics (i.e. why was this element of my teaching rated low compared to other ratings?). Yet there was some premium placed by a majority of these teachers on the mere fact that some feedback on their teaching was actually available to them, however imperfect its numeric framing. This observation was less cast as a critique of the levels of support offered by the programs, more a commentary on the reality of the growing peripheral workforce that is living in the shadows of modern academia.

The Importance of Professional Versus Institutional Interest

Clearly, the overall data suggested there were some shared practices around the use of student evaluation. One key practice was prompted by comparative analysis of student rating outcomes in student feedback reports each semester. Virtually all interviewed academics felt the imperative to act where (comparatively) negative responses were received. This tended to produce pedagogical responses designed to address perceived 'problems' either individually identified or on the insistence of others (most notably supervisors). What was characteristic was that in the overwhelming majority of instances of corrective actions being determined, the resulting actions were perceived by the teacher as being firstly without any real empirical foundation (aside from the rating score itself) and secondly were generally not perceived to have made any substantive difference in the subsequent semesters. So these deficit-driven actions were often initiated without any real clarity as to the nature of the problem itself (given the general nature of rating scales). They also characteristically tended to focus on individual teacher or course responses, in isolation from the broader program context. These realities underpinned the powerful hegemony of the layers of history, formed artefacts, rules and assumptions of an institutionalised student evaluation system.

Further, although the reactions of interviewed teachers toward student evaluation ranged from ambivalence, through anxiety to acceptance, there was a shared scepticism and unease amongst both teachers around the broadening institutional utility of student evaluation outcomes as quality assurance and performance management measures.

Initial discussions about student evaluation—both at the individual and collective level—saw the expression of strong anxieties about these developing uses of evaluation outcomes. Here it was generally considered that what were perceived to be the inherent fragilities of student opinion were amplified when its consideration is divorced from its important pedagogical context. This was particularly felt as a result of the:

(a) difficult curriculum context within which the programs operated, which was torn between high academic performance expectations, competence demands of the profession and the need to skill high-calibre practitioners of the future;

(b) drive for pedagogical innovation, which was often disruptive of student certainty and inherently difficult to get right, particularly in initial iterations (this sentiment was particularly felt by one of the programs which had introduced a controversial move to the use of online simulations); and

(c) frequently challenging teaching conditions encountered by teachers due to pressures to maintain high enrolment levels in the face of challenging content, heavy study loads and the historical reliance on deeply unpopular, exam-based final assessments in these discipline areas.

In particular, teachers with educational leadership responsibilities considered that these contextual factors were not well understood outside their local environment. This meant that the comparative analysis of student feedback outcomes across the university would be inevitably misleading. This was seen as being flawed even when comparing subjects internally within the program given differing class sizes, the effect of core or elective subjects or relative levels of curriculum complexity. Conversely, any attempt to appease student opinion to lessen this (arguably unwarranted) attention on their programs was seen as having the potential to undermine the critical academic standards on which the program's reputation was built.

Teachers generally saw things somewhat more simply: if student evaluation data and the reductive metrics it produced were made comparatively accountable in a more public form, then they would be under far greater pressure to appease student opinion rather than respond to its outcomes. In essence, in the collective mind of the teachers across the two programs, more visible and accountable forms of student feedback data would fundamentally re-define its role and its function.

In further analysing the perspectives of teaching academics on the elevating use of student evaluation data—both collected in workshops and from individual interviews—some further tensions were apparent. These tensions provide some insight into the real pressures surrounding the elevated and more public use of student evaluation data and are outlined below.

1. *Student satisfaction and learning quality*: Most fundamentally, there is a powerful potential tension between elevating expectations of student satisfaction and the need to sustain high quality learning outcomes. Although these two objectives are not automatically incompatible, heightened demands for positive student outcomes may constrain the use of curriculum, teaching or assessment strategies that are 'less popular' amongst students. In addition, often students are required to attain a series of required standards, meaning strong impositions are placed on students to ensure such standards are demonstrated (such as exam-based assessments). Such imperatives—along with other graduate expectations—may conspire to limit possible levels of student satisfaction.

2. *Student satisfaction and pedagogical innovation*: Almost inevitably pedagogical innovation results in student disruption in learning. Pedagogical habits in higher education mean there is a strong student familiarity with certain approaches to teaching and assessment. Teachers who attempt to innovate tend to face the difficult realities of trial and error as experimentation with new approaches are piloted and refined. The action of making student evaluation outcomes public (as a reductive metric) provides no real insight into the effects of such innovation. Hence, despite the potential longer-term benefit of such innovation, teachers may be discouraged from innovating to avoid negative consequences of lower student satisfaction.

3. *Student satisfaction and multiple accountabilities*: The outcomes of student evaluation—when formed as a point of accountability to the institution—creates an additional imperative to which the teaching academic needs to respond. This is additional to the responsibilities to the discipline or profession (for the maintenance of educational standards), to the institution (for the fulfillment of required practices and maintaining a suitable research profile) and to the faculty (for maintenance curriculum and pedagogical requirements). With the elevation of student evaluation as a privileged accountability measure in the contemporary institution, there is potential for heightened tension between it and these other significant accountabilities. This may result in ever-greater pressure to give students what they demand as consumers, rather than what they need as determined by discipline and other professional standards.

4. *Student satisfaction and professional judgment*: The elevation of student satisfaction is in potential tension with the use of student opinion as one source of professional insight into the effectiveness of curriculum design, teaching practices and assessment. By making responsiveness to student evaluation mandatory, there is a potential undermining of professional judgment as the significance of student opinion becomes a disproportionately important force. This may have the effect of minimising the influence of professional experience, peer advice or research literature as means of guiding professional judgments about pedagogical practices.

5. *Student satisfaction and need to grow enrolment levels*: Universities continue to be under pressure to grow their student cohorts to maintain financial viability. As a result, there are escalating pressures—primarily driven by institutional marketing and omnipresent sectoral league tables—to achieve consistently high levels of student satisfaction so as to encourage prospective students to enrol in programs. Aside from creating tensions around maintaining challenging and robust educational environments, such pressures can tend to encourage teachers to devise strategies to improve student satisfaction in ways that are not necessarily consistent with the educational interests on students.

6. *Student satisfaction and career-building*: With the extended use of student evaluation data for a range of internal university processes around judgments of individual teaching performance, teachers could be under pressure to ensure students are permanently satisfied. This may tempt teachers to identify factors that could potentially enhance (however superficially) student opinion. These could be largely benign (such as more 'entertaining' teaching approaches or building closer personal relationships with students) to more troublesome actions, such as reducing program demands or assessment expectations.

7. *Student satisfaction and impetus for improvement*: Finally, there is an elevating tension where greater stock is placed on quantitative student data about how to exactly respond to its often ambiguous (or even contradictory) outcomes. As most universities make minimal use of open form qualitative questions, most often this becomes based on largely speculative assumptions about what produced rating outcomes, without any real data being available to give life to the dimensions or scope of the student response. So teachers are forced to rely on numeric expressions of deficits, complicating their ability to respond and potentially leading to

overreactions or the compounding of genuine pedagogical problems. Worse still, incorrect assumptions may lead to further deterioration in subsequent outcomes.

These localised tensions around student evaluation reflect the broader and increasing uncertainties around its intensifying use in the higher education sector as a proxy for teaching quality. Central to this is the increasingly uncertain object of contemporary student feedback, contested as it is between the demands of quality improvement, quality assurance and individual performance measurement.

What is notable is that these tensions around orthodox quantitative student evaluation identified in this localised context well reflected what research suggests are the broader and increasing uncertainties in the higher education. This was primarily around the uncertain object of contemporary student feedback, contested as it is between the demands of quality improvement, quality assurance and individual performance measurement.

Given this, it is useful to analyse the contradictions that appeared to underpin these tensions and how these were manifested in everyday practice at the commencement of the case studies. In Table 3.1 below, the key identified contradictions around orthodox forms of student feedback identified in the case studies are outlined. This is based on material drawn from the thematic analysis of the initial collective dialogues, later individual reflections and the evaluation-related artefacts. In addition, the primary manifestations of these contradictions, as observed in everyday practice by participants are also reported.

Table 3.1 Key contradictions: conventional forms of student evaluation

Key identified contradictions	Primary Manifestations
Maintaining learning quality *versus* need for 'above average' student satisfaction levels	*Standards/satisfaction*: tough professional practice and assessment standards, contrasting with student evaluation policy imperatives
Drive for pedagogical innovation *versus* the need to meet student expectations-demands	*Innovation/acquisition*: disruptive pedagogies linked to changing professional practice domains, contrasting with student-as-consumer gaining legitimate access to professional domain
Accountability to the discipline for standards *versus* individual accountability as an 'effective' educator to institution and students	*Professional/educational*: the powerful drive of discourses of professional knowledge-practices, scrutinised by regulators, contrasting with the institutional and student perceptions of what constitutes quality teaching and learning engagement
Quantitative assessment *versus* need for broader qualitative insight and support to pedagogical improvement	*Quantitative judgement/improvement imperative*: the inadequacy of summative quantitative student assessment to provide substantial insights into successful or failed practices, contrasting with a desire to improve the quality of pedagogy
Pressure to sustain student enrolments *versus* need to challenge/broaden discipline knowledge and disrupt ingrained assumptions about effective workplace practices	*Market imperative/challenging environment*: the market pressure to sustain student enrolments at highest possible levels, contrasting with the need to provide a challenging and robust exploration of requisite discipline knowledge and workplace practice environment

What is apparent in this data is the strong reflection of the historically shaped contradictions generated by the contesting discourses around the use of the student voice. The resulting tensions have seemingly had a strong shaping effect on approaches to assuring learning quality, levels of engagement in innovation, and in producing real pedagogical uncertainty in teaching practices.

However, further apparent in these local sites was an additional contradiction that is characteristic of higher education programs that are responsive to a professional or vocational domain of practice.

Both researched programs were also under the critical scrutiny of professional and government regulators, who assess educational effectiveness from the distinct (and divergent) perspective of exiting graduate knowledge and professional competence. This scrutiny has a power in that it provided licence for the continuation of teaching and subsequent access for graduates to the professional registration. This lingering attention was significant for both programs, as they were dependent on ongoing accreditation to function. This provided considerable ongoing agency to regulatory expectations.

This was more problematic given this was expressed largely via an essentially vocational competency framework that was used to assess both curriculum design and as a form of final assessment. This had the effect of forcing a range of curriculum and assessment responses, many of which elicited negative student responses. This was most notable around the need for a comprehensive range of matters to be 'covered' in imposed competency (or standards) frameworks, which were then assured by end of program examinations set by the regulator.

This additional domain created further strong implicit tensions in the case study environments, as it further challenged the relative pedagogical autonomy of teaching academics. It also created the shared imperative of needing to 'professionally guarantee' specified knowledge and practice capabilities of graduates (in order they subsequently can meet externally scrutinised expectations), whilst also maintaining requisite levels of student satisfaction (whose significance was simultaneously being elevated).

This specific tension, along with the range of other contradictions and related complex tensions outlined earlier, were clearly influential in both shaping, disturbing and even disrupting engagement with the student voice across the two studied programs, both before and during the action research.

Multi-voicedness: Differing Teacher Responses to Key Tensions

However, just as there were some strong and re-occurring similarities in responses to these tensions, it was significant that participants perceived their impact somewhat differently. Significantly, these differences tended to reflect differing relationships of participants to discipline knowledge and to the university itself.

The analysis of the data suggests these differences (and their effect) were most notably related to the several key factors, notably:

The relative teaching experience of the academic: As noted earlier, more experienced teachers tended to recognise the need to develop pragmatic means to reconcile these tensions in some form of uneasy détente. This meant keeping simultaneous focus both these demands, essentially seeing the need to find some form of pragmatic balance between maintaining student satisfaction whilst responding to the plethora of other demands. Often this meant finding ways to modify the rigidities of imposed curricula, working more deliberately to address matters to be examined or to offer students greater levels of support than was necessarily sustainable (resulting in considerable evidence of academic overwork). Conversely, newer educators (who were primarily employed part-time) expressed consistent anxieties about the implications of student feedback on perceptions of their personal and/or professional competence. This was further complicated by their desire to pedagogically innovate, an instinct that often came from their own positive or negative learning experiences, or exposure to sites of professional work that graduates would encounter. However, this drive was tempered by the inherent dangers of pedagogical disruption, which may result in (at least) an initially negative student response. As their employment was often semester-by-semester, this became a difficult tension to navigate. For these less experienced teachers with a more precarious employment relationship, maintaining student satisfaction was critical as it was perceived as essential to maintaining employment or gaining a promotional foothold in the university.

Relationship to the discipline/profession: Where this relationship was ambiguous (such as those who had been exclusively teaching for some time), less concern was apparent about the need to concede to the expectations of the profession. It was also for this reason that those still active in the professional discipline (largely, though not exclusively, part-time academics) saw this not only as a major tension but also a matter of significant professional expectation of their dual status as academics and workplace practitioners.

The distinctive role of educational leaders: Educational leaders were navigating often conflicting imperatives of the university (primarily around the quality assurance of teaching and sustaining enrolments), the discipline (around 'appropriate' representations of knowledge and contemporary practice), teaching academics of differing levels of experience, employment status and expectations, and the actual available capability for educational development. This was all in the context of the influential demands of students in programs that were highly vulnerable to enrolment fluctuations (and word-of-mouth). Hence, educational leaders in both programs often exercised a high level of individual agency in response to student feedback, which that reflected the disproportionate demands of this complex negotiation of differing tensions.

Level of anxiety around the relationship of pedagogical innovation and student opinion: The likelihood of short-term student unease with pedagogical change and its implications for student evaluation created varying levels of anxiety. This strongly reflected the cultural traces of the increasingly dominant quality assurance discourses encountered by academics in the immediately preceding period. Some academics perceived student feedback as a threat that could reflect individually on their professional competence, whilst others identified it as a useful catalyst to build a stronger and more contemporary program. This dichotomy was most notably in the second program that had recently and significantly reformed.

These various initial dimensions demonstrated from the data represent what Engeström (2001) describes as multi-voicedness around the activity of student evaluation. Social communities like those existing in the two programs invariably are constituted around differing perspectives, conceptions, experiences and histories. Moreover, the specific division of labour within the program teams—most notably forms of employment and positional roles—creates differing vantage points from which to understand student feedback. This generated dialectic potential for contested translation, negotiation of meaning and debates around innovation to develop the nature of the activity. Considerable evidence of this dialectic interplay was apparent in the data collected around student feedback discourses in the two programs.

Epistemological Tensions Around Contemporary Quantitative Evaluation

Given the contested nature of the everyday activity of student evaluation, a key challenge is to make visible these tensions and disturbances around the increasingly complex role of student evaluation *in situated practice*. These tensions—inevitably framed within the broader context of the socio-historical influences that have provided the layers of the meaning and action of the use of the student voice over time in higher education—are produced by the increasing uncertain epistemologies around it emerging role and function.

As data collected here well demonstrated, student evaluation is often treated by academics as rudimentary and insufficient of itself to provide compelling evidence for pedagogical change, particularly where other forms of feedback about teaching are valued.

Yet elevating institutional regard for accountable and measurable student feedback to fuel quality assurance means often that change will be demanded based on its outcomes (rather than informing a individual professional judgment as was the historic role performed by student survey outcomes). This key tension effectively frames the contemporary discourses of student evaluation, more frequently forcing dialogue to move from traditional rhetorical engagement (reflecting indifference and/or uncertainty) to a more critical debate on the quality assurance potential of student feedback for teaching and learning.

The nature of this more critical dimension is more fully analysed in the table included as *Appendix*. This data, based on a thematic analysis of this situated research, provides an insight into the nature of the framing tensions and the broad shared themes that emerged from participant responses to these tensions. This table also summarises the key epistemic questions around the use of student feedback that this data suggests need to be considered. The results presented in the table are presented in the following manner in *Appendix 1*:

- *Identified tensions (first column)* summaries the key tensions emerging from the overall analysis of the data around the purpose and utility of quantitative student evaluation provided by teachers and program leaders;
- *Broad thematic categories identified (second column)* records the consolidated thematic outcomes emerging (clarified further in facilitated collective dialogue around these identified tensions; and
- *Questions emerging relating to student feedback identified (third column)* represent the range of potential epistemological questions that are implied from these tensions.

Conclusion

This chapter provided an insight into the complex realities that surround both the perceptions and the contemporary work of student evaluation in higher education. In analysing the various perspectives of teaching academics and educational leaders in situated practice, we encounter an evocative instance of the strong tensions frame the outcomes of the (quantitatively represented) student voice in contemporary higher education. This particularly pronounced when it is driven more by accountability and quality assurance discourses—which are clearly on the ascendance in modern institutions—than by its seminal purpose of guiding pedagogical decision-making.

Based on the data collected from the two cohorts of teachers, it is apparent that the relationship between teaching academics and student feedback is strongly mediated by primary artefacts, such as the nature of the student feedback system and its core tools (such as quantitative surveys and forms of analysis of these metrics).

These historically-formed artefacts impose a series of specific epistemological assumptions around the nature of appropriate pedagogical practice, with the powerfully reductive lucidity of student ratings creating a far tangible logic to implore action over other sources of intelligence that are more abstract (and seemingly less objective in form). Escalating collective and individual accountability demands by institutions—framed around student opinion—only serve to amplify this effect. This pressure also comes from other realities: the market and professional exposure of the programs and the strong divisions of labour within contemporary teaching cohorts, which increasingly reflect differing employment status and proximity to the profession.

Conversely, the key contradictions identified in quantitative student evaluation in situated practice often work to produce collective forms of indifference, skepticism and/or uncertainty about the use of student feedback for pedagogical development, as well as anxiety about how the institution may use the comparative data it collectively generates. This accords with findings of several other studies in this area, such as those by Arthur (2009), Chan et al. (2014) which identify similar patterns.

Hence, as internal quality assurance and performance management frameworks begin to rely more heavily on student evaluation outcomes, so there is a distinct danger that this may prompt a reformation in the relationship between teachers and students over time. This pressure has the potential to encourage teachers to adopt pedagogical or assessment strategies that appease student opinion, resulting in the danger of diminishing academic standards as a compensatory outcome for improving student survey outcomes. This effect is even more likely to be acutely felt by precariously employed teaching staff, whose continuing employment is likely to become more and more dependent on delivering positive student opinion.

Chapter 4
Analysing the Potential of Student Evaluation in Practice

Abstract This chapter introduces two practice-based case studies undertaken in a major Australian university centred on using the student voice as a catalyst for pedagogical development. This research was designed to provide an insight into the potential of the student evaluation formed around more qualitative forms of data and collaborative academic dialogue to enhance pedagogical practices in the ever more complex environments of higher education teaching and learning. These case studies—developed using a unique formulation of Cultural Historical Activity Theory (CHAT) and action research methodology—sought to investigate the expansive potential of the student voice to enhance professional dialogue around teaching toward the ongoing improvement of situated pedagogical practices. The chapter discusses how the case studies were established, how data was collected and the methods used to interpret the data generated from respondents. A key element of the research was the introduction of an *expansive learning evaluation cycle*, which was designed as a stimulus for collective and reflective dialogic processes, based on the elevated role of qualitative student feedback.

Keywords Qualitative student evaluation · Professional teaching dialogue · Cultural historical activity theory (CHAT) · Expansive learning

Introduction

As the quality assurance and performance management motives for student evaluation have continued to escalate in significance in the contemporary higher education environment, so the original quality improvement imperative has tended to recede. This creates a clear imperative for investigating alternative approaches to the use of the student voice that are specifically focused on improving pedagogical practices. This necessitates moving beyond orthodox metric-based forms of student evaluation that are gradually being reformed toward the demands of the educational market and corporate management needs. Such approaches may offer the

© Springer International Publishing Switzerland 2016
S. Darwin, *Student Evaluation in Higher Education*,
DOI 10.1007/978-3-319-41893-3_4

potential to not only more effectively harness the student voice, but also to incite deeper academic engagement in exploring strategies for pedagogical improvement.

In this chapter, the specific design of case study-based research to assess alternative forms of developmental evaluation using the catalyst of the student voice are outlined. This research was developed in response to the inherent limitations identified around the pedagogical implications of current dominant forms of student evaluation outlined earlier in this book. In a broad sense, the objective of the case studies was to establish if qualitative representations of the student voice might offer a greater expansive potential for pedagogical practices than those generated by conventional quantitative models of student evaluation that currently dominate the higher education landscape.

Specifically, this research was intended to systematically explore the developmental potential of student feedback to enhance pedagogical work in higher education environments. Essential to these tasks was harnessing what Engeström (2000) has evocatively described as the *ethnography of trouble*—making the contradictions, tensions disturbances and ruptures visible in this conventional 'everyday' activity—in order to engage case study participants in critical analysis toward innovation and developmental change. This provided a potential means of encouraging teaching academics to adopt a more active and critical engagement with student feedback.

Moreover, the research was designed to investigate the consequences of fracturing the traditional settlement around the individualised use of quantitative student feedback. The recent moves to use student evaluation as a comparative market-based measure, as well as an assessment of academic performativity, mean that student feedback data has moved from the realm individual deliberation into the public domain. Exactly what the consequences of this transformation have been for the regard teaching academics hold for the student voice—and what this has done the relationship with student feedback—is important question to assess.

Hence the case studies sought to assess if the developmental motive underpinning student evaluation could be successful reinvigorated using alternative forms of engagement with feedback. Importantly, the design of this research explicit recognised the critical stimulus role of the student voice, as well as the genuine desire of many teachers to respond effectively to the student learning needs and the legitimate demands of students for improved pedagogies.

Cultural Historical Activity Theory (CHAT) Foundations of the Research

Qualitative research approaches are increasingly significant in interpreting complex social experiences from the perspective of those involved, and to contextualise these in their sociocultural origins (Glense 2006; Marshall and Rossman 1999). They offer the researcher an opportunity to immerse in naturalistic contexts that provide a complex and multi-voiced perspective on individual and shared experiences. Qualitative research is centred on an emergent design, which is focused on discovery rather than diagnosis (Schram 2003).

This case study-based research was framed by a qualitative methodology, conceptually grounded in Cultural Historical Activity Theory (CHAT). CHAT is increasingly recognised as a powerful analytical tool to understand complex activity, seeking to understand and influence the nature of complex social practices through the contextual analysis of the historical layers, mediating artefacts and object-orientation of local activity.

The theory finds its origins in the cultural-historical psychology of Lev Vygotsky (1978), being subsequently developed by his student Leont'ev (1978), Luria (1976) and more recently through the work of Engeström (1987, 1999, 2007a). The pioneering work of Vygotsky in the immediate years following the Bolshevik Revolution in 1917 emerged as a reaction to the irresolvable tensions between the two dominant psychologies of the era: crude, reductive forms of behaviourism and subjective idealism centred on the understanding of an internalised consciousness (Wertsch 1985).

Vygotsky sought to give life to the materialist intent of Marxist philosophy, which cast human consciousness as being developed in a sensuous relationship to the external world. This contrasted to the notion of consciousness being a product of controlled learning, or formed in atomised and internalised mental processes. Hence much of Vygotsky's work before his untimely early death sought to understand what mediated the relationship between the individual and the social, with a strong focus on the mediating role of language and semiotics (Daniels 2008).

His colleagues, A.N. Leont'ev and A.R. Luria further developed this work by broadening the Vygotskian scientific understanding of the development of human consciousness. This was to focus attention on how such development occurs through the internalising of social relations. This was grounded in the materialist notions, which asserted the sensuous and material nature of human activity.

From this philosophical foundation, the conception of object-orientated activity was introduced as a means of furthering understanding of how the internalising of external social actions shape inner mental processes. Though sustaining an emphasis on the critical role of mediation, Leont'ev and Luria proposed complex human activity as the unit of analysis to understand the development of the social mind.

This subsequent work, constructed on the foundations built by Vygotsky, provided the framework for the later emergence of CHAT. This development understood that the 'structure and development of human psychological processes emerge through culturally mediated, historically developing, practical activity' (Cole 1996, p. 108). Therefore, as Daniels (2008) observes, contemporary activity theorists 'seek to analyse the development of consciousness within practical social activity' (p. 115).

In its contemporary manifestation, CHAT is emerging as a broadly employed conceptual framework in research. It provides a potent explanatory structure to understand the complex socially mediated and intentional processes that underpin human learning and development activity (Engeström and Miettinen 1999). It has an increasing presence in educational research, including as a means of investigating complex learning environments—including those of higher education (Wells and Claxton 2002). This increasing use of CHAT in educational settings reflects a rising recognition of its capacity to foreground the social, cultural and historical mediation of human development. In doing so, it necessarily encounters the interplay between consciousness and activity, exploring the inherent dialecticism between social and individual agency.

CHAT also stresses the dynamic, societal, collaborative and potentially expansive nature of human activity. Hence, as Cole (1996) observes, CHAT 'rejects cause and effect, stimulus response, explanatory science in favour of a science that emphasises the emergent nature of mind in activity and that acknowledges the central role for interpretation in its explanatory framework' (p. 104).

As a result, CHAT offered several compelling foundations for research on the expansive potential of the student voice on pedagogical practices. This is because CHAT allows the educational researcher to:

- analyse the seemingly disparate social practices around student evaluation, via a robust interdisciplinary framework that is explores how such practices shape the 'social mind' of individuals
- make explicit of the inherent tensions and contradictory imperatives in the activity of student evaluation, and their implications for shared academic practices
- observe of the role that social and cultural artefacts of student evaluation play in mediating and shaping complex and intentional human activity in university settings
- illuminate the expansive developmental potential of tensions and contradictions present in student evaluation, to enhance broad and everyday academic practices.

A fundamental element of CHAT is the theoretical unit of analysis it uses to understand and further develop human functioning, characterised as the activity system. This notion of social activity represents a rejection of individualist and cognitivist explanations of human development. Instead, it understands such development as collective and co-constructed, being 'embedded in sociocultural contexts and intrinsically interwoven with them' (Stetsnko 2005).

The activity system is the key conceptual unit of analysis in CHAT theorising. It is the critical means of establishing the historically, culturally and socially mediated relationship between the subject (point of observation) and the object (the orientation of an activity). In exploring the tensions and contradictions within activity, it attempts to explain the nature of the activity and the dialectic relationship between the social and individual mind.

Engeström (2001) argues the nature of these complex activity systems can be captured in five explanatory principles:

- the prime unit of activity theory based analysis is centred on these collective (rather than individual) activity systems and considers the function of historically and culturally negotiated artefacts in mediating the 'social mind'

- these activity systems are multi-voiced and multi-layered, meaning they are complex and intersubjective
- activity systems are collective, culturally mediated and object orientated (that is, intentionally toward a defined object). They and are shaped and transformed by the ontogenesis of the activity system and other activity systems with which they interact
- tensions and contradictions are both inevitable and essential to change and development in activity systems
- activity systems have expansive potential for development as a consequence of contradictions being made visible and aggravated.

Engeström (1987) developed the primary conceptual tool used in CHAT for understanding the social form of collective activity systems. This was a further development of the individually focused conception of the triadic subject-object mediation characteristic of the Vygotskian 'genetic' tradition (Daniels 2008). Essential to this representation is a broadened focus that considers integrates a range of additional social dimensions.

This evolved representation, cast as *second-generation activity theory*, considered the social rules that frame activity, the community that is interdependent in sharing social meaning and the division of labour which demarcates positions, roles and tasks (Jonassen and Rohrer-Murphy 1999). Later work by Engeström (2001) has further developed this conception, with the introduction of the notion of competing activity systems and further interest in the effect of 'boundary crossing' between such activities. This is characterised *as third generation activity theory*.

CHAT as a Form of Developmental Research

CHAT provides a robust and purposeful conceptual framework for a critical understanding of the complex social activity of student evaluation in higher education. It achieves this by systematically investigating the 'psychological impacts of activity and the social conditions and systems that are produced through such activity' (Daniels 2008).

This theoretical framework therefore provides a viable explanatory means to consider the potentiality of student evaluation in higher education, providing the capability to re-envision the potential use of the student voice.

The explanatory and developmental tools of CHAT played a central role in both developing the case studies and the subsequent analysis of their outcomes. For the research, this CHAT-based case study intervention provided an opportunity to go beyond mere observation of practice, to engage in ongoing dialogue with actors moving with the uncertain flow of impediments, affordances, disruptions and developments that characterise the realities of daily work.

As Engeström (2000) suggests, this interventionist model of research engagement is clearly aligned toward a developmental motive:

> If actors are able to identify and analyse contradictions of their activity system, they may focus their energy on to the crucial task of resolving those contradictions by means of reorganising and expanding the activity, instead of being victimised by changes that roll over them if forces of a natural catastrophe (p. 153)

This inevitably casts the researcher as an interventionist and developer, providing a toolkit of conceptual tools for generating rich data that is deeply contextual and developmental in its potential impact (i.e. having the potential to lead to the reconceptualising of pedagogical work).

These two case studies were developed using what is a novel melding of an action research methodology with CHAT. There were several imperatives for this approach. Case studies represent instances of a social activity that illuminate the complex social dimensions of the phenomenon. As Yin (1994) observes, case studies are useful in that they allow the investigation of a 'phenomenon within its real life context especially when the boundaries between phenomenon and context are not clearly evident' (p. 13).

Specifically in their use in CHAT, they also afford a situated environment to test the expansive learning potential of the area of inquiry (Stark and Torrance 2006). Given this, case studies offer a useful means of casting light on the two of the critical questions that are at the centre of this study around the contemporary condition and developmental potential of student feedback.

Action research method focused on pedagogy is used widely in education, as it affords the opportunity to 'systematically investigate one's own teaching/learning facilitation practice with the dual aim of modifying practice and contributing to theoretical knowledge' (Norton 2009, p. xvi). This orientation aligns well to the broader developmental bias of CHAT, providing the basis for theoretically informed exploration of practice (in this case using the prism of student feedback).

This approach was devised as it offered the potential to more actively and directly engage participants in the work of developing of teaching and learning using the student voice. Further, it allowed the more effectively evaluation of the more critical use of elevated forms of student feedback data to develop professional dialogue around pedagogical practice.

This CHAT-based, action research model also offered a more engaging method by which to collectively consider the contemporary usefulness of student feedback, particularly as it had further taken on a quality assurance function. It also provided the opportunity to more effectively assess the potential impact of qualitative forms of learning-focused student feedback in encouraging situated forms academic development.

Finally, this somewhat novel use of action research as a complementary methodology for CHAT had the potential to expand theoretical knowledge in the broadened conceptual use of this framework.

Selecting Suitable Locations for the Case Studies

The first task was to identify suitable sites within the chosen research site for the case studies. Given the nature of the investigation, it was determined that two differing sites would be desirable: a single site may prove overly narrow and reductive, and more than two may generate excessive data or, given the immersive nature of the work, may limit possible research engagement with the sites.

It was resolved in consultation with educational leaders in the two case study sites that a period of three semesters would be optimum (so as to be able to conduct three iterative action research cycles). This would provide sufficient time for the case studies to develop within successive action research cycles.

In essence, the two sites to be researched needed also to represent a *purposeful concept sample*, that is potentially information rich and that allowed a clear understanding of the phenomenon under investigation (Cresswell 2005). Based on this broad framing, the following specific criteria were developed by the researcher for discussion with a range of program conveners to determine site suitability:

- a coherent teaching program with a range of subjects with differing student cohorts
- a relatively stable teaching team with experience in conducting, and responding to, student opinion surveys
- a willingness for the academic teaching team to actively engage in a CHAT-based, action research project over at least three semesters
- demonstrable focus on innovative or disruptive pedagogies which may or may not have impacted on student feedback outcomes
- capacity to further develop curriculum, teaching strategies, course materials, learning technologies and assessment based on the outcome of research
- openness to further develop the individual and collective pedagogical capabilities of academics based on the outcomes of research
- agreement for the outcomes of the research be investigated and published (subject to appropriate ethical clearances and informed individual participant consent).

In order to provide a useful context for analysis of the implications of the use of student evaluation, it was also important that the case study sites had substantial experience in using the (previous) evaluation system. Aside from providing a critical context for this research, it would also demonstrate an openness to engage with the student voice. This was not as straightforward as it would have seemed, with differing areas of the university having divergent levels of engagement with the student evaluation system. Based on these range of criteria, two suitable programs were identified and subsequently offered by program conveners as case study sites for the research.

The site of the first case study was in a recently formed postgraduate program. The program—primarily focused on delivering graduate certificate and diploma programs for experienced graduates—had approximately 500 student enrolments per year.

The second case study was conducted in a program offering postgraduate programs, though with programs overwhelmingly designed for recent graduates. It had student enrolments of around 1100–1400 in recent years. Although the programs offered by this second program had existed for over thirty years, its mode of delivery had been recently radically reformed to integrate a blended learning mode (i.e. using a combination of face-to-face and online teaching).

Several further potential case study sites were identified but were discarded, as they either:

- could not effectively support the collaborative action research model being proposed
- had specific situational limitations that would prevent investigation of the current use or prospective use of student opinion
- were constrained in their capacity to develop programs or the capabilities of academic staff based on research outcomes, for a range of differing reasons.

Put simply, given the nature of the research proposed, the two case studies were selected as they afforded the best opportunity to understand the use and potential of student feedback, whilst at the same time possessing a genuine interest in developmental improvements in program design, teaching and academic capabilities.

One important aspect of the recently revised university policy framework also assisted in facilitating this approach. This was the continuing ability of individual programs within the university to develop specific local strategies to seek student feedback outside the conventional quantitative mode. This afforded this action research approach in the two selected sites, and allowed the broad exploration of different approaches to the collection and use of student feedback data.

Although these two programs sat within the same broad discipline, they embodied the policy and procedural approaches of the broader university (and the sector more generally) in regard to the use of student evaluation. Importantly for comparative analysis, standardised student opinion surveys had previously employed in both programs. Moreover, both were in the process of debating how to transition effectively to the new student feedback system.

Therefore, the relevance of these programs lay not in their specific discipline or location, but their employment of broadly standardised quantitative student opinion surveys and the related mandatory responsibility to respond to its outcomes. In addition, both programs were actively seeking to:

- improve teaching and assessment quality using a collaborative action research framework
- wished to identify and act on opportunities for substantial program and academic development
- were open to forms of development they may be generated by collective assessment of mediated student opinion.

As Norton (2009) argues, action research in university settings is most effective when it is a result of a perceived need for enquiry into what is already being done, rather than imposed as a formalised staff development initiative. For this reason, the action research was clearly framed around the history and trajectory of the individual programs rather than as a generic research initiative being bought to bear on the program for purely academic interest.

The two case studies foregrounded in this research also represent instances of the rapidly changing environment of higher education, sharing the characteristics of:

- large-scale teaching programs with complex curriculum and rigorous assessment demands in a broad discipline domain
- offering teaching and assessment in mixed modes of delivery (i.e. both face-to-face and online)
- being under considerable pressure to recruit and retain students, maintain high levels of student satisfaction and meet rigorous expected graduate capabilities in the emerging Australian higher education 'marketplace'
- operating under various demands of institutional accountability, program and academic responsiveness and broader pedagogical effectiveness, with all of which student feedback influences in one form or another.

However, they also have key differences that are important as they create a distinctive character for each case:

- one program is primarily offered via online learning with limited face-to-face orientating seminars, whilst the second carries a more significant face-to-face component (though with considerable with online elements)
- one program has highly diverse student demographics and academic entry levels, whilst the second has a more homogenous cohort with a standard academic entrance expectation
- one has a large casual teaching group (most of whom also work in professional practice) and a small core full time academic staff, whilst the second has primarily a permanent teaching workforce of full-time academics, supplemented by a cohort of casual teachers from a variety of backgrounds
- one program had developed and modified curriculum from scratch over the last five years (within a mandated competency framework), whilst the second has an accumulated history over two decades with relatively stable curricula (and has shaped the broader curriculum framework used across the sector).

In CHAT terms, these shared and distinctive characteristics of the two programs provided the opportunity for the contextual exploration of activity settings that are discrete but are also what Yamagata-Lynch (2010) describes as 'highly interrelated bounded systems' (p. 79). This provides the ability to conduct sociocultural analysis of the outcomes of the cases that is multi-dimensional, and allowing a greater understanding of the effect of individual and shared agency in activity.

The Role of the Researcher

In the research, I took the role of a *participant-observer*, allowing me to experience of the same reality as participants experienced. This also meant foregrounding my own personal experiences and reflections in order to deepen the nature of inquiry (Marshall and Rossman 1999). This approach was considered all the more appropriate given the Vygotskian foundations of CHAT that inspires an inherently developmental form of research inquiry into social practices.

This implies that the research itself forms part of the very social practices the researcher seeks to investigate. Therefore, the chosen methods were natural to CHAT–informed, action research as they were inherently immersive, highly interventionist and hermeneutic in form. Indeed, as Langemeyer and Nissen (2006) observe, rather than offering:

> …a fixed set of rules or recipes to be followed, (a CHAT-based) method is the ongoing theoretically informed reflection of the social practices in which research participates; yet method is also, still, a tool for research, a specific cultural object produced to form and transform that activity. (p. 189)

Moreover, there is a clear and productive resonance between CHAT and action research. Action research represents a complementary method, as it is orientated to collaboratively investigating situated social practices from within and developing a defined knowledge cycle to expansively improve such practices. In doing so, it also seeks to reduce the barrier between theory and practice by applying and further constructing research knowledge (Noffke and Somekh 2006).

This underpinning framework—founded on CHAT-informed action research—meant the researcher could be most productive when acting as an active *participant-observer* in this empirical element of the project.

As Glense (2006) observes, by being immersed in a social setting, researchers learn:

> first hand how the actions of research participants correspond to their words; see patterns of behaviour; experience the unexpected and develop a quality of trust, relationship and obligation with others in the setting. (p. 49)

Further, as Cole (1991) argues, this form of participant observer research, combined with a key organisational role within the actual work environment (i.e. as an academic developer), offered extraordinary access to the organisation and its everyday information networks. It allows the collection of a wide range of internal situated data that otherwise would be very difficult to access. It also permits ready access to participants, management and importantly, the everyday affordances and impediments that reflect the reality of life within the case study sites and the university more generally.

From a theoretical standpoint, this opportunity for immersion was a critical advantage in developing the frame for this research. As Sannino et al. (2009) contend:

> First, activity theory is a practice-based theory. Second, it is a historical and future-orientated theory. We argue that there are methodological issues that distinguish an activity theoretical approach from traditional approaches to research. Activity theory involves the researcher throughout the course of the development, stagnation, or regression of the activities under scrutiny, as well as in the activities of the research subjects. This deep involvement in everyday human life is a crucial resource of activity theory. (p. 3)

The posture as *participant-observer* was made more feasible (and arguable more acceptable to the action research teams) as I had extensive experience—and resulting credibility—as an academic developer and student feedback administrator in a broader university role prior to the research study (as outlined in the Preface of this book). This meant a series of established direct relationships with many participants also already existed. Given I'd also had experience prior to the commencement of the action research in advising educational leaders in the faculty on academic development matters, there was less anxiety about the potential of the action research to generate disruptive or unproductive change that may have otherwise been the case.

Engaging Educational Leaders

Following the logic established earlier in this chapter, the educational leaders of the program were initially engaged to discuss the parameters of the action research model. These leaders included the Dean of the faculty, program conveners and academics who had experience in convening key subjects.

This was arranged as a facilitated discussion by the researcher and ran over a three-hour period. The session was recorded with the consent of the group and notes were taken by the researcher of then subsequently circulated to the group for confirmation.

The educational leaders first considered the anticipated focus of the action research and the potential for the elevated use of qualitative student feedback. It was quickly apparent that there was a shared disengagement from quantitative student feedback used broadly within the university.

A broad consensus emerged that the current evaluation model, though broadly informative as a metric of relative student opinion, had failed to provide useful or consistent insights for needed program improvement. This is well reflected in this observation by one of the leaders captured in this session:

> …there is no doubt the student voice is important, however what this voice is saying and what it is expressing needs to be more explicit if it is to be acted on. Too much emphasis is currently placed on knee-jerk reactions to numbers, sometimes doing more harm than good.

Participants in this discussion drew reference to the elevating significance of student feedback surveys in the university, with a recent policy introduced requiring programs to respond where ratings were beneath the universities average level. In discussion, the comparative value of qualitative student opinion surveys was also debated. Some differences became apparent about what were the appropriate levels of accountability to student opinion that academics should have to demonstrate.

This is captured in these contrasting responses below, where the tension between educational judgment and program reputation with students is evident:

> …the reality is that students are more than capable of making judgments about teaching, however the real question is how this is understood, and by who, and what it is weighed up against…it is one important input into judging teaching effectiveness, but one of many.

> ….students pay a considerable amount of money to study programs like ours and we need to know promptly and clearly when teachers are not meeting their expectations. Otherwise, we will lose students as word-of-mouth will undermine this program very quickly.

However, there was general agreement that current quantitative student feedback surveys lacked sufficient depth to effectively and consistently guide program development decisions. A number of examples were offered where conclusions had been drawn from student evaluation reports that had proven misleading and had subsequently led to poor decisions having been made.

This was observed as a particular danger where those without an intimate knowledge of the program, its trajectory or limitations may reach forms of arbitrary judgment. This sentiment was well captured in the commentary of one participant:

> ….there is a great temptation to simplify complex teaching and assessment situations to a number and make an equally simplistic judgment about the quality of the teacher or whatever….we have subjects (like on legislation) that are challenging that are always rated more negatively because students have preferred other types of subjects.

This led to a substantial discussion around how to maintain a reputation for quality in the university, within the industry and with regulators if conventional forms of student evaluation were disrupted. This was seen as a serious impediment to the action research approach being proposed. The group also debated the divergent research on quantitative student evaluation that was circulated by the researcher in advance of the discussion (summarised in Chap. 2).

It was broadly agreed that there were grounds for the developmental use of student feedback using an action research model. However, this model needed to represent a highly credible alternative to be accepted within the institution and by stakeholders outside the university. Lingering concerns clearly remained as to how be seen to be genuinely accountable in the absence of a defined metric.

Nevertheless, consensus was reached around the need for enhancing student learning to be the primary object of the action research model, rather than just the outcomes student feedback of itself. The tone of this consensus is reflected in this observation:

> In the end, student opinion is just reflecting the student view....we need to respect it of course, but we need to focus on the primary issue of creating the context for good curriculum, good teaching and good assessment. Student reactions are the outcome, not the core of our work here.

In considering the specific nature of the action research response, program leaders returned to how vulnerable the program was to the effect of inadequate student learning. Although the student evaluation results the program had received were on or above institutional averages, some sharp anxiety about the actual quality of student learning prevailed in the group.

Based on anecdotal evidence and several significant student complaints (ironically outside conventional student feedback mechanisms), the intuitive sense of these leaders was that such elements as the design of online teaching, assessment and feedback had the potential for improvement. They also aspired to broaden the pedagogy of the program to offer more innovative forms of learning, whilst also wanting to assure the educational foundations on which the program currently rested.

Yet there was also continuing unease on the viability of an ongoing action research project and the time demand it may place on teachers. There were several reasons for this. As outlined in the last chapter, in one of the programs most academics were engaged on part-time contracts and given their predominant roles as workplace practitioners, they spent limited time at the university.

Similarly, despite some attempts at professional development, most were 'accidental' teachers, engaged primarily (though not exclusively) for their discipline expertise. These teachers were also dispersed across three capital cities outside the city from where the program was offered. One participant observed this paradox as:

> ...a fragile balance between raising educational expectations whilst keeping these teachers on board....they have the capacity to simply not continue if they feel expectations of them by us exceed what they believe to be reasonable.

Equally, there were concerns about the potential resource implications of greater developmental imperatives being identified as a result of elevated student feedback data. Several participants raised another paradox around this matter: making more visible the limitations of student learning could increase academic dissatisfaction if these issues could not be effectively addressed.

Ultimately, a shared commitment developed to test broadened engagement with qualitative student feedback as a means of potential pedagogical improvement. It was also hoped that the action research may incite further engagement of the largely part time teaching workforce in the collective task of program enhancement. It was agreed that an introductory seminar involving all program teachers would be convened prior to the commencement of the following semester.

This seminar would be designed along the lines described in the previous chapter, with participating teachers being provided material in advance on the proposed CHAT-based, action research model and its motivation to enhance student learning and provide the opportunity for situated academic development.

Engaging Teachers in the Research

All available participants in the two programs were engaged in separate orientation sessions, which introduced the broad framework of the research project. The parallel motives of localised action to maximise the benefit of student opinion and contribution to broader theoretical knowledge in this domain were subsequently foregrounded. It was ensured that participants clearly understood these dual imperatives up front.

These sessions were timed to be well in advance of the start of the first semester of the action research to allow sufficient time for deliberation, formulation of approaches and the planning of research activities. As participants were largely unfamiliar with the process of action research—let alone its potential relationship with CHAT—materials were developed and circulated in advance of the sessions to allow advance organising of this proposition and to allow clarification and debate in the introductory sessions.

A model framed as an *expansive learning evaluation cycle* was proposed as a means of practically representing a possible broader use of the student voice. This explanatory device was designed to conceptualise the nature of a possible CHAT-based, action research cycle for discussion in introductory sessions. The model melded the conventional action research cycle associated with the work of Carr and Kemmis (1986), with the expansive learning cycle developed by Engeström (2001) and later further refined by Postholm (2009). It is illustrated in Fig. 4.1.

With its dual origins in CHAT and action research, this model was introduced by highlighting its foundational elements, which included:

- the framing of a CHAT-based, action research model that is focussed at the collective action at the program level (to stress integration and enhancement), centred on a research cycle driven by the outcomes qualitative student feedback and ongoing academic reflection

Fig. 4.1 Expansive learning evaluation cycle. Adapted from Carr and Kemmis (1986), Engeström (2001) and Postholm (2009)

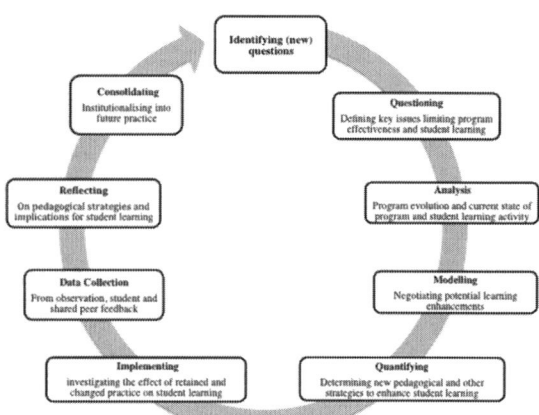

- the casting of the student voice as a potentially productive contributor to professional academic learning, through a reflective and ongoing action research collaboration with colleagues
- a focus on student learning outcomes, understood through a diverse range of professional inputs (but with the catalyst of student feedback) to identify program development opportunities
- determined attention to the perceived affordances and constraints on student learning (rather than on teachers, teaching and courses of themselves) to drive professional dialogue and pedagogical change
- a focus on situated forms of academic development, with responses designed to identified learning needs addressed collectively and individually within the potent reality of ongoing practice and tested for effectiveness in successive semesters
- a deepened recognition of the complex and often contradictory forces that play out in contemporary higher education learning environments.

An explicit protocol was negotiated with the two case study sites regarding the conduct of the research (and particularly my role as a *participant-observer*). The research was to be primarily designed as a form of critical ethnography, an approach that is characteristic of CHAT-based inquiry. This protocol clearly identified the action research teams as the primary initiators and drivers of the action research projects. The role of the *participant-researcher* was mutually agreed to be:

(a) introducing the CHAT-based, action research model and facilitating associated group workshops
(b) generating data and analysis around the qualitative student feedback data collected during the three semesters
(c) framing potential program and academic development options for teams to consider in collective dialogue
(d) providing ongoing advice during the projects (where this was sought by participants).

The teaching cohorts in each program and support staff (primarily educational designers) would form the action research teams. However, involvement would be voluntary and levels of input self-determined. This would form the basis for a series on action research cycles to be completed over three semesters, the outcomes of which would be critically assessed in comparison to the preceding use and impact of quantitative student feedback.

Based on the CHAT framework and drawing on the work of Norton (2009) on pedagogical action research in higher education settings, the primary imperatives of the empirical dimension of this research were:

- exploring and analysing the developmental potential of student feedback to influence and transform situated pedagogical practice in the identified programs
- conscious focus on the investigation of the tensions and contradictions inherent in the activity of student evaluation (and between inter-related activities that rely on its data)

- assessing the potential of this form of CHAT-based action research to stimulate developmental change and situated forms of academic development, evaluating the relative effectiveness of this approach compared to the use of orthodox quantitative student opinion data
- contributing to broader theoretical knowledge about the use of student feedback in contemporary higher education settings as a result of the action research outcomes.

Participants were introduced to, and then subsequently debated, the primary conflicts that have been identified in literature around academic teaching. This had a particular focus on where these issues intersected with student feedback. Within this broad framework, participants in the introductory seminars defined a series of critical questions they believed the action research projects should be seeking to address in the first semester of the project. These questions were refined by the researcher and returned to the teams for confirmation.

In the initial workshops, the identified tensions around existing quantitative forms of student evaluation generated considerable debate, as did their implications for the discipline-teaching context. Aggravating these tensions—characterised by Engeström (2000b) as creating *ethnography of trouble*—provided a productive framework for participants to explore the significant contradictions that were inherent in their educational roles within the College, in their relationships with the profession and importantly in their relationship with students.

These contradictions—formed in collective dialogue as abstractions and essentially at a distance from individual practice—sparked fundamental debates about the nature and significance of these relationships. For some participants, this resulted in the opportunity for the first time to understand these issues as broader systemic limitations, rather than as personal failure. This provided a potent means for contemplating new ways of working.

Others clearly saw this as an act of over-intellectualising (or at least over-complicating) the relationships between academic, students and the profession. This was memorably summarised by one participant as it being only about 'creating a lot of heat, but not much light'. This was a critique that elicited some support from experienced teachers who had 'seen it all before', offering variously sceptical (and at times cynical) reactions to the conception of teaching as a 'complex' activity.

Reflecting a strongly pragmatic approach, this perspective saw inevitable dangers in making anything more visible so as to bring additional scrutiny or judgment. Here an explicit preference was expressed for rational and explicit goals that simply offered a defined approach to identified tasks. As Engeström (2000b) notes, such a motive is inherently individualistic and acts as a brake on major change. As such, it represented an antithesis of the CHAT-based, action research approach that underpinned this work, in that it denied the fundamental collective and object-orientated orientation of the model.

This range of responses to student feedback provides a useful insight into the differing reactions it provokes in academic teaching contexts. It suggests that assumptions about the largely homogenous impact of student feedback on academic teaching may not necessarily well grounded in the complex social realities of the contemporary university.

Nevertheless, some broad (albeit grudging) consensus was reached around the key questions that these tensions implied for educational practices. Further, it was significant that across the two workshops that CHAT-informed, action research was considered to at least have some potential to generate new and expanded dialogue and develop pedagogical practice.

This outcome suggested that despite the differing perceptions of the value of student feedback, some common recognition existed across teaching academics that the student voice may have an inherent form of value. Essential to this acceptance was the re-assertion of individual academic judgment in the consideration of student feedback. This was significant as this was to largely evaporate in the new 'public' university student evaluation system, which many academics saw leaving them to either defend or ignore student rating outcomes.

The action research framework provided some assurance of a transparent and broadly democratic means of collectively considering the outcomes generated from students. In this volatile context, a student evaluation model centred on qualitative student data and collective forms of dialogue about improvement was generally regarded as a productive step.

However, early fractures developed within the action research teams that roughly mirrored differences in organisational roles and employment status (described in more detail in the last chapter).

It was program leaders in both programs who were generally more active in identifying potential responses to student feedback in the subsequent action research cycles. Sessional teachers demonstrated responses that reflected anxieties about the overcomplicating of the teaching function through the perceived over-analysis of student feedback.

Others in tenured academic roles tended to more frequently seek to rapidly distil and simplify outcomes to address apparent problems. Some lingering discord over recent contested changes to teaching approaches (particularly around the greater use of online learning strategies) further complicated this fracturing. This meant in workshops, attempts to redefine research questions tended to be dominated by program leaders, with largely peripheral input being provided by others. This forced the guiding action research questions to be formulated in very general form.

As will be detailed in subsequent chapters, this complex topology was to become more significant as the action research progressed during the three semesters. These fractures in the teams were to become increasingly influential in the later semesters, somewhat paradoxically coinciding with broad program improvements as a result of heightened engagement with student feedback and professional dialogue.

Data Collection Methods

Given the inherently interactive nature of participatory action research, the researcher is necessarily intrusive. They work with participants to frame questions, to create provocations and gather data important to the questions being explored in the broader research inquiry (Marshall and Rossman 1999).

However, as Cole (1991) observes, when the researcher undertakes this form of research within a broader organisational development role, they necessarily adopt an even greater interventionist persona. This has the effect of further blurring the demarcations between these researcher and developmental roles. This means that the nature of data collection is also inevitably subject to heightened personal subjectivities and more difficult to isolate from existing understandings of the situational context in which such data is collected.

In this research, this is further complicated by the fact that the CHAT was guiding the design of the overall research, as well as the design of the action research approach employed as a fundamental driver of the case studies themselves. For these range of reasons, the data collection process needed to be carefully conceived and managed to ensure trustworthiness and limit potential imposed subjectivities that could hinder its reliability.

Consequently, aside from establishing the protocols for the role of the researcher and action research teams outlined earlier, a series of other strategies were put in place including the:

- collection of data from multiple perspectives, including from the participants working as an action research team as well as individually, from students and from artefacts generated before, during and after the action research process (providing triangulation)
- testing and modification of key data with action research participants, such as the outcomes of action research, analysis of student feedback and individual interview responses (providing verification)
- recording and/or systematic collection of 'thick data' from student feedback, action research workshops and interviews to ensure a depth and breadth of analysis (providing complexity).

The range of empirical data collected in the case studies is summarised in Table 4.1.

The nature of the CHAT-informed, action research model used in multi-dimensional form to drive these case studies had important implications for what and how data was to be collected. Firstly, it meant an emphasis in framing appropriate data collection methods to ensure the accurate mapping of the 'structure of the transformations made (so they) can be retraced and critically reflected' (Langemeyer and Nissen 2006, p. 190). Essential to this was the collection of data that was sufficiently broad to consider what evidence of learning and change emerged with the aggravation of the tensions and contradictions generated by the *expansive learning evaluation cycle* (described earlier in this chapter).

Table 4.1 Sources of data for the empirical stage of the research

Data form	Source	Form of capture
Preliminary orientating interviews	Program leaders (Program Directors and Subject Convenors)	Field notes
Proceedings and reflections on initial orientation workshops	Action research teams	Field notes, session recording, written respondent feedback
Qualitative student feedback (over three semesters)	Student responses to qualitative questionnaires/semi-structure interviews (over three semesters)	Online qualitative questionnaires or interview records
Proceedings and reflections on end-of-semester and pre-semester workshops of action research teams (over three semesters)	Action research teams	Field notes, session recording, written respondent feedback
Individual interviews for action research teams members at conclusion of the three semesters	Action research team members	Field notes and recordings
Key program artefacts	Program documentation, minutes, reports and related actions generated during the action research	Collection of relevant artefacts for analysis

Engeström (2007a) suggests evidence of what he defines as *expansive learning* is where an activity system resolves 'pressing internal contradictions by constructing and implementing a qualitative new way of functioning for itself' (p. 24). Such expansive learning is reflected most acutely in:

(a) the broadening of the shared objects of professional work to seek to identify and respond to problems
(b) the development of new forms of knowledge and tools to engage with identified problems
(c) lived, yet invisible, cognitive trails of reformed work
      (Daniels 2008; Engeström 2007b).

Hence, in order to understand the potential expansive learning in these case studies, the framing of data collection was around these three key points of potential reformulation in pedagogical activity: reformed approaches to teaching, generation of new or modified shared objects and the 'invisible' experiences of participants in the action research.

There are clear strengths in an immersive form of research engagement for enhanced data collection as a result of proximity, access and subsequently, deepened analysis. Nevertheless, there are also inevitably weaknesses that need to be recognised and managed. The proximity and access of the researcher to the object of study means that it was consistently difficult to clearly demarcate the academic developer versus researcher role. This resulted in a series of limitations that will be further explored in later chapters.

However, it is reasonable to conclude that the organisational and positional power held the researcher demonstrably distorted some outcomes. Further, as is not uncommon in qualitative study, the effect of being studied in-depth in action (the so-called *Hawthorne effect*) inevitably changed how participants acted and responded, despite the longitudinal nature of the action research cycles. Finally, the case studies represented the reality of a specific spatial and temporal reality, which inevitably shaped and contextualised the data the case studies generated.

Forms of Data Interpretation

Consistent with the methodology of this research, data collected from participants and students was interpreted using a broad thematic coding method, which is characterised by Marshall and Rossman (1999) as *emergent intuitive*. This relies on the immersive and intuitive capabilities of the researcher to develop emergent themes for analysis of the data.

To effectively manage this, a seven-stage model for thematic analysis was designed. This is framed by the thematic analysis framework for pedagogical action research in universities developed by Norton (2009) and integrates in its stages approaches for specifically analysing CHAT data offered by Langemeyer and Nissen (2006). This adaptation took the form outlined in Table 4.2.

The samples of data presented from the two case study chapters which follow is descriptively categorised according to its method and time of collection. For example, the category *A-2-12*, indicates firstly it was the data was collected in the first program, or 'B' in the case of the second program). The second number used

Table 4.2 Data interpretation method

Stage	Activity
One	Immersion: comprehensive consideration of collected data, including its cultural-historical mediation and broad relationship to frames of expansive learning (outlined above). Consideration of broad initial categories
Two	Generating categories: initial identification of emerging categories in the data, particularly around developmental change (or its absence)
Three	Deleting categories: identifying categories where there is insufficient justification for it to be considered significant compared to other identified
Four	Generating themes: identifying and theoretically organising key themes where commonalities have emerged
Five	Checking themes: ensuring thematic allocations are reasonable and defensible, particularly from a theoretical and methodological perspective
Six	Linking themes: establishing the possible inter-relationship between identified themes
Seven	Presenting outcomes and methodological reflections

Adapted from Norton (2009) and Langemeyer and Nissen (2006)

represents the instance it was collected, such as at a workshop, in an evaluative response post-workshop or a semi-structured interview. The final number represents the respondent identifier used in collecting the data. All other data is reported according to its specific description, but is formed around the broader range of sources included in Table 4.2.

Conclusion

This chapter introduced the two CHAT-based, action research case studies designed to investigate the potentiality of the student voice to enhance pedagogical practices in higher education settings. The importance of these foundations—the sociocultural framing of CHAT and the dynamic created by the action research model—were explained for their relevance to this form of research approach. In addition, why this framework offered a viable qualitative research approach for this form of study was examined. The chapter also sought to provide a description of the specific framework adopted to define, collect, thematically code and analyse data in the research period of three teaching semesters. This underpinning provides an important context for understanding the data generated in the qualitative case studies that will be detailed in the next two chapters.

Chapter 5
Student Evaluation in Situated Practice—The Case of a Recently Designed Program

Abstract Student evaluation in contemporary higher education environments operates within the increasingly contesting activities of institutional quality assurance, individual performance management and its original objective of improving the quality of higher education teaching and learning. Moreover, the elevation of comparative quality assurance metrics across the sector and within institutions has all but assured that quantitative measurement of teaching, teachers and/or courses is institutionalised as a privileged metric in institutional, supervisor, student, academic and, even at some levels, community understandings of effective teaching practice. In this chapter, the outcomes of the first of two case studies exploring an alternative expansive use of the student voice are detailed. This case study—undertaken within a large, dynamic and relatively new teaching program—was designed to assess whether collective pedagogical practices could be enhanced using an evaluative cycle framed around qualitative student evaluation data and based on collaborative forms of academic dialogue. The outcomes of the case study reaffirm the powerful influence of orthodox quantitative evaluation, as well as the potentiality in the more expansive use of student voice as a catalyst for educational development. However, the influence of differing forms of academic employment, the disproportionate influence of the divergent motives of programs leaders and the dilemmas of sustaining the levels of enthusiasm for a more intensive model of student evaluation significantly impacted on the effectiveness of the evaluative cycles.

Keywords Qualitative student evaluation · Case study research · Pedagogical improvement · Employment fragmentation in higher education · Expansive learning

Introduction

This chapter explores the outcomes of the first of the two CHAT-based, action research case studies investigating the developmental potential of an alternative qualitative form of student feedback. This research, conducted over eighteen

© Springer International Publishing Switzerland 2016
S. Darwin, *Student Evaluation in Higher Education*,
DOI 10.1007/978-3-319-41893-3_5

months in a significant program in a major Australian university, sought to investigate whether the more collective consideration of this data had the potential to improve both professional academic dialogue and ongoing pedagogical practice.

The foundation of this action research was the *expansive learning evaluation cycle* introduced earlier, which was designed in an attempt to generate more meaningful and professionally engaging use of student feedback. This had the objective of sparking more productive collective deliberation and debate amongst teachers around prospective improvements to program design, teaching and assessment in order to enhance student learning.

The site of this first case study was centred in a department primarily responsible for offering a major and highly visible postgraduate program (with approximately 500 student enrolments per year). This program is offered in multiple sites across the country using a blended delivery model, pairing a series of face-to-face introductory workshops, online modules and ongoing online engagement.

The program was relatively recent in its formation, having only been first offered in 2006. However, given the dynamic nature of the sub-discipline and the sustained competitive pressures on the program, it had been subject to ongoing reformation of its content and modes of delivery since this time.

The program was jointly delivered by a three full-time academic staff and around 20 part-time teaching academics, most of whom are workplace-based. This academic workforce composition was a consequence of a range of factors, including:

- highly variable enrolment levels and the dispersed delivery mode, which requires considerable staffing flexibility
- the dynamic and complex nature of the discipline
- the recent establishment of the program, which essentially meant that its employment practices reflected the changing nature of academic engagement in universities
- the difficulty of attracting and retaining experienced practitioners into full-time academic work, given the income disparity between work-based and academic environments.

At the time the research commenced, the program was generally considered to be broadly successful and had retained a relatively consistent student load since its introduction. However, as was the case with other universities offering similar programs, there was considerable competitive pressure between institutions for a limited number of potential students. There was also significant regulatory scrutiny of courses by the industry and government regulators.

Hence, this site was selected as it met a range of criteria for the study (these were detailed in the previous chapter). The area offered a large-scale teaching program with complex curriculum assessment demands, seeking to enhance both its credibility and responsiveness (including from student feedback) to improve its pedagogy. It also had previous experience with the quantitative university student evaluation system and possessed an openness to engage in collaborative action research around the elevated use of student feedback.

Initial Activities to Formulate the Action Research

As detailed in the last chapter, initially the educational leaders of the program were engaged to discuss the parameters of the action research model. Following on from the consensus reached in this forum, an introductory workshop was convened pre-semester involving all 24 teachers teaching from the program.

The session was framed by an introduction to the broad research project around the use of student feedback in higher education. The *expansive learning evaluation cycle* and a supporting rationale was also circulated in advance to participants to allow some opportunity for reflection on what was being proposed.

The general reaction to this introductory workshop was characterized by some reluctance and suspicion as to the motives for elevating the significance of the student voice in the teaching process. Similarly, subsequent discussion was centred on clarifying questions and often-sceptical commentary on the proposed approach. There was little evidence of the genuine engagement essential for productive action research.

As one participant recorded in their assessment of this part of the day:

> I was really unclear about why we needed to have such an elaborate model as presented….surely just focusing on where we were falling short of student expectations and developing some thinking around this would be sufficient. (A-2-21)

It was quickly apparent that even though the approach had been framed with an action research focus, the CHAT dimensions of the model proved overly complex and somewhat confusing for most participants. This is perhaps unsurprising given the overwhelming majority of participants were part-time academics who would have had limited exposure to this epistemological sphere.

For this reason, the theoretical foundations of the approach were subsequently minimised in the remainder of the session. A clearer and more practical focus developed around the more familiar action research cycle (i.e. reflect-plan-act-observe-reflect). It was apparent from participant responses that this was a more effective orientation. A typical evaluative response was:

> …I really struggled to understand the first session, but when we began to discuss the 'how-to' of action research and what we might look at in this process, it was much clearer. I could begin to see some benefit for us spending the time needed to make this work worthwhile. (A-2-13)

Participants in this component of the introductory session were generally more engaged—exploring and debating approaches to action research based on thinking provided in advance on the developmental potential of student feedback. Much of this was stimulated by a series of provocations prepared for the workshop on the nature of the existing curricula, learning activities and assessment, and how these compared leading forms on innovative practice in the higher education sector.

Based on this analysis, participating teachers spent the final two sessions devising and then refining a broad action research framework to guide the first semester of the cycle. Teachers debated what specific issues could be researched using student feedback in order to improve the pedagogy and effectiveness of the program. The broad framework for the action research was captured on the day and subsequently re-circulated to the group and refined to until broad agreement was reached amongst participating group members. This agreed framework is reproduced below:

Agreed Action Research Cycle—Case Study One

Stage One (pre-semester): Framing the action research

- identification of the range of issues that need to be considered to potentially improve student learning outcomes
- collaborative review of existing curricula, learning outcomes, learning activities and assessment and consideration of alternative approaches to teaching and learning, including those used in other universities in discipline area and in other disciplines
- negotiation of potential learning enhancements and formulation of collaborative responses
- formulation of research questions around enhanced learning effectiveness to be individually and collaboratively investigated
- identification academic development and educational design needs for the semester
- publishing of any agreed changes and research questions.

Stage Two (during semester): Ongoing professional inquiry and dialogue

- implementation of agreed learning approaches by individual academics or group collectively
- critical action research based enquiry of student learning outcomes, using a variety of sources including professional sense, student feedback, peer input and research outcomes.
- publishing of individual research outcomes in a collective space (such as a wiki or blog).

Stage Three (end of semester): Review Conference or Seminar

- collaborative reflection on action research outcomes and determination of future responses (such as to institutionalise, expand further, modify or abandonment)
- publish outcomes and identify opportunities for future expansive potential for the program or sub-discipline (i.e. new questions).

Formulating Evaluative Questions

There was a reasonable straightforward consensus achieved around the nature of the action research framework—albeit with some reservations about additional workloads. However, there was more significant debate about the questions that would guide the action research itself (and therefore the data that would be canvassed from students).

After assessing a range of possible action research questions generated by small groups, a series of broad questions were agreed around learning enablers, impediments and program learning activities, as well as on assessment and feedback strategies. After a clarifying debate, the teaching group resolved a series of research questions are detailed below.

Action Research Questions—Case Study One

1. *Effectiveness of assessment design*

   - Have we developed appropriate structures and reliable consistency across the range of student assessment and in specific subjects?
   - What could be improved in how we assess across the program and in specific subjects to enhance student learning?

2. *Blended teaching and learning*

   - How effective have we been as blended teachers this semester: have we been clear about our roles and have we improved levels of student engagement?
   - Were we able to effectively use the potential of the online innovations to improve student learning?
   - What other online resources could we add to the online platform to improve the quality of online teaching and student engagement?
   - Are there professional development areas that would assist to improve the quality of our online learning?

3. *Future directions*

   - Are students being effectively exposed to the emerging trends in the sub-discipline?
   - If not, what may need to be added or highlighted to improve graduate capabilities?
   - With the continued discussion about the introduction of additional higher-level programs, what do we need to consider from this program level?

Based on these research questions, a series of directly related qualitative student feedback questions were to be designed by the researcher to inform the professional deliberations of the teaching group. However, considerable tension emerged in the final stages of the workshop around how student feedback data would be presented, who would draw implications from it and how the individual and institutional responsibilities for outcomes would be reported and understood.

Following this, several participants began to doubt the viability of the action research process itself. Representing this, as one participant noted in their assessment of the session:

> It is all well and good to investigate at a 'deeper' level, but the university is still going to make judgments and more extensive data may only lead to more developed conclusions about the teaching approaches….it is essential that more evaluation doesn't just lead to more blame. (A-2-17)

The semi-structured interviews with individual teachers (detailed in Chapter 3) provided a clear logic for this anxiety. A significant number of teachers reported feeling unsettled and even undermined by previous student feedback ratings they had received. For some, the demands for explanation for these quantitative outcomes by program leaders only accentuated this anxiety about student feedback.

To counteract this anxiety, program leaders (in tandem with the researcher) needed to negotiate a series of commitments to secure the confidence of teachers to engage in the action research process. These four explicit commitments included that:

- the focus of data collected would be on student learning (as implied directly by the proposed model) rather than narrowed to teaching performativity
- consideration of qualitative student opinion would be mediated by the researcher and thematically coded, so the primary issues of concern would be debated (rather than matters of individual performance)
- the professional insights of teaching academics would be foregrounded as a key mediating factor in considering student responses
- to ensure transparency, issues emerging from student feedback and related professional dialogue would be collectively considered in a similarly convened end-of-semester forum, as well as progressively during the semester via online forums.

Having broadly addressed these concerns, teachers then considered what evaluative questions may be asked of students. The researcher-facilitator provided some guidance on possible questions that may naturally flow from the earlier determined action research questions. Based on this advice, teachers devised a series of open-ended qualitative questions that would be put to students via an online survey toward the conclusion of the semester.

Initial Student Evaluation Questions: Semester One

1. What elements of this subject were most effective in assisting your learning in this <subject of the program>?

2. What elements of this subject made learning in this <subject> more difficult?
3. How effective was the assessment in developing your understanding of this <subject>?
4. How useful was the feedback you received in clarifying your understanding of this <subject>?
5. How effectively did you think this subject related to other subjects in the Program?
6. From your experience in this subject, what changes would you suggest for this subject in the future to make it more effective?
7. Do you have any other comments on this subject or the program more generally?

In addition, teachers agreed to participate in an ongoing professional dialogue with peers throughout the semester, both informally and via a blog that centred on the key evaluative questions defined in the pre-workshop. To facilitate this, the researcher established a series of blogs (using an online collaborative blogging software tool) around the three key areas identified in the action research questions.

A further development workshop was scheduled for the end of the semester where this dialogue and student opinion outcomes would be considered, developmental options and impediments identified and actions for implementation defined.

Outcomes of the First Action Research Semester

Despite the commitments given in the introductory workshop, teachers were quite reluctant to participate in online professional dialogue around the three identified areas of action research focus during the first semester. Only 16 of the 24 teachers offered posts, and the total number of posts throughout the semester was only 36.

Moreover, most commentaries were brief and not clearly related to the questions posed in the research. Instead they were largely anecdotal accounts of incidents or problems in practice. This participation was far less than anticipated in the overall research design and in the action research model itself. Program leaders speculated that this low engagement partly related to teachers working remotely and not feeling either connection with peers or the collective ambition of the original action research plan.

Ongoing feedback from teachers during the semester also suggested some frustration and/or unfamiliarity with the technology, yet improved instructions and online encouragement to participate failed to improve responses.

However, subsequent analysis of the end-of-semester workshop suggested this was instead more a result of unfamiliarity with blogging, a reluctance to publicly speculate on student learning and limited confidence in having a useful perspective to offer. Whether this was characteristic of this specific teaching group, or a more flawed assumption in the research model is a matter that became more apparent in further semesters (this will be returned to later in the chapter). However, this limited response in the first semester meant only a small amount of useful data was generated that could be meaningfully considered.

Toward the end of semester, students were asked to respond to the series of qualitative evaluative questions formulated in the introductory seminar. The survey was administered by the researcher and offered to students using the online Survey Monkey tool, with an initial email and two follow up emails all carrying an embedded link to the survey. The survey was completely anonymously.

By the conclusion of the survey period, 102 responses to the qualitative questionnaire were submitted across the four subjects of the program. This represented an acceptable response rate of around 30 % and was broadly similar to the response rates for previous quantitative surveys for this group.

However, unlike previous quantitative evaluations, the open-ended questionnaire generated a considerable amount of data—in excess of 20,000 words of student feedback on their learning. Although responses ranged significantly from great detail to superficial overview, much of the data was rich in form and usefully related to the action research questions that framed the feedback.

By coincidence, a government regulator had also decided to conduct their standard cross-university quantitative survey during this same semester. In effect, this meant students were asked to complete both a qualitative and quantitative survey for the same subjects. The outcomes of this survey, which generated 118 responses to a series of standard quantitative student evaluation questions using a Likert-type scale, were also made available to the researcher. This data provided a useful comparator in later analysis of the outcomes of the qualitative data.

The extensive data emerging from the qualitative student survey was thematically coded and analysed, along with the more modest data generated via the teacher blogs. As Glense (2006) observes, thematic analysis is the most widely accepted means of data analysis in the sociological tradition. It allows the researcher to effectively segregate qualitative data into clusters for further description and systematic analysis. To develop the analysis in this and the second case study, thematic coding was emergent in form. For instance, as a result of some difficulties in category coding, a second taxonomy was developed to assist in analysis.

This second layer employed the categories proposed by Cresswell (2005): ordinary themes, unexpected themes, hard-to-classify themes and finally, major and minor themes. In considering student and teacher responses, the themes were allowed to naturally emerge from the data without preconceived expectations of clusters, though the emergent themes were also broadly framed in the language and context of the program itself.

This provided utility for developing a report for the action research team, as well as providing a valuable data set for the broader research intent of considering the developmental potential of student opinion.

Based on this data analysis, an *Evaluation and Course Development Report* was produced by the researcher for consideration by the action research team. This report sought to illuminate the key thematic outcomes emerging from the data and the broad program and course development issues these outcomes implied. In summary, the outcomes of this analysis of the data was that:

- a significant majority of students were broadly satisfied with their learning experience in the program.
- there were clear indications that as the program and its learning approaches were maturing and that student learning was improving.
- the efforts of teachers to facilitate the program was generally highly regarded and valued, with a large number of students singling out teachers for high-level acclaim.
- most students thought that flexible access to online resources, forums, quizzes and live classrooms was a major positive in the design of the program.
- several elements of the programs were highly regarded as contributing to learning (most notably face-to-face intensives, discussion forums, assignments and quizzes).
- there were widespread reservations amongst many student as well as teachers about the value, credibility and relevance of the mandatory exams as a form of assessment that was seen seriously inhibiting the ability of the program to broaden and innovate in the learning approaches it could adopt.
- the onerous time limitations on subjects were a source of considerable student and teacher anxiety and frustration, especially around the ability of students to absorb and reflect to the level of knowledge required for both assessment and later workplace practice.
- there was also considerable anxiety over the reliability and accessibility of the multiple technologies being used by the program.
- there was some apparent tension between students with differing levels of familiarity with subject areas prior to commencement, resulting in perceptions about inequitable levels of participation in discussion questions and unrealistic entry-level knowledge expectations.

The *Evaluation and Course Development Report* also offered stimulus questions that could be usefully considered in order to potentially develop the program and student learning. These questions were developed around the issues emerging from student responses.

Course development issues identified from first semester student feedback

(a) How can forms of assessment (and the exams specifically) more reliably and validly assess the knowledge, skills and capabilities that are taught in the program and required for workplace practice?
(b) How can the limited teaching periods be further enhanced to allow students to sense they are sufficiently prepared for assessment and later practice?
(c) How can the online learning technologies used in the subjects be more effectively harnessed to enhance the student learning experience?
(d) Can we create a greater sense of a community of practice between students within the subjects as a means of allowing greater self-direction, more equitable online participation and peer support?

(e) Are there strategies to engender clearer student expectations and related teacher-student protocols that would increase student certainty around subjects and the program more generally?

(f) What changes may create the foundation for an even more positive learning environment for students to enhance their overall experience in the qualification?

Consistent with the agreed action research model, a two-day, post-program workshop was convened immediately at the end of the semester. This workshop included 21 of the 24 teachers engaged in the action research.

The key focus of the workshop was the data and conclusions drawn in this first *Evaluation and Course Development Report*. In introducing the data to the workshop, participants were encouraged to critically reflect on both their personal and shared experiences during the semester, and to identify potential program development options from this debate.

Further, consistent with the underpinning CHAT foundations of the action research model, participants were encouraged to consider the complex, and at times contradictory, expectations of pedagogical practice the report raised.

As a result, a novel focus of this collaborative dialogue was the discussion of the tensions emerging in the feedback outcomes and what would be classed in CHAT terms as their expansive learning potential. The broad primary tensions that were identified and debated included the tension between such things as:

- pedagogical expectations of professional self direction in learning and the pragmatic student drive for expedient completion of specified learning and assessment activities
- exploratory engagement in professional practice discourses and the largely rigid demands of required professional–vocational competencies at the completion of the program
- the rich and collaborative learning engagement possible via simulated learning technologies and the individualised nature of study which used inter-subjective professional contexts of judgment
- differing formal and informal pedagogical approaches designed by teachers and educational designers in the program, from simulation in a virtual environment, to scaffolded building of professional capability to assessment of student responses against 'real' interpretations of professional practice.

This formed the foundation for workshop dialogue, which also explored a range of course development options (and possible enabling pedagogies) for enhancing student learning. Further details of how these tensions were understood by participants—and the range of responses developed in response—are outlined in detail in Appendix 2.

As a result of this collaborative academic dialogue, the final session of this first post-semester workshop formalised a series of specific response strategies (in the form of a *Course Development Plan*) for implementation in the following semester. These would also frame the further deliberations of the action research teams in the following semester.

In addition, the *Course Development Plan* anticipated a series of related professional development initiatives to support these enhancements. It also envisaged longer-term educational design projects that could be productive to further improve program effectiveness.

The primary course development elements of the plan included:

(a) encouraging stronger and earlier student engagement with learning materials
(b) enhanced sharing of online discussion stimulus activities
(c) establish clearer expectations around teacher and student responsibilities
(d) more active forms of collaborative engagement with student blogging responses
(e) building a key point of assessable continuity throughout the subjects of the course
(f) ensuring online modules are available well in advance of face-to-face sessions with students to improve integration of the subject components
(g) creating a stronger online student community across all sites.

In addition, some immediate academic development initiatives were planned around the improved use of online classroom technologies, design of practical cases and more effective facilitation of blogging.

Analysis of the First Cycle of Action Research-Evaluation

In reflecting on field notes from the introductory and post-semester workshops, it is apparent the action research project was a complex and at times contrived episode for many of the participating teachers. This conclusion was subsequently confirmed in later individual interviews (this detailed further later in this chapter).

In the introductory workshop, the researcher encountered dual scepticism. This was firstly a product of lingering anxiety and uncertainty about the outcomes of previous quantitative evaluation (undertaken by both the university and the regulator).

Secondly, it arose from the complex and even more disruptive form of elevated student feedback being proposed in this project. It was also the case that few in the group had any experience or even familiarity with the action research model, let alone its underpinning CHAT foundation. What this resulted in was an action research group that was overly dependent on the researcher in its initial work (and even to some extent in its later work).

At one level, given an element of the research was to explore situated forms of academic development, this became also an opportunity to engage this action research team in critical analysis within authentic pedagogical practice.

However, at another level, as I withdrew as the semester progressed and more conclusively in the post-semester workshop, action research participants tended to retreat into more functionally driven responses to the complex and rich data that the qualitative student feedback was generating.

Despite the *Evaluation and Course Development Report* highlighting a range of potential improvement options (which would be the orthodox advice of academic developers), the team opted merely to bring forward the release of learning materials and elevate expectations of student engagement.

This example pointed to another broader limitation: though the action research (drawing on its CHAT foundation) highlighted a range of contradictory imperatives that emerged in and within the student and teacher data, solutions defined tended to be the most obvious responses and, at times, even simplistic in form.

As the primary discourses noted in the field notes for the post-semester workshop illuminated, the orientation of the action research became instrumental in focus and single loop in form—that is, 'what is the problem and how do we fix it'.

Yet the framework of the overarching learning evaluation model was orientated toward more paradigmatic objectives: the double loop learning of not just correcting problems but critically reflecting and evaluating the very frames of reference that bounded pedagogies in use.

This initial outcome underpinned the power of what Stacey (2000) describes as shared mental models in organisational practice. The disruptive effect of the action research approach was clearly insufficient to displace the more familiar shared responses to student feedback outcomes. In this first semester of CHAT-based action research, the significant challenge of disrupting the socially negotiated understandings on teaching and learning practices (and their improvement) was clearly demonstrated. The discord between the modest instrumental outcomes generated from the rich and complex student feedback data was apparent. This dissonance was also evident to participants. This was captured most acutely in an incidental conversation at the final break of the post-semester workshop, where one participant wryly observed:

> …well that was a lot of work for not much return….perhaps next semester we could streamline the process and just identify the things that need tweaking rather than look in such depth at everything. (A3-117)

Similarly, in wrapping up the final workshop, the program convener made this telling conclusion:

> …we have discovered a great deal about the program through this process, we know now what are the key challenges and we just need to now act on these few things so our future evaluations will tell the story of the changes we made here. (A-3-119)

This well reflected dissonance between the complex and even at times contradictory data generated by the evaluation-research method and the actual course and academic development outcomes resolved by the action research team. This indicated that the action research had developed an incidental rather than ongoing character. It also suggested that the form of data generated was neither sufficiently engaging nor accessible to inspire actions beyond the instrumental.

Outcomes of the Second Action Research Semester

Despite the limitations emerging in the outcomes from the first semester, at the first post-semester workshop the action research team resolved to continue the model for a second semester.

However, some reservations were emerging amongst both program leaders and participants given the now apparent imbalance between the extent of data generated and the actual outcomes it produced. Participants had agreed to use the same questions and data collection approaches as used in the first semester.

Yet in contrast to the considerable unanimity to date, this decision was not universally agreed. Several members of the action research team began to more publicly express anxiety about the limited student feedback on their individual subjects or specific issues they were concerned about.

Similarly, the program convener expressed private doubts about the loss of the ability to use student feedback to scrutinise the performance of individual teaching academics. As this pressure grew, it was became apparent that some more subject-specific data would need to be included in the *Evaluation and Course Development Report* (should this emerge in sufficient definition to be meaningful).

In the second semester, 91 students contributed evaluation responses to the qualitative questionnaire across the four subjects of the Graduate Certificate program. This again represented a reasonable response rate of around 30 % and was broadly similar to the response rates for previous semester.

Similarly, in common with the previous semester, the open-ended questionnaire generated a considerable amount of data—this time around 18,000 words of student feedback on their learning. Again responses ranged significantly from great detail to superficial overview. Ten of the 22 program teachers contributed their thoughts about the effectiveness of the program using an online blog. From this data, a second *Evaluation and Course Development Report* was generated, which used a similar format to the first (though including more subject-specific observations).

It was apparent that a range of significant student frustrations expressed by students in the previous evaluation (in regard to such things as exam preparation, alignment of activities and assessment, instructions, equitable participation and the online site) had receded considerably in this evaluation. Put simply, the student feedback outcomes in this second semester suggested the instrumental steps taken in the previous semester had seemingly addressed some of the key problems identified.

Nevertheless, some problems remained and others had emerged (with some a direct result of changes made in the previous semester). These related to course design, student workloads, quality of feedback, differential levels of teacher engagement and forms of assessment. Reflecting this, the following questions were generated for the action research team to consider from the thematic analysis of student feedback:

(a) Are there strategies to increase the time students have to review and reflect on learning materials (to militate against the relatively short teaching sessions)?

(b) Are we offering too many discussion forums, are the forum questions engaging and open enough and are they clearly aligned to student learning progress through the subject?

(c) How can feedback be improved and made more consistent to enhance student learning?

(d) Is there a need to develop a broader and richer range of case studies and related client files to provide more selection options for students?

(e) Is there a means of enhancing the online face-to-face connection by the limited introduction of tutorials?

(f) Are we developing quizzes at the right level and can these also be morphed into forms of exam preparation?

(g) Is sufficient allowance provided for a) some of the specialist interests of students and b) submission and other forms of writing?

(h) Can we provide scaffolded support for oral assessments (and can these be made more authentic)?

(i) What are the alternatives to the current online blogs and the response to the seeming unreliability of online communication software?

As with the previous semester, 19 of the 22 teachers teaching that semester met for a post-semester action research workshop. In advance of this workshop, participants were provided both a copy of the *Evaluation and Course Development Report* for the semester, and the previously developed stimulus document—*Issues, tensions and potential options identified in evaluation process*.

Program teachers met over two days and debated the evaluation report and considered options for further course development raised by the questions emerging from data. I played a limited facilitation role in the workshop; primarily introducing the *Evaluation and Course Development Report* and then allowing the action research team to further consider the data and possible responses.

As a result of this dialogue, the action research team defined a series of course development responses including:

- providing more open forms of access to intending students to allow great opportunities for early engagement
- limiting the number of discussion forums to a core that were actively facilitated by designated teachers to ensure the forums actually contributed to interaction and student learning
- developing assessment rubrics to make assessment feedback more consistent across subjects and developing associated guidelines on providing effective feedback that aids student learning

- working on the redevelopment of current case studies over the next two semesters, with an objective of stronger and more tangible alignment to the core client file assessment tool
- seeking budget support to expand the number of face-to-face tutorials in order to enhance student engagement
- redesigning quizzes so they are more aligned to the learning outcomes for each subject and the eventual assessments students will undertake
- over the next two semesters, reviewing the course as a whole to look to introduce opportunities across subjects for developing specialist interests
- persuading the regulator the need for enhanced focus on writing skills (as it is currently outside the registration requirements tested in formal assessment
- developing additional learning materials for supporting oral assessment, including the inclusion of 'model' presentations to assist student prepare for delivery
- investigating the pilot next semester of alternative online technologies for student blogs and inter-communication.

The action research team also defined developing and improving assessment rubrics and designing feedback for student learning as priorities for academic development leading up to, and during the following semester.

In this second semester, the discourse of the action researchers was again largely dominated by a similar instrumental drive to that emerging in the first semester. Interestingly, the introduction of subject-specific data created new tensions as individual participants defended or assailed particular outcomes. A noticeable breakdown in the social solidarity of the group occurred at these points.

However, there was equally evidence in the outcomes of some maturing of the collective inquiry model and some indication of a deeper level of engagement. Indeed, in this second semester, the researchers field notes suggested a greater level of engagement with the issues of tensions in the teaching and learning process (as captured and re-circulated from the first semester).

This produced a more sustained level of scrutiny of the more complex dimensions of the student feedback data. In essence, what was evident in the deliberations of the action researchers in this second semester was a greater level of responsiveness to the feedback data. This lead to evidence of a broadened professional dialogue, albeit with not infrequent retreats into more pragmatic responses.

Nevertheless, the action research team remained broadly enthusiastic about the approach and the development outcomes it generated. Demonstrating this, they planned a third semester of evaluative activity using the same framework used for the preceding two.

Outcomes of the Third Action Research Semester

The third semester of the model was developed in difficult circumstances for the program. Student numbers unexpectedly had dropped, meaning fewer teachers were engaged to teach in the semester. This had the effect of fragmenting the action research team, with only a core of 14 teachers remaining of the 26 that had been involved in the first semester.

This also meant the level of collaborative evaluative dialogue during the semester—which was already limited in previous semesters—all but disappeared in this semester. Added to this, the reduced number of students meant the responses to the student feedback questionnaire halved from the levels of the first semester, significantly reducing the breadth and depth of student input.

It was clear even from the early stages of the semester that the momentum behind the model and its developmental intent was to be defied by the contraction occurring in the program. Discussions with the remaining academics during the semester reflected a growing unease about the future of the program; meaning that thinking was more centred on survival than on the improvement imperatives that dominated previous semesters. Moreover, given the reduced numbers of participating teachers, the continuity of the action research cycle was clear disrupted to a point where it seemed to have effectively reached an end.

Nevertheless, a further *Evaluation and Course Development Report* was produced for this semester for the remaining action researchers to consider in an end-of-semester forum. The qualitative student data generated (with this more limited sample than previous semester) suggested there were further indications that the program was continuing to mature and that student engagement was improving. Indeed, in this third qualitative assessment by students it was conspicuous that the efforts of teachers was increasingly regarded, with a large number of students singling out teachers for acclaim.

How much of this development reflected the value of several semesters of action research and situated academic development was difficult to precisely assess, but it was a conspicuous feature of this semester's student response. Similarly, a significant majority of students thought that many of the core online elements of the program were working in a highly effective way to enhance learning. This represented a significant turn-around from the initial semester of the action research model.

Several specific elements of the program developed as a result of the action research were considered by students as highly effective contributing to their learning: most notably the more effective integration of face-to-face intensives and online sessions, the better aligning of teaching and assessment strategies and better facilitated discussion forums.

In addition, compared to previous evaluations, there was far less concerns expressed about the value, credibility or relevance of exams and oral presentations as a form of assessment, which suggests scaffolding developed in response to previous evaluations was proving effective. Similarly, the time limitations on subjects that were a source of considerable anxiety and frustration for students in previous evaluations were not a significant feature in this data (with the earlier distribution of course materials).

However, several issues remained problematic: there were inconsistencies emerging in the levels and timeliness of assessment feedback provided by different teachers (seemingly reflecting differing levels of engagement with rubrics and feedback guidelines).

Some new frustration also emerged from students around inequitable levels of participation in discussion forums, with a significant minority of students decidedly unhappy that some students seemed to exercise disproportionate effort (suggesting some continuing issues with either forum design or facilitation approaches).

From these outcomes, a series of course development questions for the remaining action researchers to consider. In this semester, these questions needed to be devised in the context of several new factors, including the:

- primarily instrumental focus of the action research in previous semesters (despite some limited evidence of maturing of the model),
- limited number of remaining participating teachers
- reality that the program was itself focusing on its immediate survival (and was generally in a pedagogically sound state).

In this context, more modest development questions were therefore formed as:

(a) How can approaches to feedback been made more consistent to ensure students feel this is equitable across subjects?
(b) How can more equitable participation in discussion forums be generated?
(c) How can the online learning technologies used in the subjects be more effectively harnessed to enhance the student learning experience?

In considering the *Evaluation and Course Development Report*, the remaining members of the action research team were largely focused on broader strategies to enhance student recruitment to the program, as this was the most pressing survival need felt by most participants.

This rendered matters of course development largely secondary. This resulted in the action research component of the end-of-semester workshop being reduced to little more than a half day (after being conducted over two days in the first two semesters). Despite this limitation, several improvements were defined for implementation in the following semester including:

- further professional development on rubrics and feedback
- greater access to 'model' feedback that had been well received by students
- enhanced quality assurance of the quality of feedback to student assessment by sampling of responses by the convener
- sharing and mentoring of effective online facilitation techniques between program teachers
- continuing work already commenced on improving the design of online elements used in the program.

Interview Data from Action Research Participants

Two months after the final workshop, the researcher invited all of the original 26 teachers who had participated in the action research to participate in a semi-structured interview. Of these, 13 teachers accepted the invitation.

Perhaps unsurprisingly, those who took up the offer had been involved in the three semesters of the action research. Six of the interviews were conducted face-to-face and the remaining via telephone. In order to understand the context of participant reflections, the interviews sought to initially explore the levels of teaching experience of the participant, some of the influences that had shaped their current approaches to teaching and the affordances and hindrances they perceived to initiating pedagogical change. From here, the primary focus was moved to experiences with student feedback and specifically their reflections on the action research model.

Broadly, the teachers interviewed roughly divided into two categories: teachers who had been teaching since the inception of the program in 2006 (with around six years experience in the program) and the remainder with two to three years experience. Within these two cohorts, there were differing professional backgrounds: around half were primarily industry-based who melded this role with their academic work, whilst the remainder were experienced in the field but currently only worked as full or part time teachers (as well as researchers and/or public policy advocates).

These differing origins were clearly reflected in how participants responded to most questions. An example of this was to the question of what had primarily shaped their approach to teaching. Those who were from workplace contexts were strongly shaped by the need to develop an appropriate and robust array of skills and interpersonal capability for the profession.

Alternatively, those outside immediate practice tended to focus on the need to effectively educate, inspire and/or challenge students around the role and purpose of workplace demands. It was also apparent that those who had been involved with the program from the beginning carried a somewhat more sophisticated understanding of the challenges of teaching curricula which included a difficult and regulated combination of discipline, practical and interpersonal knowledge in a blended delivery mode.

Similarly (and unsurprisingly) those teachers newer to the role generally reported the most change to their teaching approaches over time. However this was manifested more in regard to functional use of the online mode of delivery and in preparation students for assessment, rather than in broader pedagogical domains.

In further background to the specific issue of student feedback, teachers were asked to reflect on what they perceived to be the most significant constraints to improving the effectiveness of their teaching. Interestingly, practitioner-teachers universally identified a lack of teacher education as the most significant.

Conversely, those more experienced in teaching largely cited a lack of available time and resources as constraining. Both categories of teachers were however anxious about the unbounded potentiality of emerging learning technologies (including some of those currently in use in the program).

Several developed this further to express that these technology challenges—in combination with perceived onerous assessment demands—were making pedagogical innovation a fraught proposition. The dual pressures of limited time, technical skill and high regulatory scrutiny of student learning outcomes created significant apprehension and acted as a powerful constraint to innovation. One teacher (a practitioner-teacher) succinctly captured this range of anxieties and their constraining effects, commenting:

> Time limitations are a big issue - that is, the limited time for preparation for each course, in combination with the speed at which we need to move through the material in an intensive form makes changing teaching difficult. Although getting training and confidence in all the technologies available might help develop my teaching, I don't really know if I could find the time to develop and use it effectively. And the (regulator) insists on an exam at the end and this really limits what we can do…we know being a effective future practitioner is much more than this, but if the students do not pass the exam we are seen as being poor teachers. (A-8-4)

Participants were also asked to further reflect on their previous experiences with quantitative forms of student feedback following the experiences of the action research. For the inaugural teachers in the program, this experience was over six semesters (and for some longer where they had taught in other areas), and for newer teachers only over two or three semesters. Yet all but one of the thirteen participants reported negative or null experiences with quantitative student evaluation feedback. Several respondents remained sceptical:

> …a lot of surveys and not much use….it seems they were for bureaucratic reassurance rather than to improve our teaching. (A-8-4)

> …you got the impression that that as long as not too many students are complaining and everything is done on time, then the university is happy. (A-8-7)

> …the sole focus seemed to be recording student feedback as the only way to 'really' evaluate (the effectiveness of) a program…this seemed more a process than an action. (A-8-13)

Other respondents doubted their real value in providing insights into teaching quality:

> …these (quantitative) evaluations, because they were really not aggregated or analysed, have not been particularly useful in guiding us as teachers….to know how to improve the program and our teaching. (A-8-2)

> …individual comments from students give some clues, but it hasn't really been possible to know whether or not that comment is representative of many students' experience. (A-8-5)

> …as far as I knew, students completed their questionnaire and that was about it….no real impact unless a real problem was apparent. (A-8-1)

One respondent adopted a different posture on qualitative student feedback, best captured when they observed:

> …we need to hear clearly the student perspective no doubt, and understanding this in the context of what's happening in other courses and comparing results. This means teachers are forced to think hard about what they are doing, particularly if its poorly regarded by students, and whether they should do things differently. (A-8-3)

Nevertheless, what was apparent from all respondents was a genuine recognition of the important role of student feedback could perform in improving teaching and enhancing student learning. For most this was grounded in a commitment to create a productive learning environment, as well as produce graduates capable of contributing positively to advice and advocacy (though with varying emphases and characterisations). Some representative observations on this were:

> …my objective is to assist students understand some fundamentals of the practice environment. So I want students to engage in the course and appreciate what they have learnt during it. (A-8-6)

> …I really would welcome more opportunities to evaluate the program – in whatever way it needs to be done – and make changes that improve their outcomes. (A-8-10)

> ….as I spend a lot of time guiding students through the subject, answering questions, highlighting the relevance of critical components and clarifying the areas students are having difficulty understanding…it is critical I know how appropriate the judgments I make on these matters actually are from a student perspective. (A-8-3)

Respondents were then asked to reflect on the action research model they had encountered over the three previous semesters. All respondents were broadly positive about the action research model, albeit with varying levels of enthusiasm.

Six of the respondents offered a highly favourable assessment of the model. It is notable all those in this category were primarily the teachers who were part of the original group of teachers recruited to the program. They included both full-time and part-time teachers. Some observations that characterised this group included:

> …..very useful and I have taken a lot on board and changed (my teaching) to reflect that. (A-8-6)

> …it was extremely useful, part of that was seeing the evaluation of the program overall and not only the individual courses. (A-8-11)

> …of particular value was how the (action research) based evaluation identified key questions based on student responses, as well as some potential responses. These were a brilliant springboard for the review sessions. (A-8-9)

> …it was the first time that an attempt was made to provide feedback in an organised manner. It was useful in that it challenged me to consider some of the harder educational issues involved, when I hadn't really been previously aware of them. (A-8-8)

Other respondents were less certain. Although they saw the potential value of the action research model, they were somewhat more equivocal about how realistic it really was given the time limitations between review sessions and the recommencement of teaching. Some of these sentiments are represented by these observations:

> ....it was great to sit down and spend some time and discuss what worked and what didn't. However we needed more time to actually think through and implement what was decided was necessary or useful. (A-8-3)

> ...I would have liked more time to go back over the recommendations and evaluation report to see what more I might do. At times it seemed we had so much data that it was very challenging to prioritise it, let alone act on all of it. (A-8-1)

> ...it was quite useful, but for me it reinforced many of my perceptions, perceptions that have been difficult to really act on given my limited time and resources etc. (A-8-12)

Other respondents, though positive about the model, saw it as part of a useful enterprise that was more general and not necessarily unique to this form of enquiry:

> ...quite useful, though I'm not sure it didn't tell us anything we didn't really know if we had considered it at this level of detail. (A-8-2)

> ...reflection is always useful, though this work did use considerable resources and really needed someone to be co-ordinating and driving it if it was to succeed. (A-8-7)

> ...I got some useful information, for instance understanding the online lurkers and problems with our assessment and feedback. These are things that are useful to know. (A-8-10)

However, all respondents agreed that the focus on evaluating student learning (as opposed to more conventional focus on evaluating teaching) was a useful enhancement. It was also universally regarded as providing a more legitimate basis for determining the quality of teaching pedagogies than conventional quantitative ratings.

Yet respondents were more equivocal on how influential in actual practice the action research outcomes were. Around half the respondents provided substantial examples of how the action research model outcomes had impacted directly on their own teaching approaches. This is captured well in these observations:

> ...the (action research) was quite influential. I have implemented changes. For example, better setting up of student expectations and trying to scaffold and support student assessments. I now highlight the relevance of certain activities and relate learning more to workplace practice. (A-8-11)

> ...I was inspired to think more clearly about my expectations and those of the students, how to integrate the worlds of learning and practice and how to ensure students were learning for assessment, and what is the most feedback, like rubrics. (A-8-8)

> ...it did change the way I looked at myself as a teacher and forced my to reconsider habits I had developed. (A-8-6)

Other respondents were less convinced about the actually impact of the action research on their teaching approaches. Notably most of these responses came from those who were part-time teachers simultaneously engaged in professional practice.

> ...it was only moderately useful. It certainly raised issues but the question was how much could realistically be achieved in the time available. (A-8-1)

… reasonably influential I guess, but having said this I found it actually reinforced the way I was headed anyway, so it didn't provide a direct impetus for change, but a motivation to continue. (A-8-3)

….it has been useful to better understand the process and the impact of teaching and supporting students. But I also think it put a lot of pressure and maybe unrealistic expectations on those of us who weren't here all the time to do more in our own time. (A-8-7)

Conclusion

In this first case study, data suggested that the CHAT-based, action research model used over three semesters had proven moderately effective in sustaining engaged professional dialogue and in generating some tangible developmental change. The three cycles had generated three substantial *Evaluation and Course Development Reports* of around 60,000 words of qualitative student feedback. From the deliberation and debate flowing from this feedback data, there was some significant evidence of pedagogical improvement and a modest range of situated academic development initiatives.

Equally, the *expansive learning evaluation cycle* could not be considered fully effective either. The original model proposed engaging teaching academic reflections alongside that of students reflecting on their learning. This proved largely ethereal during the three semesters, with reflective dialogue by teaching academics was largely confined to the pre and post semester workshops. Further, as was reported in participant reflections at the end of three semesters, there was some uncertainty about how influential the model was in practice. Some of this was clearly related back to the nature of its initial introduction, which proved challenging due to the complex conceptual framing of the model. Its broad collective nature also created some early reservations with the lack of specific focus on individual subjects and teachers.

In addition, the fragmented nature of this teaching workforce—involving a small core of conventional academic teachers and a second larger group of practitioners from the field engaged in teaching—had divergent responses to elevated student feedback. This also appeared to limit its potential developmental impetus. Moreover, the significant time and resource limitations of the primarily part time teaching workforce, in tandem with an unexpected fall in enrolments and staff in the third semester, made it difficult for the action research to gain genuine momentum.

Chapter 6
Student Evaluation in Situated Practice—The Case of an Established Program

Abstract In this chapter, the outcomes of the second case study centred on the elevated use of qualitative student evaluation data are detailed. Unlike the first case study, the program under investigation in this case was a well-established program with a long history of broadly successful educational outcomes. However, the program had recently undergone significant change, with its exclusive face-to-face mode of delivery disrupted with the introduction of a blended form of delivery, which incorporated significant online components. This disturbance—in an established program with a comparatively high level of tenured teaching staff—created considerable anxiety and produced a volatile pedagogical environment in which to elevate the significance of the student voice. This context provided a robust environment for testing the value (as well as the limits) of collaborative pedagogical discourses in a time of major education change. Overall, the case demonstrated that a deeper and more strategic engagement with the consequences of major education change can be effectively driven with the use of an elevated qualitative form of student feedback. However, although this can produce important pedagogical improvement, the histories of programs can mean this also may come at considerable cost to ongoing cohesion of teaching groups.

Keywords Qualitative student evaluation · Case study research · Pedagogical improvement · Pedagogical change in higher education · Expansive learning · Online learning

Introduction

The second case study was undertaken in a teaching area that offered specialist programs for postgraduates, centred primarily on development for professional workplace practice environments. The core teaching of the area was built around a qualification that had a thirty-year history and was well established and highly regarded in industry. However, shortly before the commencement of the case

© Springer International Publishing Switzerland 2016
S. Darwin, *Student Evaluation in Higher Education*,
DOI 10.1007/978-3-319-41893-3_6

study, this program was radically redesigned. It abandoned its conventional face-to-face teaching approach and adopted a blended learning model based on a combination of intensive workshops and online learning modules (including the use of a simulated learning environment). In addition, the previous fixed two-semester program was made more flexible, so it could be completed in a minimum of five months, or in up to a three-year period.

Over the period of the case studies, the program had between 1100 and 1400 student enrolments per semester. Given this scale, the program had a substantial core of 18 full-time academic staff, most of who taught primarily on this program (with some academics undertake other postgraduate teaching). However, in contrast to the program considered in the first case study, this program had a well-established structure with a relatively large cohort of permanent full-time academic staff and more conventional peripheral workforce of tutors directly responsible to subject conveners.

The program retained a considerable network of around 180 part-time tutors who were responsible for working with students in a variety of forms across the component elements of the program. These tutors tended to be roughly divided between recent graduates and more experienced workplace practitioners. Most of the teachers involved in the program were currently engaged in part-time teaching and in other work in the discipline field. Moreover, despite its recent move to a blended mode, the program retained an explicit reliance on a largely conventional formulation of curriculum, rather than relying the inherent expertise of practitioners-in-practice to drive the learning process.

The program was also offered by a small number of other universities, as well as by one large private institution. Despite the limited number of providers, the level of competitive pressure on the program had grown significantly in recent years. This had been primarily a result of the growth in more time-flexible study programs and the more expansive use of technology. This had meant students no longer needed to re-locate to undertake study at a particular institution (as had been historically the case).

As was the case with the previous case study, this program met the range of criteria established to be a suitable site for this research. It was a substantial program, with a complex range of curriculum, teaching modes and academic engagement. Academic staff also had previous experience with using the quantitative student feedback model.

The educational leaders of the program were broadly open to the proposed development action research cycle centred on an elevated use of qualitative student feedback and the use of a collaborative deliberation of its outcomes. Indeed, given the considerable competitive and internal pressure the program was under to sustain learning quality—particularly given the disruptive impact of these recent pedagogical innovations—educational leaders felt this was a highly desirable intervention to deal with the plethora of challenges thrown up by the changed mode of delivery.

Initiating the Action Research Project

After some preliminary discussions with the Program Convener and individual subject co-ordinators, the broad notion of a CHAT-based, action research project was proposed to a meeting of the Program Committee. This committee included representatives of academic staff, administrative staff, academic developers, students and a representative of the professional body covering the discipline area. In this second case study site, I adopted a similar research orientation as a *participant-researcher* similar to that described in the earlier described case.

This meant proposing the *expansive learning evaluation cycle* (introduced earlier) and exploring its broad theoretical and methodological foundations. Although the Program Committee enthusiastically embraced the broad proposition, there were some reservations around the whole-of-program ambition of the action research (particularly given the realtively large scale of the program).

From this discussion, it was agreed that the action research should instead focus on the primary core element of the program that was most radically redesigned. It had been transformed over recent semesters from a traditional face-to-face lecture/ tutorial program, to a blended learning model based on an initial one-week intensive orientation and a range of semi-structured learning activities undertaken in a simulated learning environment.

Following further dialogue, it was agreed to seek support of the teaching cohort for engaging in the CHAT-based, action research model. However, given the extent of recent pedagogical disruption in the program, it was decided by this group that a more structured form of action research than was adopted in the first case study site was desirable.

A framing document that proposed a specific action research strategy was designed and circulated to program teachers prior to the workshop. This framework suggested a model aligned to the still-evolving change occurring in the program as it moved somewhat uneasily from a traditional to simulation-based learning environment. As was the case with the first program, an initial one-day introductory workshop was convened which involved the core academic teaching workforce (18 academics) and the key part time academic conveners of tutors working in the differing subject areas of the program (a further 12 staff). In addition, two academic developers and three administrative staff attended the workshop.

The workshop was initially introduced to the action research model and its theoretical underpinning. In the subsequent discussion, a number of significant issues quickly emerged. Firstly, the level of enthusiasm for the enhanced use of student feedback by participants in the workshop was limited to a small number of individuals, and most of these were those co-ordinators who had been involved in preliminary discussions. Based on the comments offered, it seemed this limited enthusiasm was primarily revolved around two related reservations:

- that the level of change and disruption that the program was already going through made it poor time to be assessing the quality of student learning

- whether the elevated use of student feedback would only serve to aggravate existing tensions, frustrations and external perceptions about the effectiveness of this pedagogical transition.

From the earliest discussions in this workshop, it was apparent that participants had endured a significant and challenging transition from a traditional learning environment to one that was largely framed by an online simulation. Many participants gave life to the challenges of this transition: dramatic and uncertain curriculum reformations, unfamiliar technological demands, untried and radically altered pedagogies, as well as fundamentally different forms of student engagement, assessment and feedback. The most substanial elements of this change had been progressively introduced over the twelve months immediately preceding the workshop. These lingering anxieties were well captured by several participants when related to the proposed action research:

> ….is this really the right time to be asking for more student feedback or assessing student opinion more directly?…it has been a difficult and sometimes not entirely successful transition….I am not sure we or the students are actually convinced it (will work as intended. (B-1-05)

> ….aren't we already committed enough, this has all been pretty tough going for us all and I think that our energy is best used in trying to make things actually work rather than adding new ways of discovering how they are not. (B-1-09)

> …there are already many people who have serious doubts about the effectiveness of this change and I am really having enough trouble keeping things together….this is probably something we should do when it is all bedded down. (B-1-12)

Conversely, there were a significant minority offering a differing perspective on this same question:

> …we have made some very major changes, of course it would be crazy to simply make a standard judgment on student evaluations…however I can tell you from my perspective we definitely need a clearer understanding of how to make student learning more effective in this environment. (B-1-16)

> ….if we show we are on the front foot, asking the hard questions of students and ourselves, then surely that demonstrates that we are serious teachers working in a difficult changing environment. (B-1-17)

These samples characterised the core of a prolonged debate. In essence, this came down to two key propositions. The first was whether it was wise to provide more extensive evidence on the apparent fragilities of a new and immature learning approach. The second was whether a higher level of student insight and related academic debate would maximise the potential to improve the effectiveness of the program.

For many academics, the current outcomes of student opinion surveys were not as problematic as claimed by program leaders. In debating this matter in the workshop, it emerged that overall the program in its earlier (more traditional) form had generally received consistent sound student feedback ratings. A significant minority believed that this was a highly successful and well-regarded program that had gone off the rails with the dramatic change of teaching mode.

According to this assessment, it was actually the case that previously achieved student opinion survey ratings tended to exceed university averages. Other academics reported generally low concern with student surveys until the introduction of the new simulation-based teaching model (as ratings had fallen in implementing the new model).

However, further reflecting on the recorded dialogue in this element of the workshop, it appeared this response was more complex than it initially seemed. It represented a mixture of satisfaction with the previous achievement of good 'student numbers' and lingering and largely unresolved dissatisfaction with the recent change in the mode of pedagogy and resulting forms of student (dis)engagement. Several experienced academics, who'd noted their previous student survey scores 'ticked the boxes' for management, captured this general sentiment most effectively when they declared:

> …why on earth would we now move to extend our evaluation efforts when we aren't even sure we have the teaching right….how can students possibly favourably review such an obvious work-in-progress? (B-1-25)

> …we knew this new simulation model was a radical departure and we may just be giving further ammunition for how radical, and probably foolish, it actually was. (B-1-27)

What was conspicuous in this part of the discussion was the intensity of the unresolved dissatisfaction with this move. Clearly a significant number of teaching academics felt that a successful program had been injudiciously replaced with a speculative, and thus far unsuccessful, flexible model. As a result, it was difficult to unravel concerns about the developmental use of student feedback from these lingering concerns.

This inevitably meant a reprise of the ferocious debates that led up to this recent change. Program leaders, other academics and academic developers countered with their belief for the need for the program to evolve and adapt to changing student, technological and market demands. This generated a further broader ranging debate about effective pedagogies and valid epistemologies in the discipline. However, little of this debate troubled matters of student feedback.

Nevertheless, following an uneasy form of détente agreed around these polemics, it was seemingly resolved that a trial of a CHAT-informed, action research model would be at least of some value to the program. This however was only on the basis that the learning evaluation model was to carry an explicitly developmental character (given the relative immaturity of the program). Similarly, there was recognition that given the challenging adaption required by many academics teaching within of the program, and the continuing fragility of the technology being employed other modifications were necessary.

Firstly, student feedback outcomes were to be confined to the teaching group and not subject to the broader scrutiny of the faculty or university prior to this being agreed by a similar forum. The outcomes of the action research would also remain internal to the group.

Secondly, action research questions would centre on the broad improvement of the program overall and the related identification of further program and academic development needs. That is, it would not focus on individuals or specific elements of the modules as such. Essentially, this acted to lessen concerns of some teaching academics that they may be negatively reflected upon in something they were not convinced by. This provided an uneasy yet important foundation for the research, but also enhanced the broader prospects of the program winning greater acceptance amongst the experienced academics teaching on it.

As a result, the developmental evaluation became inextricably linked to the fate of the program. This created a distinctly different dynamic to the first case study site. The assessments of the day by participants remained highly mixed, ranging from enthusiasm to little less than a sense of impending doom (and much in-between these two poles). For instance, one academic wrote:

…I really think this is the right time to look hard at what we've done with the program and actually analyse our claims about simulations and flexibility. (B-1-66)

Whilst another cast a darker shadow over proceedings:

…I'm sure there are good intentions behind improving how we evaluate it (the program), but it is all about timing…airing your dirty laundry may create some good outcomes, but it also has the potential for some pretty negative consequences for individuals as well. (B-1-74)

A third offered a somewhat more ambivalent take on proceedings:

…I guess we will just have to see what comes of it, we are all feeling a bit battered by the change, but maybe understanding how we can improve the program with the help of some experts here could make things better. (B-1-65)

In liaison with program leaders, a summary of workshop outcomes was subsequently circulated to all participants for feedback. Aside from some minor changes of emphasis, this summary was largely unchanged and was subsequently endorsed by the Program Committee for trial implementation in the coming semester, and for potential use in subsequent semesters subject to its effectiveness. The model negotiated took the following form:

Agreed Action Research Model: First Semester

Stage One: Early Semester/Ongoing

Regular teaching team forums

- identification the range of issues that need to be considered to potentially improve student learning outcomes
- collaborative review of existing curricula, learning outcomes, learning activities and assessment and consideration of alternative approaches to teaching and learning, including those used in other universities in discipline area and in other disciplines

- negotiation of potential learning enhancements and formulation of collaborative responses
- formulation of research questions around enhanced learning effectiveness to be individually and collaboratively investigated
- identification academic development and educational design needs for the semester
- publishing of any agreed changes and research questions

Stage Two: During Semester

Action Research team (teaching team and educational design team)

- implementation of agreed learning approaches by individual academics
- critical action research based enquiry of student learning outcomes, using a variety of sources including professional sense, student feedback, peer input and research outcomes
- publishing of individual research outcomes in a collective space (such as a closed wiki or blog).

Stage Three: End Semester

Review Conference or Seminar

- collaborative reflection on research outcomes to determine future responses (such as to institutionalise, expand, modify or abandonment)
- publish outcomes and identify opportunities for future expansive potential for the program or sub-discipline (i.e. new questions).

Outcomes of First Action Research Semester

Given the significant reservations evident in the introductory workshop about the possible outcomes of a more determined canvassing of student feedback, it was agreed in consultation with the teaching team to use semi-structured interviews with students to generate data for this first semester of the action research.

This decision was prompted by the concerns of several participants that a survey-based model of student opinion—even in the more qualitative form proposed—would not illicit sufficient depth to allow the primary objectives of this evaluative work to be met. These primarily objectives were established in the often turbulently negotiated consensus of the introductory workshop reported in the last section.

The key challenge arising from this encounter was to ensure the action research constructively contributed to program development. Internal speculation by some suggested the *expansive learning evaluation cycle* would only generate negative data that could be used (inadvertently or otherwise) to diminish the efforts of academics engaged in a recently introduced and radically different pedagogy.

Hence ongoing communication was essential around the collaborative nature and developmental intent of the model. Throughout this initial semester, the action research team was also regularly convened as part of scheduled forums, with a specific focus on analysis of the pedagogical effectiveness of the program and identifying areas for reform and targeted professional capability building for teachers and tutors working on the program. This was to some extent framed by the reflections of teaching academics during the semester, which was intended to inform both ongoing and summative professional dialogue about their work during the semester (as a mediating dimension to the outcomes of student feedback).

At the conclusion of the first trial semester, the researcher and two research assistants interviewed 63 completing students (representing roughly 40 % of the cohort) using the agreed semi-structured interview method. The sample size was chosen so as to be sufficiently large to offer significant data outcomes, whilst the range of students was defined opportunistically based on their availability and willingness to participate. The interviews were based of three primary semi-structured questions which were defined so as to product a broad range of qualitative data on the affordances, limitations and potential of the program from a student perspective. These questions were:

(a) What did you find effective in the course?
(b) What didn't you find effective?
(c) Is there anything else about the program that you would to provide feedback on?

A rich array of data was collected from these interviews, with over 40,000 words of data transcribed. Based on the same logic described in Chapter Four (and used in the last case study), this data was systematically analysed using a multi-leveled thematic coding model to establish the primary issues that emerged. This was further refined to generate the outcomes for the first *Evaluation and Course Development Report*.

Overall, students participating in the program expressed strongly divergent opinions around their learning experiences in the program. These ranged from:

• strongly positive reflections on the simulated practice based nature of learning
• mixed responses that while broadly supportive of the approach, disputed the quality of its implementation by the university
• highly negative reactions that saw the flexible teaching mode as completely ineffectual way of completing this type of program.

These divergent responses meant developing generalised outcomes from the semi-structured interviews was unrealistic. As a result, the thematic analysis inevitably tended to privilege these majority perspectives of respondents, rather than those with more equivocal or novel opinions. This outcome meant the data in the eventual *Evaluation and Course Development Report* for this first semester were far more polarised and contradictory in form than was the case with the first case study. This in turn tended to render it more a chronicle of debate, without a distinct developmental trajectory being implied.

Undoubtedly this disparate response reflected the similarly divergent student responses to the changed mode of delivery of the program. However, distinguishing how much of this was about the effectiveness of the mode itself and how much was about the pedagogical quality of the program became a serious challenge to this new model in its first iteration. This was difficulty was only amplified by the existing volatility of the teaching group.

The key major positive themes to emerge in this first collection of student feedback were around the:

- levels of program flexibility
- value of a simulated rather than abstracted environment for considering issues of professional practice (although this view was by no means universal)
- value of group collaboration (amongst functioning groups)
- the contribution of practice mentors (i.e. teachers).

In addition, less significant positives identified by the students included the use of authentic artefacts and 'real' time expectations, variable completion periods and peer mentoring. However, it was evident from the feedback data that the negative observations considerably outweighed the positive in the majority of interviews. In considering the range and intensity of the most significant negative responses, it can seen that these related broadly to:

- unfulfilled student expectations
- inadequate orientation
- loss of more familiar approaches to learning
- a functionalist drive in enrolling in a program toward admission
- inconsistent and/or unreliable responsiveness by teaching academics.

Other student frustrations included the lack of timely or consistent feedback, inadequate communication at a range of levels, inconsistent forms of program and assessment design, unreliable technology and program signposts. Several other minor negative factors were identified including excessive workloads (particularly in comparison to more confined conventional teaching models) and the dysfunctional (and on occasions dystopian) state of a small number student groups.

In regard to the third development-focused question in the semi-structured interviews, the following primary themes emerged as areas for potential improvements:

(a)   increased face-to-face seminars in the orientation phase of the program to more clearly set expectations and clarify assessment requirements
(b)   increased online scaffolding to provide more detailed instructions and guidance around the 'how to' of the program
(c)   mandating feedback practices to improve assessment usefulness to students
(d)   introducing step assessment that allow formative activities to be assessed

(e) establishment of clear professional standards to enhance the expectations of the behaviour, collaborative inclination and dispute resolution in practice firms

(f) provision of more resources to relieve the workload of practice mentors

(g) reduced groups to pairs.

From this data, *Evaluation and Course Development Report* for the semester was produced. In reporting on these outcomes, it was noted that earlier concerns in the teaching cohort about the likelihood of considerable student dissatisfaction were to some extent realised. In order to provide a constructive basis for considering these outcomes, the significant tensions and contradictions identified in student responses were further distilled to assist this debate. These were reported as the:

- expectation of the program as a straightforward educational program akin to previous learning experiences (that is, built on a familiar pedagogy) *versus* the educational objective of the program to be a challenging and highly self-directed program, centred on the development of autonomous skills for workplace practice
- ambiguity of expectations of skills demands within the simulated learning environment *versus* the objective of students drawing on undergraduate education to build capability for individual and collaborative professional actions
- individualistic and conventional nature of preceding education experiences *versus* the collaborative and virtual demands of this program
- built expectations of the engagement in actual environments of the discipline *versus* the under-developed or unconvincing program artefacts deployed in a necessarily generic and contrived simulated learning environment
- framing of academic staff as mentors and advisers in the online environment *versus* the reality of these staff also assessing the quality of student performance based of fulfilment of assessment criteria (i.e. rendering authentic forms of 'trial and error' problematic).

Clearly the implementation of an essentially online learning program represented a significant pedagogical re-alignment. Inevitably, most students would have had little real experience with online learning, high-level simulated learning environments or even effective group collaboration. It was conspicuous that many of the students most hostile to the new approach had expressed deep frustration about the online simulation as a form of learning (and its radical difference from that which they expected to encounter). Others had endured ongoing group dysfunction.

The volatility of student responses, in tandem with a fractured teaching group, meant identifying productive questions that could be (re)considered by the teaching team for the next iteration of the program was challenging. Nevertheless, from the qualitative student data several clear themes emerged which framed the following stimulus questions:

(a) Given the overwhelming majority of students have undertaken a conventional forms of face-to-face higher education, how can the expectations for autonomous learning in a largely virtual environment be better framed?

(b) How can students be more effectively scaffolded in the transition to this very different learning environment?

(c) How can the relevance of the program to workplace practice be enhanced?

(d) Are there means to improve how dysfunctional student groups can be assisted?

(e) Are we (and therefore students) clear on the relationship between a simulation and the actual environments of practice? Can this resonance by improved?

(f) Is assessment doing the work of enhancing learning given the obvious tension between staff as guides and as assessors?

(g) Do we need to regulate academic responses into a standard form to better reflect what we see to be sound professional response approaches?

(h) How do we know that the program is achieving its objectives? Is it in student engagement, is it developed artefacts they develop or is in the assessment outcomes?

Initial Post-semester Workshop

Consistent with the agreed action research model, a post-semester workshop was convened approximately a fortnight after the circulation of the *Evaluation and Course Development Report* that included the data outlined in the preceding section. Given the relatively complex divergence in student feedback, the Report also included a tag cloud reflecting the range and intensity of student opinion on the positives, negatives and ideas for innovation. In total, 16 academics, 11 tutors and five support staff attended this first post-semester workshop.

At the commencement of the workshop, consistent with the CHAT-informed model in use, participants were encouraged to consider the complex and contradictory nature of the student feedback. This was offered as a potentially useful basis for constructive professional dialogue around the state of the program, and particularly where improvement was clearly necessary.

Some brief discussion had already occurred about the Report in the regular team discussion, as well as in the corridors of the faculty. Hence, it was quickly apparent that the *Evaluation and Course Development Report* had also already created considerable debate amongst program teachers, leaders and designers. This meant that the workshop rapidly developed a combative atmosphere, primarily around the usefulness of student feedback, the program's current pedagogical construction and the value (or otherwise) of this form of student feedback. For most participants, this meant defending their individual efforts or alternatively doubting the value of the pedagogy. Little early focus emerged toward overall program improvement issues.

Perhaps as a result, this workshop was largely unsuccessful in reaching any depth of analysis. The divergence in student feedback responses, rather than presenting a potential dialectic force, instead offered opportunities for advocates and detractors to offer their various perspectives on the program. As one academic poignantly observed in their end-of-workshop feedback:

> The only thing really achieved here today was to again rehearse the various pros and cons of moving from face-to-face to online. The feedback from students served primarily as evidence to support pre-existing views one way or the other. (B-2-8)

However, as one of the program leaders also observed slightly less pessimistically:

> I guess we at least brought all the tensions in the group into the open and we did ensure that the difficultly of the change we have gone through was clear. But the student feedback allowed us to actually debate issues in a more tangible and less rhetorical way, so I suppose that's a step forward. (B-2-21)

The notes taken during the workshop reflect that the level of professional dialogue was a dramatic departure from what was anticipated in this action research process. Instead of a collaborative engagement around key professional issues, the workshop was dominated by dichotomous thinking that reflected the seemingly unresolved tensions in the group.

Again, as was the case in the initial workshop, this was contested on the familiar ground between those who were aggrieved about the relatively recent move from conventional teaching and those who had embraced the new blended model. Consistently this was further aggravated by the ambivalence of other teachers (most notably recently engaged tutors). In addition, the persistent failures of the online resources and tools in use in the program to effectively deliver a high quality platform for quality teaching and learning proved a highly distracting issue. This dilemma was captured in the following exchange recorded in notes taken during the workshop:

> *Speaker One*: One of the key issues to be improved that was identified in the Report was orientation and ongoing support for students in their online work.
>
> *Speaker Two*: Well, if we actually knew what we could usefully orientate them to and support them with, then we might be able to do something.
>
> *Speaker One*: What do you mean...we need to give students a clear understanding of what to expect online and then build better support to ensure this actually happens.
>
> *Speaker Two*: But we ourselves have no real understanding! We knew what to teach when they were here, but now it's all open and uncertain. Anything goes...what is a simulation meant to do anyway?
>
> *Speaker Three*: but don't we have to do it, so isn't it better to just get on with it, but as a newish tutor I do have to say I agree with (Speaker Two)...I really am not sure what I am meant to support.

As a result of this dynamic, combined with the reality that few teachers had seemingly engaged in any productive professional reflection during the semester, meant that the workshop descended into a pragmatic, and at times tense, exchange about specific remedies to largely superficial issues raised in the *Evaluation and Course Development Report*.

In essence, many of these debates simply resulted in imposed outcomes being defined by program leaders, as no real consensus could (or would) be reached even at this level of base-level engagement. The workshop outcomes were consequently modest in form and largely without a clear relationship to the broad matters raised in the *Evaluation and Course Development Report*. Some of the more fundamental tensions emerging out of the student data were disregarded for what was cast by wry participant as 'short-term wins'. In summary, the broad outcomes were:

- Technology *(largely agreed)*: improve site navigation and make 'look and feel' more sophisticated, explore use of Skype (as a replacement for failing Wimba), make use of RSS feeds, create a single sign on and develop and internal email.
- Student support *(largely imposed)*: develop a new online orientation (as no consensus on this being in the face-to-face orientation); develop guidelines on appropriate communication protocols, standardising artefacts (as no consensus on what would be authentic artefacts), and review of student workloads across subjects.
- Staffing *(largely agreed)*: increase co-ordination of online component, produce position descriptions for various staff roles, more training on working in online environments (nature not specified, as could not be agreed), greater mentoring and debriefing of tutors, consider manuals to guide work of specific roles.
- Educational structure and design *(largely imposed)*: introduce form of compulsory individual assessment, improve capacity for more timely feedback, audit next course for consistency of assessment feedback, consider how to lessen student workload where considered excessive.

Hence, the first semester of the action research model ended as it had started, largely mired in the unresolved controversies about the move to a blended delivery model for the program. Although the elevated level of data had created some tentative debate, it had functioned primarily to amplify existing dissent or to harden the defiance of those leading the changed pedagogy. The range of course improvements, partly agreed and partly imposed, were modest and pragmatic in form, characterised either by low-level action or abstract intent. In considering the participant feedback at the end of the workshop, we see these various sentiments reflected in the commentaries provided on the effectiveness of the workshop:

> Good try, but this issue is bigger than a semester of student feedback. Little can be resolved until (Program leader) finally realises that students don't want this sort of amateurish online stuff and come here for a decent and well organised teaching program. (B-2-1)

> I think we made some progress, some people are still struggling with the change and I understand that. The main thing is that we plough on and improve what I think will be a great program once we iron out the teething problems that must always be part of a new approach. (B-2-6)

> It was a bit frustrating; being new I have only experienced conflict about this program…I enjoyed trying to work online as a teacher and as a mentor for students. It does take a bit of getting used to but I think we also just have to recognise it takes time to move from something standard to something very new. I think the problem is that some people don't want to leave what they know well and I respect that. Maybe they need to look at moving into other teaching, I don't really know. (B-2-19)

> This is beginning to look like a pretty dangerous program to be involved in…one thing I realised from today's workshop is that we have some pretty serious problems and these are both practical and educational. I'm just not sure looking at student feedback in greater depth is actually helping, it seems to be just inflaming the two sides of this argument further. (B-2-3)

Although the collaborative action research model had generated considerable data during this first semester, it was hard to argue it had achieved much more (and particularly enhanced collaboration). Rather than work as action researchers, the group had appeared to further fracture. It seems the unintended benefit of more compelling evidence simply made the fissures more acute, in that it could be used to further support unresolved arguments for and against the changed pedagogy.

Yet it was still likely some elements of the program would be improved based on student feedback, and it was hoped by program leaders that this dialogue, however flawed, may have moved this debate on in some more material form (that is, beyond its characteristic rhetorical form). However, it was evident that program leaders needed to deal with the broader unresolved issues about the program's redesign if a serious professional dialogue centred on student feedback were to be effective in subsequent semesters.

Outcomes of Second Action Research Semester

The period between the first and second semester of the project was significant, with a number of disgruntled staff exiting the program, a number of the tutors opting not to continue. The number of students enrolling also fell from the level of previous years.

The tumultuous level of debate generated by action research was generally credited with encouraging departing academics to leave the program, whilst the problems with the online simulation was seen as the primary reason for falling student numbers. Anecdotally, it was reported student word-of-mouth had created considerable anxiety amongst potential students and many of these had opted to study elsewhere.

Hence, the second semester was destined to present further challenges no only to the program, but also to the action research model itself. Given this context, and the experiences of the first semester, the Program Committee became more active in debating how the performance of the program and how it could be most productively improved. This inevitably intersected with the action research project, with greater expectations placed on it to drive program enhancement. This heightened the anxieties of some of the remaining program academics that student feedback may be used more directly to assail academic performance.

It was in this more complex context that a slightly reduced number academics and program support staff (14 academics, 10 tutors and four support staff) reconvened to consider the design of the second stage of the action research. The researcher provided a critical assessment of the outcomes of the first semester project, highlighting the limitations in the outcomes given the then profound tensions in the group about the shifting pedagogical foundations of the program. Put in CHAT terms, this had meant the assumed shared object of the action research (i.e. program improvement) had been supplanted by a fundamentally different object orientation: the appropriateness of the change from conventional to a blended learning model.

Similarly, the distinct vantage points of action research participants meant neither was there a shared subject perspective. In essence, this meant its developmental potential to improve teaching and learning was seriously hindered. Perhaps its primary contribution was to further aggravate the tensions around pedagogy, as well as to identify some pragmatic options for short-term enhancements. Program leaders then introduced the changes that had been made to the program for the coming semester as a result of the outcomes of this work in the previous semester.

They also aired concerns expressed in education committees regarding the decline in program enrolments and the consequent significance of improvement that could be identified through further collaborative action research efforts in the subsequent semester.

As discussion about the next stage of the project developed, it was quickly apparent that the departure of several key protagonists and the urgency of the situation confronting the program had engendered a different disposition in the group. Recognising the limitations of the first semester, there was a productive debate around modifying the action research model to ensure it legitimately did the development work expected of it in its initial manifestation.

A strong consensus emerged that the experiences of program teachers and tutors needed to be a more significant element of the research process and this should accord with the expectations of the model proposed in the first semester. This meant greater ongoing reflection during the coming semester and all participants agreed to a semi-structured interview at its completion on these reflections so this could be directly fed into the action research.

Ironically, there was also a strong desire of the group to 'balance' the broader student feedback data with some very specific questions to ensure that the largely minor changes put in place for the current semester as a result of the previous semesters' research had actually proved effective.

Moreover, given the strong pressure that academics were encountering regarding problems in the program, there was a universally agreement that there was a need to supplement the qualitative thematic coding of student data. The group resolved to introduce a quantitative scale and several forced answer responses from students. These were seen in the mold of quality assurance: providing the potential capacity to market program improvement more effectively to those external to it. This resulted in a new series of student and academic questions being negotiated during the workshop. These questions were:

1. Student Questions

- What do you think worked effectively to support your learning?
- What do you think was less effective and hindered your learning?
- In your opinion, what aspects of the program need improvement?
- Forced answer questions with ratings (with area for explanation of responses)
- How effective were the simulations in developing your understanding of practice?

- How effective was the group-based firm structure in assisting your learning?
- How effective did you think the virtual firms were in simulating a workplace environment?
- How useful did you find the online simulation?

2. Academic questions (End semester semi-structured interviews based of captured reflections during semester)

- What do you think worked effectively in supporting and expanding student learning?
- What do you think was less effective and constrained student learning?
- What specific elements of the program need to be further developed to be more useful to further student understanding of workplace practice?
- How effective were the range of learning activities (such as group activities, mentoring and reflections) used in your subject area?
- How effective do you think the group structure worked effectively?
- How effectively did students perform in assessment and are there any issues that arose from it?
- How effective do you think the online site and simulation were?
- Were there specific issues this semester that you think needed to be further considered by the teaching group?
- Do you have any other observations you'd like to make?

In post-workshop feedback, participants generally expressed much more positive sentiments on the action research process than in the previous semester, albeit with some lingering reservations. Characteristic of the primary responses are the excerpts from responses highlighted below:

> I think we are more on track this semester, we are clearer on what we need to do and that we all have to get involved if we are going to made the program work as was intended…. if we can get a better balance between student and academic input maybe we can avoid a situation where we are defensive, but are able to really take on what challenges we find. (B-3-13)

> The negativity of last semester seems to have faded and it seems we know we are more cohesive…I just hope the action research gives us what we need to develop and improve the course and that it doesn't come back to haunt us given the efforts we are all trying to make this semester. (B-3-1)

> If we can't get this right then our student numbers will fall further and we will find it even harder to make the program effective, so the challenge for all of us if to work to understand what will make this program a success, both in the short and the longer terms (B-1-22)

Given the heightened anxiety about the program and possible student feedback, it was agreed that the research process and associated academic reflections of teaching would be a standing item for discussion at team meetings. In addition, academic development activities scheduled during the semester were centred on areas identified as challenging from the earlier student feedback. These various forums were used during the semester to focus the attention of teaching staff on professional reflection and dialogue. This action proved broadly (though not universally) effective in elevating the level of analysis of the program as it evolved during the semester.

At the end of semester, all students were asked to complete an online questionnaire designed on Survey Monkey. An online questionnaire, rather than the previous approach of student interviews, was employed for several different reasons.

Firstly, as noted earlier, there was a desire amongst the group for the introduction of quantitative questions and it was reasonably considered these would be most validly responded to with some greater level of anonymity.

Secondly, there was a consensus that the very extensive data collected from students via interview in the first semester had proved overwhelming for the process of deliberation of the teaching team, particularly in the absence of a reflective response from teaching staff as a countervailing force. Finally, given the related desire for more direct academic input, resources were required for what would be time-consuming semi-structured interviews (hence meaning insufficient resources could be provided for similar student interviews in the narrow window of time available).

At the end of the data collection period, 113 students responded to the online survey (representing an impressive response rate of around 60 %). This response rate was achieved by the use of a series of direct emails from the Director of the Program who highlighted the critical role student feedback was to play in the future improvement of the program.

In addition, semi-structured interviews were undertaken with all 28 academic and administrative staff directly involved in the program in this second semester in Semester Two, in either one-on-one interviews or in extended focus group discussions. The data gathered in interviews, focus groups and via the student surveys was systematically analysed using similar thematic coding methods described earlier to establish the critical themes that emerged from data. These again were then further refined to generate the outcomes for the Semester Two *Evaluation and Course Development Report*.

In summary, this second evaluation of the program suggested there had been:

- a substantial improvement in student opinion from the first evaluation, with a much higher level of satisfaction with the program overall, a more positive tone in responses and lessened anxiety about several key impediments identified in the Semester One evaluation around group work, communication and expectation setting
- considerable student dissatisfaction remained around the online design, primarily the complexity of the overall online site, the limited sophistication and low quality of the simulation and unreliability of inter-communication tools;
- with the benefit of greater academic input, it emerged there was considerable epistemological confusion evident amongst staff (and to a lesser extent, students) regarding the overall objective of the program: put in its most simple form, was the program intended to replicate or simulate workplace practice environments and is it to prepare students for professional practice, or assess capability for it (or even toward further academic study)?

- uneven workloads were still problematic both for students and teachers, with some thought needed to reduce the emphasis on the enabling administrative/procedural tasks to enhance the terminal objectives of professional practice capability
- improvement was still needed in the quality of orientation and ongoing guidance provided to students. Clearer communication protocols between teachers, students and groups were also necessary.

In a significant turnaround, the majority of students and teachers responding identified the collaborative work with mentors and other students as a key positive element of the program. Students reflected on the benefits of working collaboratively, frequently observing they found it useful to learn from each other as well as the lecturer.

Academic staff broadly expressed that a positive group experience for students improved the overall learning experience and there was a general consensus that the overall quality of final work submitted was of a much higher standard than in the previous semester.

Group work was also seen by most staff and students as an effective means of developing interpersonal, time management and other general professional skills, which would transfer well into professional environments. This was a particularly significant outcome as it was a critical underpinning of moving to a simulated and collaboratively based learning environment.

Although some residual concerns remained around several dysfunctional groups and some individual students were concerned about equitable workloads, these were relatively isolated examples and starkly different from the level of dissatisfaction around this issue that emerged so strongly in the Semester One evaluation.

Moreover, academic staff observed that those student groups that worked exceptionally well together were much more proactive about organising weekly meeting times and often had face-to-face meetings, as well as using the online tools. Additionally, some staff indicated that they themselves benefited from working with a team of teachers and sharing ideas and problems, though this was tempered by concerns that communication between staff needed to be further improved.

Despite some lingering concerns about the form and quality of the simulation, its authenticity was considered to be higher by most students and teachers than in the previous semester. This was an area of improvement identified in the Semester One evaluation that had been worked on by both Program leaders and educational designers. Clearly, this design work that attempted to better replicate realistic work practices (i.e. that reflected the pressures and daily ups and downs of professional practice environments) had yielded this improved response.

Staff felt that this more practice-focused approach to learning made students much more 'practice ready' as they had to face real challenges in their prospective work. The exposure to 'real' documents was also considered to be useful in supporting the overall authenticity of the tasks and there were suggestions as to how resources could be further developed to enhance the authenticity of future iterations.

It was also generally considered by teaching staff that an authentic approach was a good way to transition students from the traditional forms of learning in undergraduate to real work practices. This was embodied in a new model (introduced this Semester following the earlier evaluation) that attempted to bridge learning in practice and assessment.

This approach—characterised as *feed forward*—assisted students in that they could now make mistakes in a safe environment and learn from these mistakes without immediate implications for assessment. Both staff and students felt that reviews of draft work—providing advice but not an assessment grade—could form an effective scaffold and to have considerably reduced some of the anxiety around the eventual assessment of these tasks.

To give students more than one attempt at getting a task right, to provide ongoing monitoring of students' work (and providing early intervention when things appeared to be going wrong) was clearly positive for the overall learning experience.

The students also appreciated the constant feedback and online communication with lecturers that allowed for fast turnaround of feedback. They viewed feed forward as a constructive way to improve on what they already know and a useful way to learn to do certain tasks better. Critically for the success of the new blended mode, students also felt that the authentic tasks helped to bridge the gap between the theories that they learnt in undergraduate with the practical nature of real practice. In addition, it was apparent that other key areas of the program subject to improvement following the previous semester, such as clarifying the function of tutors as mentors, improved online scaffolding and improvements to the online site, had generally improved the student learning experience.

As noted earlier, the student response in this evaluation was considerably more positive than the initial evaluation conducted in Semester One. It is also notable that the intensity of feeling so evident in the first evaluation around group work, communication, and unmet student expectations were not apparent in this evaluation. This meant student opinion was more diffuse and less clustered around specific concerns. Similarly, staff feedback offered quite diverse and even divergent perspectives on program improvements in the next iteration.

However, what was perhaps most significant from a program development perspective emerged around the significant uncertainty about what actually was the shared educational mission of the program. In the *Evaluation and Course Development Report* this was cast as the question to the action researchers: What is it we are trying to create (or what is the program epistemology)?

It was evident in a range of staff and student responses that there was considerable ambiguity about what form of learning environment that the program was actually trying to create. This ongoing ambiguity impacted in a variety of ways on the design of the program, forms of interaction and on ill-determined student responses.

It was to some extent apparent in the Semester One evaluation, but was overwhelmed by the more immediate and pragmatic matters that distracted the developmental drive of the research. On closer analysis of the data, most notably that generated from the semi-structured interviews with teaching staff, it seemed there were strong tensions around the educational work range that the program was actually meant to be doing (or should be doing). These tensions were also explicitly manifested in a variety of program artefacts: in the differing conceptions embodied in program marketing, in orientation, in learning materials, in expectation statements of interactions between academics and students and in how students were assessed. These tensions were centred on differing epistemic conceptions of the program, which variously emerged around beliefs that the program was:

- offering a 'safe' simulated environment for broad learning about the nature of professional practice;
- a program for the preparation of graduates for prospective professional workplace practice; or
- an actual professional practice environment with its authentic expectations and demands.

The specific nature of these tensions are explored in more detail in Table 6.1, which outlines how these epistemological tensions manifested themselves in

Table 6.1 Differing epistemological assumptions manifested in practice

Assumed function	Manifestations
Simulated learning environment (mentors/students)	*Teacher-student relationships*: strongly mentored and highly context dependent
	Pedagogical orientation: discovery learning based on trial and error
	Learning activities: generic based on perceptions of professional environment
	Assessment: against a predetermined academic-professional standard
	Terminal Objective: supported experience in a generic practice environment
Preparation for professional practice (teachers/student practitioners)	*Teacher-student relationships*: professionally informed with developmental motive
	Pedagogical orientation: scaffolded learning - transition from known to unknown
	Learning activities: scaffolding toward professional entry level expectations
	Assessment: progressively focussed on building professional capability
	Terminal Objective: broad entry level capability for professional practice
Professional practice environment (practitioners/ employees)	*Teacher-student relationships*: aloof and representative of professional expectations
	Pedagogical orientation: authentic engagement in realities of practice context
	Learning activities: replicating actual professional activities and practices
	Assessment: based on prevailing professional standards/expectations of practice
	Terminal objective: capability to operate in professional practice environment

practice, based on the data provided by academics, educational designers and students.

This outcome then provided a lens for considering some of the issues that clearly remained problematic in the program, including:

- significantly differing relationships being established and/or expected between teachers, students and groups
- differing levels of support, guidance and feedback in learning activities
- significant variance in the workload demands in differing elements of the program
- adoption of differing teaching personas (and resultant uncertain student expectations) from the role of an engaged mentor, to strategic guide, to unforgiving sage
- some frustration about the appropriateness and adequacy of the online platform and simulation design that underpinned the program
- distinct variation in the focus, design, standards and forms of assessment (and related feedback provided).

Consistent with the learning evaluation model, a post-semester workshop was convened several weeks after the issuing of the *Evaluation and Course Development Report*. This workshop was attended by broadly the same group who attended the pre-semester workshop. Perhaps unsurprisingly, given the more positive nature of this evaluative outcome, this workshop proved highly productive with staff actively engaged in debating the outcomes of the research and its implications.

The primary focus of the forum became the issue of epistemological tensions identified in the data and the implications of this ambiguity for the program. Notably, several participants sought to reprise of the seemingly redundant CHAT framework that underpinned the action research model, recalling the relevance of its conceptions of a shared object and mediating artefacts and its exposure of tensions within and between differing activity systems.

From this framework, the workshop discussed the implications of lacking a shared epistemic object and the related uncertainty in the teacher and student mind as to the overall educational objective of the program. It was generally agreed that this had far reaching implications for the design of learning activities, forms of interaction, simulation design and the nature of assessment.

Given the three different perspectives in evidence (i.e. the 'safe' simulation, practice preparation and replication of 'real' practice) some resolution to this tension was seen as necessary. All were seen as potentially valid, but in uncertain combination they tended to create considerable pedagogical confusion.

For teachers, this framed their relationship with students, how expectations were formed and the way assessment was used. For students, it was fundamental in a simulated environment as to the capability they were expected to acquire and demonstrate, as well as the reciprocal form of relationship they had with teachers.

It was agreed that this lack of clarity had led to specific concerns of teachers and students as to the appropriateness of the design and facilitation. This had also resulted in quite different forms of learning activities, varying expectations of student engagement and interaction, roles of teaching academics and most significantly, uncertainty in assessment and related feedback. Therefore the strong consensus of the workshop was that there was the need to clarify, and more clearly articulate, the program epistemology. This epistemology then needed to be more clearly used to align approaches used across the program.

The changed tone and significant outcomes of this post-semester workshop compared to the preceding semester were reflected in feedback provided after it. Some representative excerpts included:

> I finally think we are getting down to the important questions...instead of dealing with this problem or that problem; we are looking at a deeper level, at the cause rather than the symptoms. (B-4-10)

> It has been a very useful discussion and it has made me think much more about what I have been doing and what approach I have been taking to my teaching...I think I have been focused on the 'preparing for practice' space and it was clear from colleagues that we aren't all in that space. (B-4-5)

However, despite the broad consensus, not all were entirely convinced:

> Although I understand that it may be useful to clarify the teaching approach (and I certainly don't oppose that) we only have a limited time before the next semester and I won't be able to revise everything...I think this is something we need to work on over time. (B-4-16)

During the period leading up to the next semester, program leaders convened a number of forums to consider further this epistemic ambiguity and its implications for the program. This resulted in several teachers researching this matter further, producing a collaborative research paper titled: *What is our epistemology?*

From subsequent discussion of this work by members of the action research team, it was agreed that the program needed to be collectively understood as a program that prepared students for entry to professional practice (as opposed to a simulation of practice or alternatively 'real' practice).

This development had a significant effect over the coming semesters in clarifying and reshaping collaborative and individual efforts to align course pedagogies, artefacts and assessment with this refined epistemological framework.

This commonality also assisted in building a shared perspective in pedagogical discussions between teaching staff and educational designers, easing the transition of learning materials and assessment in reformed artefacts. Moreover, this debate was also to further influence broader faculty and institutional discussions around the nature of learning design for programs preparing students for professional practice environments.

Outcomes of Third Action Research Semester

Prior to the third semester of the action research, considerable re-design work was undertaken collaboratively between teaching academics and educational designers. This sought to improve the alignment of the program, its artefacts and assessment strategies with the renewed educational focus of the program as preparation for entry to professional practice. This proved a challenging process, as it involved significant further critical debate amongst the teaching team and supporting educational design staff.

Substantial professional dialogue occurred in the action research team during this intervening period around what specifically demarcated this orientation and what this would mean for the pedagogy of the program. It also debated the nature of the relationship of teaching staff to students and the nature of valid assessment.

This refocusing raised the difficult fundamental questions of what was the actual nature of professional practice that students were being prepared for (given it was not a unitary object) and secondly should this be a current or prospective reality of professional practice given the rapidly transforming nature of workplace environments. Although many questions proved polemic, most were constructively resolved.

It was within this ongoing dialogue that the action research team met to debate and plan the use of student feedback and evaluation strategy for the final third semester. This workshop was characterised by determined but practical debate about the re-focusing of the program and its likely implications. It was notable that attendance at this workshop was considerably smaller than in the previous two semesters, with a significant number of academics and tutors giving their apologies (with 9 academics, 6 tutors and 4 support staff participating).

Unsurprisingly, participants were keen to ensure this semester's evaluation was designed to ensure the effect of the clarification of the program's epistemology proved effective and that the coherence of the program was sustained in this renewal. It was apparent from the debate that the teaching group had now moved well beyond the seminal debates of conventional versus blended teaching and was broadly motivated to deal with the maturing of the blended model so as to maximise its potential. Perhaps reflecting this, the debate in the workshop was less referential to preceding semesters, being more future focused and sophisticated in form.

Fortuitously, improving student enrolments for the upcoming semester added a renewed sense of optimism to the group in its deliberations (particularly after the decline of the previous semester). What was apparent in this final semester was that the learning evaluation model had been normalised to the point where it was accepted as a legitimate process.

Unfortunately, this also meant to some extent that some participants seemed to be traversing the action research process merely as a necessary ritual, tending to re-adopt previously used strategies without significant question as to the effectiveness of preceding outcomes. This was most notable amongst program leaders. This included the continued use of quantitative questions (in addition to the range of qualitative questions).

The group had seen this as improving the recognition of the success of the program by key stakeholders, both within and outside the faculty in the preceding semester. It was also felt that a similar online survey, using the same questions as posed in semi-structured interviews in the previous semester, would suffice for academic and support staff (with the related commitment to ongoing professional reflection throughout the semester, appearing more aspirational than real). However, it was agreed that a series of questions would be added to both student and staff surveys to assess the effectiveness of the renewed focus of the program as preparation for entry to professional practice.

In this third evaluation, only 59 students responded to requests to complete an online survey (representing a lower response rate of around 35 %). The reasons for this lower participation are unclear, but it would appear from the data that students might not have felt the same drive to contribute this semester given the improving trajectory of the program. It may have also reflected the diminished levels of encouragement to participate by program leaders.

In addition, 19 academic and support staff responded to the new online academic survey. The data gathered in interviews, focus groups and surveys was systematically analysed and thematically coded to establish the critical themes that emerged, which were then refined further to generate the outcomes for the third *Evaluation and Course Development Report*.

The student feedback in this third semester demonstrated continuing improvement compared to preceding surveys undertaken post-implementation of the blended model. Broadly the student feedback demonstrated an elevating level of satisfaction with the program overall, with a more diffuse range of lower level concerns emerging than the more clustered and intense concerns characteristic in early stage evaluations.

Its outcomes tended to reflect the consensus struck in the pre-semester workshop of a growing maturation of the program, with an increasingly more satisfied student cohort. Having said this, students continued to identify further improvement potential in the program. Some student dissatisfaction remained in regard to technology, primarily revolving sophistication and relevance of the online simulation and uncertain reliability of online communication tools. It was becoming clear over the semesters that those students currently in workplace practice in particular found the simulated learning environment quite unconvincing and lacking in authenticity.

Aside from feedback provided by program leaders and educational designers, the responses by teaching staff was disappointing, with the few survey responses providing brief and largely superficial insights. Therefore, unlike the rich data generated by the semi-structured interviews in the preceding semester, this data offered little beyond broad generalisations (though such generalisations tended to accord with the perspectives offered by students).

A clear and important conclusion drawn by the *Evaluation and Course Development Report* was that there was a defined lessening in the level of epistemological confusion evident amongst staff and students in the previous two evaluations. This suggested the initial work to clarify the knowledge focus of the program via three strategies—collective dialogue, pedagogical re-orientation and reformed artefact design—had proved effective. For instance, the areas identified by students as improving their capability for workplace practice were more eclectic and less concentrated than in previous evaluations.

This third evaluative cycle suggested that as the program has matured, the design has offered a more coherent learning experience (as opposed to earlier evaluations more polarised around more defined strengths and weaknesses). Students identified the practical nature of program activities and artefacts as representing its major area that contributed to the improvement in their disciplinary skills.

In the various areas of the program, the relevance of tasks that were providing the opportunity to engage in activities that replicated practice environments were strongly valued. It was notably that this was most consistently recognised by students in areas where they had had no previous exposure to the discipline. Related to this was a clear and frequently expressed recognition of the value of the real-world artefacts on which many of the activities were hubbed. Having said this, some of these artefacts used, in the view of those with experience in specific areas, may have needed further review to ensure their continuing contemporary application to practice.

For the first time in this survey, a significant number of students positively reflected on the benefit of undertaking a range of practical writing and drafting tasks. Many students observed such tasks provided a highly useful and relevant precursor to this form of work in practice environments.

Others also drew on the challenges and learning of writing within and to other groups as it provided the opportunity to more rigorously assess the quality of individual writing and drafting tasks.

Again, for the first time, all of the various elements of the program received differing forms of recognition from students for improving relevant practice-based skills. Staff identified an extremely diverse array of positives, without any clear dimension dominating comments. Generally staff felt efforts to improve professionalism and communication were the most effective elements of the semester's activity.

Although a series of minor irritants were identified by a number of students, it was conspicuous that a series of issues that have featured prominently in previous student feedback in the two preceding semesters (and had received considerable attention as a result) did not significantly appear. These included concerns about group work, student workloads, quality of feedback, quality of instructions and the online platform.

The significant majority of students felt that the program was effective in encouraging professional conduct amongst colleagues. Many students spoke very positively about their experiences in establishing professional relationships with peers. Those who did not think the program effectively encouraged professionalism cited the failure of individual group members, the limitations of the simulation or the inadequate replication of real practice in-group work.

Staff were largely unanimous in the view that in this semester's students engaged more professionally than previous, albeit some feeling this was constrained by continuing problems with the quality of this simulation and online communication tools. There was no doubt from the data that this third evaluation demonstrated a continuing improvement trend.

As was the case in the previous semester, it is apparent that the significant implementation concerns of students have faded considerably, as has the intensity of student dissatisfaction that characterised earlier rounds of feedback. There was still clear development potential in the uneven quality and sophistication of the online simulation, in the intermittent unreliability of online communication tools and greater definition in the functional relationships that underpinned the program.

The end-of-semester workshop to consider the third *Evaluation and Course Development Report* was scheduled twice and subsequently cancelled due to significant staff unavailability. Given this, the Program Committee (made up of conveners, designers and external representatives of the profession) instead considered the report as part of their regular business at their next scheduled meeting. The report excited little debate and its broad recommendations were discussed in general terms in less than an hour. It was agreed that a series of further refinements would be made to the program for the following semester and these would be the responsibility of the program leaders and educational designers to design and implement.

Interview Data from Action Research Participants

Two months after this final committee meeting, all teachers and support staff were invited by the researcher to participate in a semi-structured interview around their broad experiences with student feedback and their specific reflections on the use of the CHAT-based, action research model used over the preceding three semesters.

Despite repeated requests, only ten academics agreed to participate. It is notable that all those responding worked full time on the Program and no casual or sessional staff volunteered to participate (although two had previously been engaged in program teaching as sessional staff).

The semi-structured interviews were conducted face-to-face and the questions posed mirrored those put to the respondents in the first case study site. Again, in order to understand the context of responses, the interviews initially explored the teaching experience of the participant, some of the influences that had shaped their current approaches to teaching and the affordances and hindrances they perceived to initiating pedagogical change. From here, the primary focus moved to their previous experiences with student evaluation and their experiences and reflections on the use of the, action research model.

Given the domination of full time staff in the sample, it was perhaps unsurprising that all but one of the respondents had in excess of five years teaching or design experience in this program. The only exception was one teaching academic whose arrival had coincided with the introduction of the blended teaching model two years before.

Respondents offered a diverse array of influences that had shaped their approach to teaching in the program: mentoring with program, personal learning experiences in discipline education (both positive and negative), experiences in workplace practice, a personal motivation to generate productive learning experiences and professional development and research on teaching. Only a single teacher (and almost as an afterthought) nominated student feedback as a shaping influence on teaching.

Indeed, it was conspicuous that more generally in responses that little reference was made to students (aside from they being the beneficiaries of teaching work). More consistently expressed was the influence of teaching peers or mentors, personal experiences of higher education or the professional drive to adequately prepare students for effective workplace practice.

In considering the question of what had changed in their teaching over time, respondents with less teaching experience (that is less than five years) tended to suggest fundamental changes following particular experiences or professional development, whilst conversely longer-term teachers highlighted the effects of the recent moves to online teaching and what adjustments to their teaching methods had been required.

Moreover, strong distinctions emerged between newer and more experienced teachers. Newer teachers tended to cast their trajectory toward improving their ability to support and mentor student learning. Longer-term teachers were more concerned with ensuring professional practice standards were clearly articulated, taught and assessed. This consistent dichotomy is well captured in these two counter posed excerpts:

> I have begun to include more reflective tasks in my teaching as I have begun to understand how important it is for students…and myself…to continually learn from what we are doing and identify what else we need to learn as we develop. I see my role as supportive where I can encourage students to work well, work effectively together and develop an ability to reflect….so they can continue improving skills throughout their careers. (B-7-3)

> I redesigned my online course materials to make them hang together better, modified the form of the seminars to fit them into the simulation and I have encouraged students online to get more early feedback prior to any submission to prevent the substantial failures we were getting on key tasks. I am focused on issues such as consistency, setting the right tone, co-ordinating with my colleagues and other important structural considerations of the program. (B-7-9)

Similarly, in reflecting on what was currently constraining them in making further changes to their teaching practice, the same broad dichotomy emerged. Whilst some respondents felt the constraint of expectations of professional education practice, others were dissuaded by more pragmatic realties of changing learning materials in an online environment:

> I require further time to read and synthesise material on teaching, formulate a course design to discuss with the educational designers and my peers, as well as revise and develop it in practice. I would also like to better understand other teaching methods that students have experienced and develop strategies that allow a smoother transition for students. (B-7-1)

> There a significant numbers of constraints in the locked format of the online elements of the program…one simple change you want to make can take an awful lot of mucking around, it can involve the convener to ensure it is consistent with the overall strategy,

the educational designers to make sure it can be done and the technical people in order to actually make it happen. It sometimes seems easier to just work with what I've got. (B-7-4)

When asked to consider previous experiences with the conventional forms of student feedback used previously, responses were considerably more varied. These ranged from the very positive, to ambivalence, to the hostile:

Positive and more positive. I really benefitted from the great student feedback I received and it certainly seem to make others understand I was a teacher committed to student-centred learning. I'm also sure it was central in getting recognised via my teaching award. (B-7-1)

The evaluations were often useful in isolating some of the detail that needed improvement. It was always nice to get good feedback. However there was always one or two students who were vitriolic in their feedback, but I generally tried to not let this affect my teaching practice. (B-7-7)

Evaluation was just forms handed out at the last minute in the last lecture. The value of responses therefore was always limited by low student motivation and insight. Yet when I received a high student satisfaction I was told I was putting too much effort into teaching rather than my research! I got very little useful that I ever took seriously. (B-7-9)

All but one respondent positively reflected on their experiences working with the new learning evaluation model over the preceding three semesters. There was a clear consensus that considering qualitative student feedback incited discussions of the broader structural issues of the program (although, as noted earlier, the experiences recorded particularly in the first semester didn't appear to necessarily reflect this in reality). Some representative observations of these sentiments included:

I found the new evaluation process highly effective for reflecting on my approaches to teaching. I was required to give deep thought to what I did and articulate these views. The process allowed other thoughts to crystallise and also allowed me to identify some patterns in my teaching, both good and undesirable. (B-7-6)

I reflected on my approach to sharing with my colleagues and placing greater value and priority to communication with my peers. I discovered more about the teaching experiences of my peers that really helped me understand what I did. (B-7-9)

It was so much more informative than the previous model…the combination of qualitative and quantitative data worked really well. Also very important was the staff view – especially since we have significant numbers of casual staff who are removed from the design process. (B-7-10)

It was excellent. The synthesis of the divergent outcomes and their presentation in a clear format with choices and strategies for discussion was priceless! (B-7-3)

However, the sole dissenting respondent raised an important alternative perspective that was occasionally in evidence in other interviews (albeit largely implicitly):

I didn't find the process particularly useful, it took a lot of time and resources, encouraged disagreement and in the end, like I think most teachers, I wanted to know what they (the students) learned from my course and whether it was what I was trying to teach. (B-7-2)

Broadly similar sentiments emerged when respondents were asked to consider the usefulness of the *Evaluation and Course Development Reports*:

> The reports provided a useful basis for a very animated and exciting discussion (and subsequent actions) regarding our objectives with this new teaching model. It highlighted that whilst we thought we were all approaching the course from the same perspective, this consistency of approach was not evident to the students. (B-7-9)

> The reports were highly influential on my subsequent approaches to teaching and working with colleagues. In fact, I would go as far as to say what I learnt from them has directly shaped my course design. (B-7-10)

> Very useful as it provided important clarification of our professional objectives and how effective we'd been in achieving these. The fact the second program came out much better than the first was a significant boost to morale, and it was good to get positive feedback we could trust and how this generated informed discussion amongst staff. (B-7-8)

However on this question, there was also evidence that the reports were not as influential for some academics:

> To some degree they were useful, although I had already started of thinking of new ways to approach my teaching regardless even before these evaluation reports were issued. I tend to revise my approaches as I receive the immediate feedback of colleagues and my sense of how students are responding. (B-7-2)

> Not very much…because in the end I remain unconvinced that this model of delivery is actually effective and like the reports I don't believe that creating 'real' tensions via group work and online simulation is necessarily the best way to learn practice skills. (B-7-4)

When asked to consider the overall effectiveness of the model, a similar pattern emerged with most academics identifying it as a valuable enhancement, but a minority not sharing this perspective. Some exemplar observations of this range of views included:

> I have generally found the evaluation model to be far more effective than any other evaluations I have been involved in. The way the data was given to us really allowed us to focus on some of the broad issues we needed to address rather than get stuck on individual staff/student popularity based comments. (B-7-6)

> It (the model) seemed to provide much more depth and therefore it resulted in much more useful insight and change. I think having all staff engaged directly in face-to-face discussions about the feedback is great. Combining the student and staff feedback provides a much more holistic understanding of what worked and what didn't and how to improve. (B-7-10)

> I think this new evaluation model offered great potential as a tool for aligning teaching philosophies while allowing for many diverse methods that utilise the strengths of individual teachers to emerge. (B-7-4)

Less enthusiastic commentary revolved around two important matters - direct relevance to individual subject areas of teaching and time limitations to enact change:

> Although I found the evaluation outcomes reasonably interesting, they lacked clear relevance to the course I was teaching. I needed much more specific material that gave me a better insight into what the students felt they learned in my component and what helped

and hindered this. It was hard to understand this from the broad form in which the data was produced and presented. (B-7-4)

Time is a constraint in this mode. We unfortunately have very little turnaround time between beginning and end of these courses. And the clear expectations are that we act on the feedback regardless of the demands on our time. So we were always prioritising and compromising on what we could actually develop. This is even a more significant problem where it involves changes to the online simulation or the platform. (B-7-2)

Conclusion

This second case study proved to be more demanding and considerably more volatile than the first site. The research commenced in the context of strong unresolved tensions over the move from a conventional teaching model to a blended approach using an early generation online simulation and communication forums. For the process, this inevitably meant that the participants in the action research did not have a shared object of inquiry, with this being fragmented between the value of the blended model and its further development.

Similarly, debates about the way the program was designed and the related artefacts that supported it were initially mired in more fundamental tensions about whether this was an appropriate form of pedagogy for the learning of professional practice skills. This had the related impact of intermittent and uneven academic participation in the action research process. It also produced a disproportionate and arguably further polarising influence of a large amount of student feedback data.

As this strong tension began to fade, the research was more centred on some of the immediate and largely superficial problems that were hindering the effectiveness of the online elements of the program, including orientation for the online environment, communication protocols and artefact design.

Although for the third semester more fundamental issues around program epistemology emerged (perhaps reflecting the development of a genuinely shared object of inquiry), the level of academic engagement with the research process had faded to the core group directly responsible for the program.

Nevertheless, there is reasonable evidence from the data gathered during the action research cycles that the heightened use of qualitative (and later some quantitative) student feedback generated an elevated level of professional dialogue and effected some productive change in this program.

However, as one academic pondered in the interviews at the conclusion of the third semester, would this have had to have happened regardless of this intervention, given the turbulent state of the program and the urgent need for its development? Although it is impossible to answer this question, it is apparent that the qualitative nature of the derived student feedback forced a collective dialogue that may not have occurred with more reductive quantitative data.

This debate forced the group to move beyond the ferocious differences about new teaching modes, to more fundamental questions of student learning. The action research outcomes also demonstrated that such productive dialogue, prompted by critical engagement with qualitative student feedback, could be rapidly normalised and future focused—regardless of the serious limitations imposed by program histories.

Equally, it can be also observed from these same outcomes how rapidly this collectivist perspective can retreat into the more familiar and less critical patterns of individualised concerns, as can the corollary: the re-imposition of the hegemonic drives of educational leaders. Finally, it was also notable that as was the case with the previous case, this experience similarly raised further questions about the viability of a CHAT-informed, action research model in the real environments of academic work, particularly beyond its potential value as a short-term interventionist (or conflict resolution) tool.

Chapter 7
Assurance or Improvement: What Work Can Student Evaluation Most Effectively Perform?

Abstract In this chapter, the use of the expansive learning cycle—centred on elevated use of qualitative student feedback data—will be critically analysed drawing on the empirical data generated by the two CHAT-informed, action research case studies reported in the preceding chapters. Specifically, the value of more collective forms of academic dialogue, based on qualitative student feedback will be assessed to determine if this acted as a productive disturbance toward collective pedagogical improvement. In the light of this analysis, the developmental potential of an elevated use of student feedback as a tool for expansive learning for teachers in higher education will be further assessed. This exploration will consider evidence that indicated the realisation of new ways of individual and collective functioning, the creation of new forms of pedagogical knowledge and of transformed approaches to academic teaching based on an expanded understanding of student learning. The chapter will also consider those factors identified in the research which served to limit the potential of this developmental approach.

Keywords Cultural-historical activity theory (CHAT) · Qualitative student evaluation · Sociocultural analysis · Case study analysis

Introduction

In this chapter, the substantive outcomes of the two case studies reported in the previous chapters will be analysed for their implications for the elevated use of the student voice as a catalyst for pedagogical improvement in higher education settings. Using a well-established tool for sociocultural analysis, the data produced by the use of the *expansive learning evaluation cycle* will be critically analysed.

Specifically, the chapter will assess whether this use of qualitative student feedback, in tandem with its consideration with a collective form of professional dialogue, proved effective in enhancing pedagogical practices and producing positive developmental change. Further, how sustainable such change proved to be in the

© Springer International Publishing Switzerland 2016
S. Darwin, *Student Evaluation in Higher Education*,
DOI 10.1007/978-3-319-41893-3_7

121

robust realties of situated practice will be further explored. This exploration will consider evidence from the case studies that indicated new ways of individual and collective functioning, the creation of new forms of pedagogical knowledge and of re-formed approaches to academic teaching.

In order to critically consider the levels of agency afforded by the CHAT-informed, action research model, an analytical tool developed by Rogoff (1995), and subsequently developed in the analysis of activity systems in education by Yamagata-Lynch (Yamagata-Lynch 2010; Yamagata-Lynch and Smaldino 2007), will be used. This tool offers three interrelated and mutually constituting planes of sociocultural analysis in order to understand the mutuality of development between the individual and the social environment. These planes of sociocultural activity recognise that development occurs at multiple levels: at the community/institutional level, at the interpersonal level and at the personal level.

The community/institutional level will frame understanding of the extent of personal engagement in shared activity, the interpersonal level on evidence of collaborative participation in social activity and the personal on evidence of change through involvement in such activity.

Rogoff (1995) argues that these three planes are reflected in inseparable concepts that are inherent to their form. Personal engagement is linked to the conception of *apprenticeship*, in that it analyses the processes by which less experienced individuals come to participate in sociocultural activity toward the development of more mature forms of engagement. Interpersonal actions are aligned to the concept of *guided participation*, which considers the analysis of communication and co-ordination between individuals in various processes and systems, be they face-to-face, in collaborative activity or in more distant forms of guidance. *Participatory appropriation* is the conceptual underpinning of institutional and community processes. This considers how individuals change through interpersonal engagement in activity and become capable through this involvement to change their approach to a later situation.

The first component of this analysis will consider the form and extent individual participants in the case studies engaged in the collective action research process with qualitative student feedback. This will assess what evidence emerged that this process led to a more mature form of engagement with the student voice. Secondly, the extent of communication and co-ordination between individuals is assessed to determine the nature of collaborative development that occurred as a result of the action research. Lastly, evidence of change in participants as they engaged in interpersonal activity is explored to assess whether experiences in socially-mediated activity resulted in an internalising of changed approaches to the use of, and regard toward the student voice.

The First Plane: Personal Engagement in Shared Activities (Apprenticeship)

At the broadest level, substantial evidence emerged over the three semesters that action research participants generally engaged in an elevated form of professional dialogue. The catalyst provided by thematically framed, qualitative student feedback demonstrable prompted this response. This conclusion is supported by evidence of the critical investigation and reformation of a range of pedagogical practices, in collaborative approaches to educational design and in enhanced use of learning technologies. Much of the generative activity in the collective workshops, particularly those in the two earlier semesters, sparked extensive (and at times highly animated) dialogue around what students reasonably could and actually did observe about the two programs. From this dialogue, a series of tangible developmental outcomes were devised in response.

Further, evidence indicated that the changes negotiated collectively for programs were generally supported and enacted by individual teaching academics in practice (albeit with considerably differing levels of enthusiasm and collaboration). In addition, as the action research progressed during the semesters, the level of maturity demonstrated in dialogue demonstrably elevated. This was reflected in the transition from initial uncertainty and defensiveness to a more constructive—yet contested—developmental discourse.

In the case of the first program, this meant participants who sensed a peripheral right to engage (due to their part-time, practitioner status) moving more centrally into key educational debates generated by student feedback and exploring their legitimate academic perspectives and associated development needs. In the case of the second site, this was most starkly manifested in the defined move from largely polarised dialogue around the value of moving to a blended learning model into fundamental questions about program epistemology.

Such personal engagement also emerged with the need for greater research on the educational objectives of the program and how this could be reflected in program design and teaching. However, although this maturation was reflected in dialogue, it was less certain in levels of engagement and action in changed practices.

The nature of this broad evolution in professional dialogue and related action for both programs is captured in Table 7.1. This table maps the maturing of key dialogue foci on entry and across semesters. What is notable about this data is the transformation from a focus on what could be broadly characterised as *what the teacher did* to the more significant developmental drive of *what the students were doing*. Undoubtedly the elevation of qualitative student feedback data (and the inherent contradictions it generated) had a significant impact in focusing the debate on student learning.

As the analysis in Table 7.1 illustrates, the elevation and exploration of student feedback did produce an evolving and maturing collective focus on how to most effective enhance student learning. Evidence generated in the case study environments suggests this maturation was a consequence of the thematic organisation and pedagogical ordering of qualitative student opinion. This then drove

Table 7.1 Maturing of key dialogue across the semesters

Stage	Program one	Program two
Entry	• Assessment reliability • Blended teaching • Graduate capabilities	• Value of blended teaching model • Danger of critical exposure with more evaluative data
Semester One	• Student engagement • Student expectations • Integrated assessment • Strategies to build more engaged online communities	• Improved online sophistication • Improved student orientation • Staff role clarification • Improve group cohesion • Compulsory individual assessment
Semester Two	• Strategies to build early/ongoing student engagement • Building online dialogue • Curriculum alignment • Designing innovative assessment	• Epistemological uncertainty: developing simulated practice, preparing students for practice, and replicating 'real' practice? • Implications for the design of learning objects, simulation and assessment
Semester Three	• Development of consistent assessment rubrics for consistency/student learning • Consistent feedback • Improved online facilitation	• Further review of program artefacts • Further improve sophistication of the online simulation

heightened forms of professional discourse during the semesters. This conclusion was reinforced by the reflective data collected after the three semesters from participants. In broad terms, this data affirmed that this collective maturation was recognised by participants in the action research.

Further, many individuals identified that this shared dialogue also served to develop their own understanding of the complex challenges of teaching and learning in the specific disciplinary environment. Unsurprisingly this effect was uneven, with differing levels of impact related to levels of prior teaching experience and levels of engagement in the action research process.

Although this reflective data was somewhat limited by the number of respondents (particularly from the second program), it—in combination with workshop data—broadly suggested that:

(a) participants with limited previous teaching experience tended to realise this maturation in terms of a deeper understanding of specific techniques to improve student learning and their potential relationship with environments of the discipline

(b) participants with more teaching experience tended to realise this maturation in terms of collaboratively designing pedagogies to enhance student engagement and learning, as well as confronting epistemological ambiguities in preparing students for the demands of future workplace practice

(c) participants with greater proximity to current practice environments tended to progressively elevate the need for more developed alignment between the contexts of education and practice settings, particularly in the formation of program artefacts and assessment strategies.

However, what is equally significant was the real difficulty encountered in the case study sites in securing and sustaining individual engagement in the action research throughout the three semesters. As was reported in the last chapters, there was evidence of the limited and, at times forced, reflections of teaching academics during semesters outside the introductory and post workshops.

Despite the clear framing of the action research as an ongoing professional engagement throughout the three semesters, this in reality failed to materialise. This resulted in professional dialogue that was almost exclusively centred on the student voice. This was also despite the persistent attempts of the program leaders to facilitate and encourage this ongoing dialogue between teaching academics during semesters.

This had the effect of limiting the developmental potential of the action research. Not infrequently it led to somewhat destructive debates based on superficial consideration of the affordances and hindrances to effective student learning generated by the *Evaluation and Course Development Reports*. The largely exclusive focus on student feedback meant that the sophistication of discussions was frequently limited and often functional or surface level solutions were developed (as reflected in Table 7.1). This effect was even more pronounced in the more established second program, where participation of academics in workshop dialogue was patchy and in the early stages highly fragmented.

However, some of this disengagement also went beyond the limited contributions made by academics to ongoing reflection during semesters. In observational data collected in workshops, it was apparent this was, for a significant minority of participating academics, more fundamental.

This differential level of engagement appeared to reflect diverse motives, ranging from a sense of professional illegitimacy (with an identity of practitioner rather than educator, particularly evident in the first program with a higher proportion of part-time teachers) to outright hostility (based on frustration with the activity given external factors, most evident in the second program). Obviously within these dichotomous poles of illegitimacy and hostility lay most of the participants in the study.

Nevertheless, the impact of individuals with a part-time and/or peripheral teaching role and those who reflected the traumatic impact of moves to blended forms of learning inevitably created social learning environments that were at times not only complex in form (given the limited participation of some participants), but also tension-laden as a result of the divergent object focus of these individuals.

This complexity tended to lead to too much of the action research effort—as well as the subsequent interpretive dialogue—being dominated by program leaders (and vicariously, by me as the researcher). At one level, this domination proved effective in driving the pedagogical developments identified with the elevated use of student feedback. It also demonstrably produced improvement in student engagement and learning over the study, given the evidence of improving student feedback outcomes throughout the three semesters.

However, at another level, it also meant that the levels of participant engagement were necessarily constrained and the levels of involvement (and potential maturation) more limited than may have been otherwise possible. This was particularly evident in later stage workshops in both programs, where group numbers declined and notions of consensus tended to be more imposed than real.

Reflecting this reality, as Table 7.1 graphical illustrates, the outcomes of both programs deteriorated in the final semester as a result of falling academic participation and the growing hegemony of program leaders that tended to fill this vacuum. Although this outcome was partly related to reductions to academic staff levels with falling enrolments and changed teaching staff in both programs, it also reflected a broader decline that was clearly a result of individuals becoming disengaged from an action research model that was proving less productive, democratic and inclusive in its evolved form.

In addition, it was significant that the discourses around the action research changed in the second and third semesters with a rising surety that the programs had reached a 'threshold point' of acceptable quality. Although this sentiment was represented in differing forms, it seemed to indicate the lingering strength of the quality assurance motive of student feedback.

This effect also tended to be reflected in a shared intent in both programs to demonstrate to the university that the programs were indeed meeting expectations (or perhaps desirable quality standards). This was particularly strongly expressed in the second more established program, where real concerns about perceptions of the impact of changed pedagogies on learning quality were live issues of debate outside the program.

Conversely, these powerful traces of these residually powerful quality assurance discourses also seemingly had the effect of stifling the momentum for substantial attempts to improve and develop the program. Essentially, this seemed to be based on the assumption that once identified problems were broadly addressed, efforts to interrogate the student voice could be curtailed.

Unsurprisingly, observational data gathered from the action research during the semesters suggested it was the program leaders who demonstrated the strongest evidence of maturation. This was further confirmed in data derived from the post-action research interviews.

In CHAT terms, this reflected the strong, culturally ascribed function of such educational leaders in a university, who are engendered with considerable authority and responsibility to act. Characteristically, such leaders tended in the practical level of pedagogy and assessment to mediate the collective sense of how teachers should relate to students. This form of mediated action was further framed by powerful, historically developed discipline and academic discourses.

Similarly, although the case studies were disruptively framed within the paradigm of participative action research, they progressively were more reflective of the established divisions of labour within programs and the faculty more generally as this activity was normalised.

Hence, aside from the formative workshops where participation was broad, the primary developmental work tended to be framed and driven by program leaders and conveners rather than the collective group. Data indicated that this was a retreat to the pre-existing roles that existed in programs, where because of staff being disengaged (be it in an educational or employment sense) the tasks of development conventional fell to these leaders and conveners.

This effect was intensified by short timeframes between semesters, which meant the development work tended to become centralised and controlled. This was further amplified by the disruptive challenges of online learning technologies which created another distinct and disempowering division of labour between those most capable of analysing and developing responses in the online environment (most often, the program leaders) and those who merely enacted the outcomes of this change in teaching.

On a broader cultural level, this divide reflects the increasing intensification of academic work within universities, where the conflicting pressures of teaching, research and service are limiting opportunities for collective labour.

In these case study sites, data from participant interviews suggested this reality also tended to sharpen the divide between roles, particularly the capacity to innovate and develop in teaching. This meant educational leaders were also 'expected' to take broad responsibility for student learning and drive opportunities for its enhancement, whilst teaching academics carried the manifold responsibilities as teachers, researchers and faculty members (in the case of full time staff) or as expert practitioners with discipline currency (in the case of part time and adjunct staff).

So ironically, the move to collective consideration of broad student feedback appeared to further amplify, rather than lessen, this division of labour. So pronounced was this division in the second more-established program, that program leaders (and not teachers as was the case in first program) insisted on the re-introduction of subject-level data to create a broadened imperative to act.

In practice in the two case studies, the level of personal engagement was highly variable and also evolved within fractured academic teaching communities. As a result, the development imperative was met with diffuse forms of personal agency. This created considerable tensions that remained unresolved and eventually produced significant levels of disengagement.

The Second Plane: Interpersonal Engagement (Guided Participation)

The level and extent of interpersonal engagement in the action research teams was highly variable and reflective of significant external and internal forces that were shaping each of the programs. The introductory work in both programs evolved fundamentally differently, with the formulation of the action research projects themselves.

The first program, as a relatively new and successful program with a small core and large peripheral academic workforce, saw a broad and generally enthusiastic engagement with the prospect of the use of extended qualitative forms of student feedback data. On this basis, strong interpersonal dialogue was the foundation of the introductory workshop, albeit with a somewhat loose connection with orientating CHAT-informed, action research framework.

Data indicated that this was built on an existing and established professional dialogue, centred on the objective of high quality learning for prospective workplace practice. This reflected the strong roots the first program had in the profession (given the number of sessional practitioner-teachers engaged) and the powerful need to sustain student enrolments in a market of other competing universities.

Existing tools and processes were evident on entry and these provided a substantial foundation to build further interpersonal engagement in workshops around potential program improvements driven by dialogue around student feedback. Yet it was equally notable that several participants clearly identified this development potential was often constrained in the action research, as the limitations of the student feedback data derived from the former quantitative student evaluation system continued to engender uncertainty around innovative practice.

Nevertheless, the program was an amenable site for this form of study and the affordances provided by this established professional dialogue enhanced the potential of the action research to generate significant development. Yet it nevertheless proved difficult to sustain the level of interpersonal engagement over the full life of the action research. Moreover, given the relatively high levels of peripheral academic staff, interpersonal cohesion suffered as a result of inevitable personnel changes and cyclical staffing reductions.

Finally, as noted earlier, as it became apparent that improvement had occurred in the program and students were generally satisfied, the intensity for further change seemed to recede in the minds of many participants.

Conversely, the second program was a long established program with a strong central cohort of academic staff and a significant, but relatively small, sessional group. As the research was undertaken at a time of turbulence for the program—following closely on significant and contested pedagogical reformation—interpersonal relations (along with the systems and processes that supported them) were disrupted and seemingly even disconnected.

Additionally, the program itself was struggling with this transition, magnifying the inevitable interpersonal tensions this change had generated. This played out even before the introductory workshop, with the need to carefully frame the approach to the action research with a clear recognition of these strong tensions. This was necessary to clearly recognise these tensions and contribute strategies to rebuild interpersonal relations around program development.

The action research was both framed and largely conducted within this social environment of disconnected interpersonal relations. This encouraged a centralising drive by program leaders, leading to significant ambivalence and disengagement by many participants in the workshops and the research more generally.

Student feedback outcomes inevitably formed potent ammunition to support or contest the change of teaching mode. Perhaps this would have occurred regardless of the actual form of student feedback, however the collective form of engagement no doubt provided a rich platform for determined debate.

Initially, the outcomes of the action research seemed to create more polarised outcomes, tending to strengthen the dissonance of those who opposed the change (whilst also encouraging the advocates that improvement was possible). Indeed, evidence collected in the workshops and in subsequent individual interviews suggested that student feedback had effectively inspired stronger processes and systems of communication between those carrying similar perspectives.

Over the life of the action research, this meant elevating engagement by some and disassociation by others. As was reported in last chapter, by the end of the third semester, only the program leadership remained actively engaged in the action research in any real sense. Similarly, the agreed development of shared processes arising from the action research teams reflected these different program trajectories. In the first program, a broader range of collective responses was defined (particularly during the first two semesters of the research).

In the first semester, these included developing strategies and systems to enhance levels of student engagement (by collaborating on design elements and common earlier release dates), agreeing and more clearly articulating learning expectations, developing a collective capability to online facilitation and communities and a common core of assessment throughout the program. Some of these responses were developed as situated forms of academic development, with small groups and individuals being mentored and supported in improved practices.

However, regardless of the efforts to build interpersonal co-ordination amongst academics, they largely failed to materialise as co-operative forms of development, tending to be implemented in isolation by individuals (often under direction) and largely with a superficial response to the identified issues. Evidence that emerged in subsequent workshops and in the artefacts produced suggested that there were limited co-operative responses and more manifestations of mandated approaches.

Perhaps the most telling evidence was that the fact that, despite the clear imperative of the action research model, little real reflective dialogue developed amongst teaching academics during the three semesters to inform the later debates around the meaning of student feedback.

Yet it was also apparent that the changes enacted by these means did actually produce improvements in student feedback in subsequent semesters in this first program. However, paradoxically this result then worked to produce more framed and imposed developmental strategies in the following semester. Examples of this included limiting online discussion forums to a specific form, developing standard assessment rubrics, the adoption of a core assessment object for all subjects and attempts to push for changes to the assessment standards of the regulator. In the final semester, this further retreated to strengthened modelling, quality assurance and professional development around rubric-based feedback, sharing 'effective' online facilitation techniques and improving the technology platform further (again on the basis of positive student feedback in the preceding semester).

The reasons for this specific evolution of the critical interpersonal dimension of the activity would appear to be manifold from the data collected. Firstly, the realities of a small core of full-time academics, with primary responsibility for the program and a significant part-time practitioner-teacher group, inevitably created differential levels of power and engagement in the action research.

This was most clearly reflected in the data in the generally high interventionist methods and accountability demands of the core group. This was fuelled by this group's anxieties about the limited time, capability and, at times, engagement of sessional staff. This was further accentuated by the relative stability of the core group in comparison to the peripheral teacher-practitioners, who experienced some turnover during the three semesters.

In essence, this produced three different sets of interpersonal relations: two within each cohort and a third between these two groups that reflected their highly uneven power relations and relative capability to act. Although a democratic sense was employed to frame the action research, the interpersonal dialogue and actions in, and beyond, the workshops suggested the effects of this fragmentation were significant in shaping the nature of the outcomes of the action research and how they were subsequently implemented.

In the second program, the strong tensions within the group meant that it was difficult to identify genuinely shared processes developing between teaching academics during the life of the action research. From the highly tentative planning process with program leaders and throughout the introductory and subsequent workshops, ongoing divisions prevented any broad or effective interpersonal engagement.

These fundamental divisions overwhelmed any prospect of a collective framing of (or response to) student feedback. Instead, the fracturing meant that those opposing the recent program changes tended to develop a strong interpersonal alliance during the workshops and beyond, with a determined focus on the limitations and lost potential of the former orthodox model. This essentially served to undermine, rather than develop the program.

A second group, primarily the program leaders, similarly coalesced around the imperative of further development of the new blended learning program. A third group, largely sessional and other part-time staff effectively became disengaged as this conflict raged around them (particularly in the formative stages of the action research process). The effect of this was to undermine any real shared processes or systems that could have developed as a result of the action research.

Reflecting this, the outcomes of the post-semester workshops were a mixture of generally agreed abstract developments and largely imposed specific strategies. Although some staff turnover and improving student feedback did gradually lift the level of shared dialogue (particularly around the issues of program epistemology in the second semester), the trajectory was firmly toward the action research outcomes informing the decisions of program leaders, rather than as a generator of collective professional dialogue.

A further indicator of a lack of interpersonal connection was the fact that virtually no substantive reflective dialogue was generated by teaching academics during the last two semesters, despite the explicit imperative of the action research model. The data generated by semi-structured interviews of teaching staff tended to confirm the scale of the inherent divisions in the group. Finally, as noted earlier, the final workshop in the second case study site was never scheduled; suggesting by the end of the three semesters the level of interpersonal relations had essentially evaporated in any real sense.

The Third Plane: Community (Participatory Appropriation)

Rogoff (1995) describes the notion of community as the externalised outcome of the enhanced agency that comes from involvement in activity that prepares individuals for future, object-orientated activities. For this plane, evidence of the externalisation of the experiences of learnt activity becomes significant as a form of participatory appropriation. In considering this plane for the outcomes from the first case study site, the most useful data was derived from the participant interviews at the end of the action research. It was apparent from this data that the framing of action research around qualitative student feedback was generally influential in encouraging greater reflection on the nature of individual pedagogical practice.

At a basic level, making visible the affordances and constraints to student learning was identified as significant in confirming or defying existing pedagogical assumptions held by participants. More sophisticated responses suggested that the action research was similarly influential in redefining teaching identities and fundamentals of professional practice.

Unsurprisingly given the earlier observations, this effect was varied according to the form of engagement teaching academics had with the program (and by extension with the action research itself). The ability of participants to more clearly identify significant issues in student feedback engendered a more authoritative sense of action and an enhanced belief in the value of the student voice.

Equally, the considerable commitment of intellectual effort and time required in order to effectively engage, respond and further evaluate student opinion weighed heavily on even those who saw future potential from the learning of the action research. The declining level of genuine engagement in the action research over the semesters and the receding significance of identified developmental actions, suggested that the level of actual appropriation by participants was generally modest at best. It may have been somewhat more significant for the program leaders who possessed the direct responsibility for pedagogical improvement and quality assurance of the program.

Interestingly, a broadly similar outcome can be identified in the levels of appropriation identified in the second case study. Again, the most useful data emerged from the semi-structured interviews that were conducted after the completion of the action research.

Although the number of respondents was relatively low (given the overall participants), the same broad responses emerged. Most participants identified the developmental potential of making elevated use of qualitative student feedback and the action research model more generally. This was recognised as both affirming and disrupting previously held assumptions about what proved effective and less effective in individual pedagogical practices. This inevitably intersected with lingering issues about the early move to blended teaching, but the relative improvement of the program along with staff turnover meant that this was not as significant as the desire to enhance things like online facilitation, the quality of simulated learning environments and attuning assessment to this new pedagogical domain.

Conversely, some frustration was apparent amongst several more experienced teachers about the collective nature of the action research outcomes, as they tended to provide only limited insights into the specific subject they were teaching. For these teachers, the sense was that the former model of subject-specific quantitative evaluation held clear attraction, though this was tempered by some of the value seen in more macro forms of student feedback.

As was the case with first program, evidence from the workshops suggested a declining level of engagement over the semesters of the study. Participant interviews suggested much of this again was a result of broader dissatisfaction with the directions of the program, as well as the time and intellectual energy required to invest (and some scepticism that the development was inherently 'top-down' in design. This latter perspective was confirmed by the actions observed in end-of-semester dialogue and implementation strategies, which generally reflected this entrenched hegemony.

Indeed, program leaders acknowledged throughout the action research that this was an essential strategy to overcome ongoing resistance and 'get things happening' (so the program's ongoing viability was not threatened). Inevitably, this limited the shared meaning that could develop and the levels of appropriation that could be reasonably been expected to be an outcome of the collaborative action research model.

Conclusion

In this chapter, three interrelated planes of sociocultural meaning to were used to assess the effect of the action research and the elevated use of qualitative student feedback. This demonstrated that the existing cultural and structural foundations of the programs were fundamentally important in shaping the development potential of the approach, particularly beyond the initial intervention stage.

Factors such as the existing levels of collaborative professional dialogue, the divisions of labour, the nature of the teaching community and the rules which guided assumptions about program development were all significant in how the action research model evolved in response to the aggravating effect of the elevated use of the student voice.

In both case study sites, sustaining academic engagement in the action research (and therefore its developmental trajectory) was quite challenging, unexpectedly resource intensive and confounded by often tense pre-existing divisions of labour. This outcome reaffirms the well-understood challenges of securing real ongoing academic engagement in program development tasks, given the intensifying and multifaceted work demands of the contemporary university.

It also illustrates the difficulties of creating a compelling logic for the continuation of a demanding, and times confronting, process of professional dialogue framed by student feedback within this environment. In these cases, this was further complicated by the strong lingering traces of the culture of quality assurance (manifested as deficit and defence), which persisted in framing many responses to qualitative forms of student feedback. This tended to produce a more determined focus on addressing identified problems (i.e. deficits), rather than commitment to ongoing cycles of broader-based development.

In the next chapter, more specific attention is given to the developmental potential identified in the use of qualitative student feedback in this CHAT-based, action research model. This centres on evidence of the expansive learning (or otherwise) that was generated from these case studies, as well as the implications this may have had for the development of improved pedagogical practices and for rethinking the approaches used to harness the student voice.

Chapter 8
Assessing the Developmental Potential of Student Feedback

Abstract Does the student voice have the potential to encourage improved forms of collaborative learning among academics? Can the elevated use of student evaluation become a productive generator of professional knowledge or situated academic development? In this chapter, evidence that emerged in the case studies about the developmental potential of student feedback—as an expansive tool for collaborative professional learning—will be analysed. Specifically, the chapter will consider whether the outcomes of the case studies demonstrate that the elevated use of student voice was genuinely influential in shaping individual and collective academic learning (as reflected in changed or transformed pedagogical practices). To explore this, the analysis will use the four key criteria for assessing expansive learning advocated by Engeström (2007a): evidence of the broadening of the shared objects of professional work, the related development of new forms of knowledge and tools to engage with identified problems and evidence of cognitive trails of re-formed work.

Keywords Expansive learning · Cultural historical activity theory (CHAT) · Qualitative student evaluation · Collaborative academic dialogue

Introduction

A fundamental dimension of CHAT-based research rests in its developmental orientation, focused on the notion of active intervention to make visible the historicity, contradictions and tensions in everyday, shared activity. This forms the foundation for generating innovative disturbances in collective work, toward generating expansive solutions in order to resolve pressing internal contradictions historically accumulating in social activity (Engeström 1999).

Such expansive solutions re-organise (or re-mediate in CHAT terms) work to make it more capable of achieving the outcomes being sought. This is the foundation of the theory of expansive learning, which asserts qualitatively new ways of functioning and enhanced professional practice arise from the expansion of the object of the activity. This forms as a result of the:

> creation of new knowledge and new practices for a newly emerging activity; that is, learning embedded in and constitutive of qualitative transformation of the entire activity system (Daniels 2008, p. 126).

Therefore, given the clear developmental focus of research based on a CHAT-informed, action research framework, an analysis of evidence of expansive learning is an important means of assessing the overall effectiveness or otherwise of this interventionist use of qualitative student evaluation. To develop this summative analysis, the three central characteristics of expansive learning defined by Engeström (2007a) are be employed as an analytical tool. These characteristics can be summarised in the following form:

(a) *transformative learning*: learning that radically broadens the shared objects of work by means of explicitly objectified and articulated novel tools, models and concepts.
(b) *horizontal and dialogical learning*: learning that creates knowledge and transforms… by crossing boundaries and tying knots between activity systems.
(c) *subterranean learning*: learning that blazes cognitive trails that are embodied and lived but unnoticeable…anchors and stabilizing networks that secure the viability and sustainability of the new concepts, models and tools.

(Engeström 2007a)

Using this exploratory taxonomy, the overall outcomes of the case studies will be considered to provide further insights into the expansive learning impact of this CHAT-based, action research-led intervention.

Transformative Learning

There was reasonable evidence from the case studies that the re-mediating impact of a qualitative student feedback was responsible for broadening the shared object of the evaluative activity and generating significant developmental change in programs. Essential to this outcome was the broadly shared conceptual understanding of participants around the increasing ambiguous function of student feedback within the conflicting activity systems of quality improvement, quality assurance and individual performance assessment.

There was evidence that the model also reconciled some of the pre-existing tensions around the role of student voice and the quantitative model of student feedback in use prior to the research. The effect of removing the quantitative comparator intrinsic to the quality assurance uses of student feedback was to elevate its developmental potential during the three semesters.

Paradoxically, this also had a potentially reductive effect, tending to create further tensions around how to externally demonstrate teaching quality within the rising institutional accountability discourses. This resulted in some retreat to the more familiar approaches of subject specific and quantitative data during the research.

The very emergence of the tool of elevated qualitative student feedback data, codified via thematic framing, was sufficient to spark critical and important debates within the action research teams around important matters of pedagogy, assessment and the relationship of programs to sites of professional workplace practice. It also generated a subversive dialogue that engendered serious doubts as to the actual developmental value of quantitative feedback previously in use.

In addition, the foundational *expansive learning evaluation cycle* was generally effective in inciting some critical, collective dialogue around differing pedagogical approaches. This was particularly evident around the integrative use of online technologies and in improving the quality and relevance of student assessment and feedback. At a broader level, the cycle also provided a tangible framework for enhancing cycles of reflection and action.

This suggests that the model and conceptual tools it generated worked in some form to transform the shared objects of work. Yet how radical and sustainable this transformation actually was is less certain.

There was evidence that a series of specific, situated developmental responses within the individual programs were the demonstrable outcomes of the disturbances of the elevated use of qualitative student feedback. However, given these were built on the specific historical and cultural foundations of each program, they were of differing scale and eventual effect.

Further, this processes of disturbance made visible contradictions in the everyday activity of teaching, resulting in the exposure of tensions that otherwise would have remained implicit and largely unrecognised in the programs. Examples of these more visible contradictions included:

- conflicting conceptions of the respective roles and appropriate forms of interaction between educators, the university, professional environments and professional regulatory expectations
- often pragmatic intentions of students to expediently complete a qualification, the expectation of designing high quality learning experiences and the capability limitations on program improvement
- uncertain epistemological constructions of discipline education for professional practice contexts: whether it is to engage students in preparation for professional practice, to educate students around the expectations of current (or prospective) practice, or for the actual realities practice itself
- the complex tensions created by the demands of the student-as-consumer, institutional demands for rigor and accountability, external scrutiny from the profession and the maintenance of appropriate academic standards
- implicit tensions in responses to student feedback around what were desirable, necessary and possible given the specific histories, trajectories and resourcing of the programs.

The pre and post-semester workshops provided a broadly effective mechanism to generate significant developmental discourse, at times producing a genuine depth of analysis that led to substantial insights and resultant change. The form of this professional dialogue took differing forms in the two programs for the contextual reasons detailed earlier. This meant in the first program, the model generated such development as re-formed student assessment and feedback, strategies for improved student engagement, reframing of student expectations and enhanced authenticity of program artefacts.

Evidence indicated these outcomes were clearly a result of the developmental imperative of the *expansive learning evaluation cycle*. In the case of the second case study site, the legacy of its recent transition to a blended learning model and its structural differences to the first site produced a fundamentally different developmental trajectory.

Nevertheless, in the case of the second program the CHAT-based, action research orientation provided a robust framework to critical (and extensively) debate the largely unresolved and volatile tensions about the recent reformation of teaching mode. Although it was not the sole impetus, evidence suggested these processes of collective debate assisted in resolving limitations in the online element of the program, and more generally in reconciliation of the strong differences in the group over time.

Reflecting this reality, the outcomes of student feedback generated high-level conceptual debate around ambiguity and inconsistency in program epistemology, as well as a range of related developments in response. At another level, this developmental dialogue drove significant improvements to the integration of the largely disparate online elements of the program, as well as improved forms of virtual communication with, and inter-communication between, students.

However, the broader CHAT-based, action research framework was more limited in broadening professional dialogue beyond structured discourses. Despite persistent attempts to encourage the formation of functional action research teams, there was little collective intentionality or research inquiry beyond that framed by the workshops actually developed. Aside from some intermittent and isolated instances, no substantial professional dialogue was formed to provide a more critical context for the eventual consideration of student feedback at semesters end.

Moreover, these limited instances of dialogue outside the structured workshops were often rudimentary in form. Indeed, as has been detailed earlier, by the third semester the components of the action research model had all but disappeared as an explicit focus in the collective process. This suggested the broadening effect of the model was possibly more incidental—rather than a significantly transformative—form of learning. The reasons identified in the data for this limitation included the:

- absence of a culture of collective professional dialogue or tools suitable to appropriately facilitate it during the action research (with semi-structured workshops, teacher blogs and wikis all failing to broaden engagement)
- relative complexity of the model and the considerable resources needed to sustain it (and the related over-reliance on the facilitative work of program leaders and the researcher)

- belief that a 'threshold' point of quality had been reached (notably after the second semester in each program), reflecting the powerful traces of a quality assurance rather than development paradigm
- effect of the fragmentation of the groups—most notably around employment status and proximity to the professional discipline contexts—which mitigated against the development of shared meanings
- lingering discontent, or conversely over-confidence, in the trajectory of the action research which led to disassociation
- serious time and resource limitations of academic teachings in a context of rising and conflicting demands
- progressive domination of the action research process by program leaders, building on a pre-existing hegemonies.

This absence of a stronger collective academic voice also had the negative and unanticipated consequence of amplifying the focus on the distilled thematic analysis developed around student feedback. At times, this resulted in workshops becoming largely dependent on the developmental options presented in *Evaluation and Program Development Reports*.

This narrowing dependence vicariously created the opportunity program leaders to (re)dominate the deliberations around development options as the semesters progressed and levels of engagement further receded. However, this domination was not merely because of the limitations of the model itself. Evidence from workshops and post-interviews with leaders suggested this heightened intervention also reflected anxiety of the program leaders about:

- the need for rapid developmental change in the program given the competitive environment in which they were operating, in tandem with the more visible nature of the imperfections identified via qualitative student feedback
- the inability of many part-time sessional staff to enact change in a timely way, given their differing responsibilities (often in demanding professional practice environments)
- elevating concerns about quality assurance and personal accountability as program leaders increasingly felt the absence of 'localised' evidence normally provided by quantitative student evaluation
- some lingering distrust over the level of commitment of those originally opposing the change in teaching mode (particularly evident in the case of the second program).

It was also notable that participants during workshops and in subsequent semi-structured interviews identified that the histories of program development preceding the action research were also a critical factor in this failure. It was apparent both programs had been operating without a culture of collaborative dialogue. This meant that there was general acceptance preceding the research that teaching academics would be largely isolated from the key decisions to enact program changes.

Therefore, for some participants the collaborative nature of the action research model lacked both authenticity within the culture of the program, or did not possess a sufficiently legitimacy to represent a convincing framework for ongoing professional dialogue. These range of factors appeared to have significant contributed to the largely disengaged response of most participants outside the structured dialogue of the workshops.

Even within the workshops, these realities tended to conspire to produce some responses from participants that were more contrived than real, whilst others simply withdrew and remained in the background. This would appear in CHAT terms to call into question how effectively the *expansive learning evaluation cycle* genuinely broadened the shared objects of work or incited a transformative form of learning.

Interestingly, one further important factor was in evidence. For most participants in the action research, their preceding use of conventional quantitative student feedback had not proved necessarily productive in inspiring pedagogical development. However, its focus on the individual outcomes of teaching meant that participants felt they gained some specific and local insights into the subject they were teaching.

The conventional quantitative ratings-based form of student feedback forced students to assess individual teaching agency. Therefore, teachers were largely responsible for addressing issues raised by students (however oblique these issues may have been in their actual nature). The move to a more collective, qualitative, and program level student feedback meant this effect was diluted, meaning for some a loss of direct relevance (and sense of individual agency). This effect— combined with this domination of the process by the program leaders and the researcher discussed earlier—seemed to result in a heightened sense of disenfranchising and subsequent disengagement.

Similarly, both directly in interviews and indirectly in workshop sessions, frequent anxieties were also expressed about the ability of academics to effectively demonstrate their individual worth to student learning. The data generated within the *expansive learning evaluation cycle* potentially limited the personal evidence that could be provided for appointment to tenured positions, for promotional processes or simply to affirm teaching quality in performance management dialogue.

Conversely, this absence also frustrated program leaders who wished to assess the quality or performance of individual academics. These dual pressures led to the gradual introduction of the seeking and reporting of some student feedback data related to individual components or subjects within the programs.

Although this individual data did not play a significant role directly in the workshops, it appeared to have an implicit role in changing the object-orientation of a significant minority of participants away from reconceptualising collective activity (i.e. the development of the program) to the more narrow pursuits of individualised development gestures in component parts of the program.

This all indicated that the model and its conceptual tools may not have sufficiently disrupted (or radically broadened) the existing cultural frameworks of meaning to be legitimately considered transformative in nature.

Horizontal and Dialogical Learning

A critical outcome of both case studies was the imperative created by qualitative student feedback to cross boundaries and engage with other activity systems to create new intersubjective forms of knowledge and to transform practices.

The most significant examples of such boundary crossing was manifested within discipline teaching which were reformed to more closely align with the demands of workplace practice. At entry, the relationship between the programs and workplace practice was largely abstract in form. Its primary representation was expressed subjectively through forms of regulatory imposition—most notably in mandated graduate competencies and summative assessment.

This imposed drive was seen as a critical reason—though by no means the sole reason—that both programs employed part-time staff engaged in professional practice to support the work of the full-time tenured academic staff. The more fluid context of professional practice in first program meant more part-time staff were engaged in the teaching of this program than the second (though this equally reflected the differing histories of the programs).

In essence, the spatial dimensions of the programs prior to the case studies were largely fixed. Professional dialogue that was generated with the elevated use of qualitative student feedback encouraged collective critical reflection centred on to the perceived relevance of the programs to practice environments. This heightened recognition represented tangible evidence of horizontal and dialogic learning around the actual and prospective nature of professional practice.

As a result of the issues identified in both programs in the action research model, greater legitimacy was also engendered in practitioner knowledge. This effectively dissolved the established spatial boundaries between education and practice settings. This was largely achieved by the enhanced recognition of the voice of those part-time teachers engaged in workplace practice, who'd previously worked largely at the periphery of educational discourses. This elevation also had the effect of increasing the proximity of the program to the environments of professional practice. From this boundary crossing came the integration of more authentic learning environments, artefacts and assessment into the design and teaching of both programs.

In the case of the more established second program—which had radically reformed to an online mode—this boundary crossing was a direct consequence of the strong student rejection of the simulated learning environment in the first semester. It was further forced by as ongoing scepticism about the relevance of online artefacts, as well as the adopted forms of group activities and assessment.

This rejection necessitated the action researchers adopt a form of horizontal engagement with the contexts of professional practice; so as to better understand how practice contexts operated and knowledge was formed within them. This was facilitated by more direct dialogic engagement with the part-time practitioners teaching in this second program.

It was further afforded by the highly critical feedback on the learning simulation and its related artefacts by those students currently in practice environments (whose dissonance was most acute). The simulated environment, related artefacts and assessment were significantly reformed over the life of the action research to align these elements more closely with real demands of practice. This provided further tangible evidence of this boundary crossing activity.

Moreover, the critical dialogue around program epistemology was also fundamental in dialogically transforming the activity further. In CHAT terms, student feedback (and to a lesser extent teacher reflection) in the second more established program revealed that the program was encountering fundamentally differing object-orientations.

This dialogue, which centred on what the program was educating students for (i.e. real practice, entry to practice or learning in simulated environment of disciplinary education), was incited by intersubjectivities produced by this boundary crossing between the program and the profession. This horizontal form of learning was demonstrable transformative, as it redefined the crucial elements of the program.

Making these contradictory orientations explicit and defining shared responses significantly improved student responses to the program over the following semesters. It is unlikely this would have occurred without the action research model, as the differing subjectivities of the activity systems of education and workplace practice were invisibly (but firmly) enforced by regulatory, cultural and physical boundaries. Instead, the model incited negotiation and exchange across these perimeters, transforming the activity through expansive learning.

In the case of first newer program, the larger number of current practitioners in the action research teams meant a more natural crossing of the boundaries between education and practice. This was especially the case once critical questions of relevance emerged from student feedback. The workshops identified the need—largely derived from student feedback outcomes—to respond to demonstrable anxieties expressed by students about the relevance of the program for their eventual roles once graduating. This revelation proved more acute as most practitioners worked alone in the field, and therefore needed to be able to work largely without oversight and guidance once completing the program.

Further affordances were provided by close regulatory interest in the shaping of graduates. This was also elevated by heightening public scrutiny of the profession following a series of well-publicised failures of professional conduct in the sub-discipline focus of the program.

These forces acted to transform such things as curriculum design and core program artefacts to more closely align these with those familiar in professional practice environments. This was also somewhat reflected in reformed pedagogical practices, which were redesigned to offer more authentic representations of, and engagement with practice environments. Finally, it was also demonstrated in the significant reforming of the model of assessment across the program toward the use of more authentic objects of practice, which captured the differing dimensions of professional work.

Evidence suggested that this transformation was not as significant as that of the second program, primarily because the boundary crossing was a more familiar part of the work of the program. It was also the case that the number of part-time practitioners teaching on the program made for more porous boundaries with the profession. This meant that the form and outcomes of this professional dialogue was more sophisticated and ultimately, more pedagogically effective.

A second significant boundary crossing emerging from the case studies was between the activities of teaching and online educational design. On entry to both programs, tensions were apparent between the pedagogical intentions of teaching academics and the affordances and hindrances presented by online technologies. Unsurprisingly, given what has already been outlined, this tension was most profoundly apparent in the second program where the orthodox teaching had been supplanted by a blended mode. With this change, a team of online educational designers had engaged to develop the online components of the new program. This included a developed online simulation, an embedded online site and online communication capabilities.

Given the ongoing divisions around this move to an online environment, a strong boundary was established between the activities of teaching and educational design. Generally those supporting the change tended to divest responsibility to this specialist educational design expertise—and those not disassociating themselves from it.

As the outcomes of student feedback around the inadequacy of online elements became apparent, the model gave licence for academics to cross this boundary. This was in the form of direct engagement and dialogue around the various design issues constraining the success on the online program. This form of expansive learning was not universal by any means, but it did involve a significant number of academics developing new knowledge around the complexities of online design.

Conversely, the educational designers also developed significant learning around the expectations of online pedagogies in this specific type of program design. Here again there was an intersubjectivity that progressively transformed an online environment poorly regarded by students, into one that generally proved effective as a learning space by the third semester. This involved educational designers being directly integrated into the action research model, actively negotiating and trading with teaching academics on prospective approaches. Arguably, by the beginning of third semester this boundary crossing had become an integral and largely natural element of program development.

Somewhat differently in first program, the online focus of the program was an integral element of its design from its beginning. This meant there was a less tangible boundary between it and the activity of education design. Indeed, having not been created with an orthodox face-to-face component (aside from introductory intensives), the program had significantly relied on educational design capability.

The more fluid and challenging realities of online teaching forced regular review and redevelopment of its component elements. However, the effect of the action research was to make this boundary largely invisible. This was achieved by support staff within the program taking on the co-ordination of education design, and individual academics working collaboratively on the reforming of online elements of the program. Here instances of situated academic development were apparent, with small groups and individual teaching developing the capacity to design more autonomously within the online environment.

Hence, as the semesters progressed, more developed understandings of student feedback encouraged academics to become more directly involved around the broader dialogue around online educational design. This boundary crossing work resulted in demonstrable pedagogical development that enhanced the learning effectiveness of online artefacts, communities and forms of assessment. This suggested the effective dissolution of the boundary between teaching and educational design not only improved the program itself, but also the capability for responsiveness to feedback and the educational insights of those who had previous saw this function as largely ethereal in form.

However, the action research model failed more broadly to traverse several other important boundaries. Most significantly, neither program was satisfactorily able to work dialogically with the quality assurance activity within the broader faculty and the university more generally.

There can be no doubt that the recent discontinuation of the university student evaluation system and the opening of a new quantitative student evaluation system provided an ideal catalyst for reconsidering conventional approaches to student feedback. In hindsight, without this imperative, it is likely the research may have not been able to be undertaken as the pressures built within the university for heightened quantitative scrutiny of student opinion. However, for this same reason, an unresolved and uneasy relationship developed between the action research and this coinciding strengthening of quality assurance within the institution.

In essence, this saw fundamentally different object-orientations develop during the life of the research. While the action research was orientated to improving the quality of the programs, the new university policy on student feedback was accentuating its role as a tool of assuring the quality of teaching.

As the role of feedback became foregrounded in university discourses around institutional and individual performance, the dissonance between the two activities became increasingly apparent. Attempts to bridge this widening gulf were made by program leaders and the faculty more generally. However, this merely resulted in a fence being drawn around the approach and the remainder of the conventional evaluative work of the faculty being reported as normal.

By the second semester in both action research cycles, genuine unease began to emerge about the potential individual and collective risks of solely relying on broad forms of qualitative data. This came with various motives: how to demonstrate the effectiveness of the program to internal and external stakeholders, how to target particular shortfalls in individual teaching performance or the need to demonstrate personal effectiveness for the processes of performance, promotion and awards. Concerns even emerged in both programs about how to replace the conventional marketing signposts of student satisfaction, fearing the loss of quantitative expression may act to weaken student recruitment.

These sentiments reflected the strong historical dimensions of accountability that had been layered around the validity of quantitative student feedback, and its continuing perceived legitimacy as an institutional proxy for teaching quality.

However, the inability to traverse this boundary successfully was most acute around the potential inability to undertake effective performance management of academics seen to be underperforming, given the insufficient personalised data to with which to challenge them. This absence became the catalyst for the re-introduction of more subject-specific focus and—to a limited but significant extent— quantitative data. This tended to only alienate, rather than engage, those staff subject to its outcomes within the broader collective imperative.

Conversely, the absence of subject specific data tended to embolden program leaders to initiate more interventionist steps of their own in specific localised dimensions of the program. This further facilitated the progressive domination of the action research in its latter stages by program leaders. What was significant about this discord was the broad perception that the action research model could not horizontally interact with this quality assurance activity, aside from uneasily adding it to the model. Essentially, the two activities remained contradictory and no real options could be devised to reconcile this during the life of the study. This boundary remained firmly drawn.

Secondly, the boundary with institutional academic development was not traversed by either program, despite this being a potentially critical resource in addressing issues arising from student feedback. There were several reasons for this, including the:

- limited time and inclination amongst participating academics to undertake structured academic development
- role of the researcher and experienced teachers as 'situated' academic developers that provided some strategies locally
- broad range of existing educational capabilities of staff, that allowed an 'on-demand' conception of academic development.

Nevertheless, further significant academic development needs emerged in both programs during the three semesters. These needs were only partially addressed by informal and unstructured academic development responses. In fact, most such academic development occurred in 'just-in-time' form or in response to a serious problem that had been identified.

However, this form of situated academic development tended to work more effectively for those in full-time academic roles. The result of this boundary not being crossed was that professional capability development generated by the action research was generally patchy, ad hoc and at times, ineffectual beyond the level of engendering a functional response to a specific problem.

Subterranean Learning

Engeström (2007a) defines subterranean learning as that which 'blazes cognitive trails that are embodied and lived but unnoticeable….anchors and stabilising networks that secure the viability and sustainability of new concepts, models and tools' (p. 24). It represents the forms of learning move from externalised social meaning to the internal forms of thinking, guiding innovative actions of individuals and driving transformative practices in social activity.

The evidence provided by the case studies suggests that at the broadest level, there was pedagogical development from disturbances generated by the elevated use of student feedback that reflected the emergence of some forms of subterranean learning. This learning was most apparent in evidence of the laying of discernable cognitive trails as a result of the disruptive effect of the action research.

The dialogue analysed in program workshops, the actions that followed them and the individual responses in subsequent semi-structured interviews, provided various forms of confirmation that participants recognised that a more systematic and analytical engagement with student feedback provided new ways of professionally engaging and re-forming pedagogical work.

The *expansive learning evaluation cycle* incited an ongoing evaluative dialogue that was not reductively framed around individual performativity or metrics. Instead, it encouraged the identification and reconciliation of key tensions in student learning. As Table 8.1 illustrates, this outcome was most clearly reflected in the key developmental responses across the three semesters in both programs to the primary contradictions identified in the initial workshops. Here the responses to disturbances are seen both in terms of the substantial actions that attempted to respond to these identified contradictions and the related tensions reflected in elevated student feedback.

The success of the action research in generating some productive change in both programs clearly provided a stronger incentive for its underlying concepts to be recognised as valuable by a majority of participants. Reflecting this, the overwhelming majority of participants in first program and a slimmer majority in the second, rated the model as valuable and influential during its life over the three semesters.

Further, evidence provided by the level of dialogue during workshops suggested that participants acquired a relatively sophisticated appreciation of the interaction between student feedback, educational design and pedagogical development. For more experienced academics, this was in the form of critical engagement around the nature of curriculum, assessment and even, in the case of the second site, program epistemologies.

For those less experienced as teachers (or designers of student learning), it was often the first opportunity they had to consider teaching and assessment questions in the context of student learning. This prompted a significant number in this sub-cohort to seek out literature and/or professional development to further their understanding of effective pedagogical practice, as well as situated academic development. Moreover, the discernable fragments of the learning evaluation model and the tools it employed continued to be used in one form or another in both programs. There is also evidence that the actual developments occurring during this period generated from the action research were sustained beyond its direct life.

Table 8.1 Identified primary contradictions

Primary contradictions	Key responses during the three semesters across programs
Complex-heterogeneous expectations of graduate learning outcomes	• Reframing student expectations • Redesigning artefacts/simulation to better reflect practice • Aligning assessment to better reflect realities of professional practice • Making representations to professional bodies re nature of competency-assessment expectations
Differing expectations between the desired and possible outcomes of student learning	• Reframing student expectations and making these more consistent across the program • Improvements to the quality of online facilitation, communication and simulations to address most serious concerns of students • Scaffolding students where they have limited experience working online • Improve small and larger group cohesion • Reconsider program epistemology: what are we trying to do? (second program)
Ambiguous/precarious position of academic as educator and expert practitioner	• Reframing student expectations • Use more authentic artefacts of contemporary workplace practice, including as forms of authentic assessment with 'real' implications • Further integrate knowledge of sessional teacher-practitioners into the student learning experience via mentoring • Ensure regulators more clearly understand distinction between education and practice
Growing uncertainty around the rights and responsibilities of academics, students and institutions	• Improve orientation and initial engagement for students • Strategies to build student engagement (expectations, online facilitation/communication) • More consistent criteria/rubrics for assessment • Clarify the roles/responsibilities of academic/support staff more clearly
Heightening demands for accountability in academic practices	• Introduction of clear student expectations, assessment criteria/rubrics • Ensure students are aware of the role of their feedback in further development • Provide *Evaluation and Course Development Reports* to program and faculty education committees • Supplement collective feedback with subject specific data

However, there was far less evidence that the concepts, models or tools generated by the action research were genuinely 'embodied or lived' by most participants in the two programs. Analysis suggests that this outcome was for a number of critical reasons. Firstly, the complexity of the CHAT-informed, action research model and the collective and multidimensional form of data it produced did not well assimilate well to the often pragmatic motive of participants to simply ensure their specific subject was ready to teach. A significant number of participants were various confused, sceptical or disengaged in the introductory workshops with the CHAT framing of the action research.

Similarly, many expressed frustration in subsequent workshops (and the evaluations of them) about the lack of immediacy and clarity of the thematic student feedback outcomes, prompting the progressive need for the categories used to be broadened and then the focus move to more (accessible) functional questions.

Secondly, the fragmentation of the academic workforce in both programs around employment status and program role tended to lead to the action research being progressively dominated by program leaders, meaning it largely failed to realise its collaborative potential in either program.

The volatile environment in which both programs operated further compounded this effect, producing unpredictable forces during the three semesters. This affected staffing levels, available resources and, importantly, the level of support for specific development options. This resource limitation also influenced the relative time and resources available to participants. This meant a dissonance developed between the identified desirable levels of program development and what were actually possible responses to student feedback. At times, this meant participants reported a sense of being overwhelmed by the demands or anxious about not responding to student expectations.

Thirdly, the unfamiliarity of participants with the level of analytical engagement with student feedback meant much of the discussion tended to fall into more familiar tracks of functional problem solving, rather than focus clearly on more significant issues of ongoing pedagogical development. This form of response, combined with the powerful shaping effect (for experienced academics) of previous experiences with conventional quantitative student evaluation outcomes, meant that the action research largely was formed around specific gestures for improvement, rather than more expansive pedagogical conceptions.

Fourthly, the ongoing controversy about the reformed mode of teaching in the second site seeded a deep level of alienation amongst some participants that proved almost impossible to overcome during the early stages of the action research. This left strong conceptual traces in subsequent semesters, which produce a defensive assessment of the viability of new approaches and tools. For some in this program, scepticism about the value of the program changes was conflated with student feedback more generally, making substantive judgments about program development from such feedback more polemic.

Finally, it proved extremely difficult to sustain the action research model over the three semesters. As positive developments had occurred in the programs and student feedback had generally improved, the imperative for ongoing analysis faded in the minds of participants to the point where, by the third semester, participation had largely evaporated. This offers perhaps the most powerful evidence that rather than the learning of the model having been embodied, its primary outcomes had been instead to serve the largely utilitarian purpose of successfully reforming the two programs so that significant explicit problems were resolved and students were generally satisfied.

Conclusion

In the last two chapters, the key outcomes of the case studies were critically considered using a range of analytical tools drawn from CHAT. This provided an analysis of the levels of collective engagement and expansive learning in evidence as a result of the use of the *expansive learning evaluation cycle* in practice. This analysis demonstrated that the social dimensions of the two environments were complex and multi-voiced, with the understanding of elevated forms of qualitative student feedback strongly framed by the historically formed pedagogic traditions of the respective programs.

Further, critical differences emerged in levels of individual agency exercised in response to the outcomes of the elevated qualitative student feedback. These differences tended to broadly correlate to teacher employment status, positional role and proximity to professional practice environments.

The overall effect of making contradictions visible through the elevated use of student feedback in the action research sufficiently disturbed the activity in both sites to result in some demonstrable change from its initial state. Most significantly was a clearer focus on the shared object of improving student learning. However, a critical limitation was that this focus tended to be largely of the immediate realities (i.e. next semester's program), suggesting some limitations in the level of expansive learning generated by the student evaluation model.

Having said this, the elevation of student feedback data across the three semesters did result in some significant improvements in both programs. On notable foundation for this change was a gradual refocusing from what the teacher was doing to what students were doing (or not afforded to do). There was also evidence that the level of professional dialogue matured across the semesters—although the differing levels of agency mediated this effect and positional power individuals brought to the debate.

Reasonable evidence was also found to suggest that their was some broadened understanding of the use of concepts, tools and models to reform pedagogy as a result of this critical dialogue—although again this was restrained by the pre-existing layers of history in the programs and the (re)strengthening of divisions of labour throughout the three semesters. There was also substantiation that horizontal forms of learning occurred with productive crossing of the previously invisible but powerful boundaries with professional practice and educational design.

While there was some evidence that the action research took root (particularly in the early stages of the case studies), limited academic engagement outside the structured workshops meant this was less embodied and more reactive and orientated toward the derived imperatives of student feedback. As the semesters progressed, program leaders exercised ever-greater levels of control to the point where, by the end of the third semesters, little sustainable action research activity was evident.

Hence, though the action research certainly prompted significant developmental improvement for both programs, the model on which it was based did not become fully embodied in the shared life of either program in any authentic sense. This meant the actual object-orientation was most often centred on pragmatic immediacy. Once the imperative of explicit student dissatisfaction receded, so did the levels of engagement with the model.

Seemingly the pressures of elevating university quality assurance demands and the fragmented and fluid nature of the workforces fueled this progressive disengagement. However, in addition the complexity of the approach implied in the *expansive learning evaluation cycle*—in tandem with the limited capability with which programs had to respond—also clearly contributed to some of the limitations identified here. In the next chapter, these outcomes are considered as part of a broader analysis of what may constitute a viable developmental alternative to conventional quantitative approaches to the use of student feedback.

Chapter 9
Charting New Approaches to Student Evaluation

Abstract This final chapter considers the future potential of student feedback in higher education. With the relentless rise of neo-liberalist, market-based models in higher education, there has emerged a powerful and seemingly irresistible demand from students, institutions and even socially for survey outcomes to assure the quality of university teaching. Quantitative student evaluation has become a fundamental—though inherently flawed—proxy means of determining teaching quality. However, the arguably more important foundational imperative of student evaluation—that is, to provide a valuable impetus for the professional (re)consideration and improvement of pedagogical practices—is increasingly forced into the background as these other more powerful motives escalate in significance. This has had the effect of rendering student evaluation as an increasingly unwelcome fringe dweller and essentially an intrusion in the professional domain of the higher education teacher. Therefore, it is critical that new tools and approaches to ensure the student voice remains a meaningful contributor to the professional and pedagogical dialogues around academic teaching are formalised. The chapter proposes a potential new approach to student evaluation that attempts to restore its seminal objective of pedagogical development through the elevated use of the student voice and collaborative professional dialogue.

Keywords Student evaluation · Neo-liberalism in higher education · Quality assurance · Quality improvement

Introduction

This book set out to consider the foundations, contemporary function and developmental potential of student feedback-based evaluation in higher education. Using a sociocultural lens afforded by a CHAT framework, this analysis explored the social forces that have shaped the specific evolution of student feedback and that influence its contemporary form. This analysis sought to go beyond the more

© Springer International Publishing Switzerland 2016
S. Darwin, *Student Evaluation in Higher Education*,
DOI 10.1007/978-3-319-41893-3_9

familiar and thoroughly researched debates around quantitative student evaluation—such as the design of reliable feedback instruments and how it can be used to influence the work of academics. Instead, it explored the fundamental assumptions on which student feedback models are based and their distinctive social origins. This meant also seeking to understand the nature of the complex sociocultural mediation that has shaped—and continues to shape—this increasingly important activity in the environments of higher education.

The systematic consideration of the situated contemporary relationship between student feedback and academic teaching reported earlier in this book made visible both the contradictions and ongoing tensions which exist around contemporary student feedback. Of particular significance in this analysis were the tensions between originating academic development discourses of student feedback (centred on improving the quality of teaching) and later competing drives to use the student voice for academic merit assessment, systemic quality assurance and performance management purposes. These tensions—when considered within their historical context—were a reflection of the changing social relationship between the university, academic staff, students and to some extent, the community more generally.

These have the effect of creating increasing the levels of ambiguity in the academic mind about the actual function of student feedback, precisely what orientation they should adopt toward it and how (if at all) they should change their pedagogical practices in response to it. These tensions are being further aggravated under the mounting pressures of public exposure and comparative analysis of student feedback outcomes, as well as the prospective use of this data in individual performance management discussions.

The rich explanatory potential of CHAT provided a situated analysis within two programs in an Australian university that allowed us to better understand the developmental potential of student evaluation. This assessment of the development potential of collaborative engagement with qualitative forms of student feedback suggested some real potential—albeit not fully realised in the case study research—to spark deepened professional dialogue and improve pedagogical work. However, there was undoubtedly value in attempts to improve the levels of collaborative professional dialogue around the student voice, particularly when it was made more coherent and intelligible by the use of interpreted qualitative student feedback data.

In this final chapter, the implications of this research for the current role and future potential of the student voice to influence pedagogical practice questions will be explored.

The Emergence of Student Evaluation in Higher Education

As we have seen in this book, student evaluation has undergone a relatively rapid transformation over the last three decades. It has rapidly moved from an isolated and idiosyncratic fringe dweller in a small number of US universities, to its current condition as a largely universal and highly regarded institutional citizen in institutions in the United States, the United Kingdom and Australia.

We also saw that the roots of current approaches to student feedback in higher education are deep. They can be traced from the behavioural psychology work of Remmers and his colleagues in the 1920s, through its widespread adoption half a century ago in the US under the weight of student dissent, to its tentative use in early academic development through to its assimilation as a legitimate proxy for assuring the quality of university teaching. Similarly, whilst still performing some of its earlier academic development function, student evaluation outcomes are increasingly prominent in institutional discourses around performance, marketing, auditing and reviews (Barrie et al. 2008; Davies et al. 2009).

So the emergence of the contemporary form of quantitative student feedback is only a relatively recent phenomenon, yet during this time it has transformed from its originating purpose as a localised teaching development tool to a high-utility institutional metric for the comparative assessment and quality assurance of teaching. The elevation of comparative quality assurance metrics across the sector and within institutions has all but assured that quantitative measurement of teaching, teachers and/or courses is institutionalised as a privileged measure in institutional, supervisor, student, academic and, even at some levels, community understandings of effective teaching practice.

Therefore, it is important to recognise that the current state of student evaluation in higher education strongly reflects these complex historical and cultural forces that have effectively mediated its contemporary form and function. As research presented in this book has aptly demonstrated, student evaluation in higher education operates within the increasingly contesting activity systems of institutional quality assurance, individual and institutional quality improvement and individual performance management.

We are also now experiencing the further intensification in the use of student evaluation data as its becomes a core method of ranking inter-institutional performance for international ranking scales and in the case of the UK, a public policy tool to permit (or deny) university fee increases. There seems little doubt that this amplification in the use of student evaluation data will continue as the technological capability to capture and disseminate student opinion strengthens.

Unsurprisingly, the rising significance of student evaluation has most pronounced in higher education systems reformed in recent decades around market-based, neo-liberalist principles. According to the logical of neo-liberalism, by making these performativity measures transparent, 'consumers'—in this case, be they students, governments or other customers for education services—could make a rational choice on what was in their best interests to fund.

This elevation correlated with the escalating pressure on universities to measure and demonstrate their value with the broadened use of explicit market mechanisms in the sector. This is because the outcomes of student evaluation—in forming a critical metric to inform the student marketplace around institutional and program quality—also has a role in potentially shaping the future funding of universities.

This has become the catalyst for escalating levels of inter and intra-institutional competition for resources, that are then steadily re-allocated based on comparative attractiveness in the emerging educational marketplace. This fundamental ideological shift has progressively redefined the social and economic relationships institutions have with government and students. It has forced institutions to demonstrate their economic, educational and social value through quantifiable performance indicators and accountability measures, of which student evaluation data is now an indispensible part.

In an environment increasingly crowded by comparative institutional rankings and league tables, the quantitative foundations of student evaluation has meant it has been easily transformable into a global performance measure of rising influence. Reflecting this trend, global student evaluation outcomes increasingly appears as a core element of institutional marketing, framed as a reliable assessment of the comparative quality and relative value of institutional teaching and learning. This effort is particularly pronounced in institutional campaigns to recruit international students, where student evaluation outcomes are wielded in often in definitive forms as evidence of teaching quality.

Echoing this escalating sectoral significance, student evaluation is relied on to perform ever more critical internalised quality assurance work in contemporary higher education. For instance, as data presented in this book demonstrates, student feedback now more frequently guides significant internal institutional judgments about teaching and program quality, teaching appointments, individual performance and academic promotion.

Student Evaluation as a Contestable Activity

As student evaluation has progressively become more institutionally and socially prominent, so arguably its power to potentially shape pedagogies and other educational practices has grown. The outcomes of student evaluation now inevitably shapes—either explicitly or implicitly—shared conceptions of what is understood to be effective teaching, sound curriculum design and effective (or at least appropriate) forms of student engagement.

This has meant that in the contemporary university, student evaluation has become a complex and contested intersection between academic, student, discipline and institutional interests (Blackmore 2009). This also means the objectives and the outcomes of student evaluation are subject to increasing contestation across the higher education landscape, as it is a site of significant volatility, with its inherent subjectivities fundamentally challenging the professional identity and actions of teaching academics. For instance, should the focus of student feedback be on improved student learning, is it about improving prospective student rating outcomes or about legitimising or assailing individual academic performance?

Flowing from these questions come other issues: for instance, should academics be engaged voluntarily, compulsorily or as needs for individual performance evidence emerges?

This ambiguity around the potential role and function of the student voice leads to considerable uncertainties around what actual rules frame its use in practice, which appear as increasingly contested between academic development discourses, quality assurance systems and performance management drives. This is reflected in related uncertainty as to exactly for whom student evaluation is actually designed for: that is, it for academic consumption, institutional assurance, current or potential students-as-consumers, or for broader social assurance of the efficient use of public funding (or a combination of these).

Moreover, questions also increasingly developing around divisions of labour that frame the deployment of student feedback systems at a local level. For instance, is it transacted between an academic and an academic developer, between academics and students, between students and the institution, between the academic and the institution or an academic and a supervisor (or selection panel)? These range of uncertainties form the basis of further tensions in the activity of student feedback, creating rising ground-level debates about its contemporary role and function.

However—as was demonstrated earlier in this book—despite this escalating significance, student evaluation has received surprisingly limited critical scrutiny. Its foundational epistemological assumptions remain largely undisturbed in scholarly research, which remains dominated by studies of instruments and assimilation of student feedback outcomes. Yet, as student evaluation has experienced elevating institutional and social status as an essential proxy for teaching quality, the reconsideration of these assumptions has become a more significant matter. It was within this critical epistemic space that this book sought to debate actually function of orthodox student feedback in practice, as well as its potentiality as a tool of pedagogical improvement (rather than merely a methodology of institutional quality assurance).

The evidence presented in the two case studies provides some localised—but nonetheless significant—insights into these debates. These outcomes reinforced the contention that the effect of these ambiguities is creating strong tensions around the student feedback, as the object of activity is increasingly contested. In considering this data and that generated by other related research, it can be argued these tensions are specifically manifested in higher education in contemporary debates around the value of such things as the:

- voluntary or compulsory participation in student evaluation
- private, semi-public or public consumption of student feedback data
- alignment of student evaluation to professional concerns of academic teaching and learning, or to key points of comparative sectoral or institutional scrutiny
- value and validity of individual, faculty and/or institutional benchmarks for comparative assessment of levels of student satisfaction

- use of outcomes to encourage individual critical reflection on teaching, or for the monitoring and directing of pedagogical change based on a deficit analysis of student-perceived shortfalls
- contextual consideration of semester student responses, or the comparative measurement of individual or collective performance over time.

The case studies revealed that these tensions indeed create a complex and uncertain relationship between quantitative student feedback and contemporary academic teaching. Mirroring this complexity, student feedback generates a diverse array of responses from teaching academics regarding its function and the value of its outcomes. These responses range from strong cynicism, through scepticism and disconnectedness, to strong beliefs that student opinion makes a critical contribution to the consideration of prospective pedagogical strategies (and understandings along this continuum). The case study data suggested that these beliefs are most frequently shaped by personal experiences of positive or negative experiences of student feedback, which may or may not have a demonstrable connection to the quality of individual work.

Most academics participating in the research described in this book almost naturally recognised the limitations of quantitative forms of student feedback. Yet most also volunteered reflections of the significant emotional impact of positive—and especially negative—student opinion outcomes at the end of semesters, often even where these were isolated outcomes. This suggests that despite its recognised intrinsic limitations, student evaluation also holds considerable informal and affective power over the work of the contemporary teaching academic, irrespective of the tension-laden environment it operates within.

In the case study sites, this effect was demonstrated at a number of distinct levels. One of the early fears about the research expressed by educational leaders was that it would displace quantitative student feedback, potentially limiting the ability of programs to provide evidence of teaching effectiveness to university management (or for student marketing) or to diagnose particular problems with individual teachers. For individual participants, the loss of quantitative data concerned a significant number of participants, as it would lessen the focus on their individual contribution and their ability to demonstrate personal agency in teaching. Unsurprisingly, this effect was most notable in those seeking appointment, promotion or other forms of recognition in the immediate future.

The experience of the case studies clearly demonstrated the characteristics of the uneasy and unsettled relationship teaching academics have with student feedback. Early dialogue around the use of elevated levels of qualitative student feedback, even in a consolidated form, would be characteristically greeted in both action research groups with almost instinctive defensiveness. Depending on the experience of the group, either multiple diagnoses were reached as to why students responded in certain ways, or urgent attempts were made to provide a placating response. It took time for these types of reactions to recede and for more reflexive forms of professional engagement to emerge. As the data suggested, this was similarly reflected in the level of responses defined, which moved from the functional to the more sophisticated as a more dispassionate understanding of student feedback evolved in the action research teams.

Paradoxically, both action research groups exerted considerable pressure to ensure the outcomes of the student feedback were made more broadly known with the faculty and beyond. This was an apparent means of addressing the cultural gap left by the absence of quantitative student opinion (even in the case of where this was agreed to not happen, due to the anxiety over the negative effects of a recent pedagogical reformation). This reinforces the contention that student evaluation tends to live a ironic life in contemporary institutions: occupying institutional centrality as a legitimate proxy for teaching quality, whilst simultaneously being a powerful and disturbing fringe dweller in academic teaching contexts.

Research presented in this study also reminds us that ratings-based feedback is susceptible to the subjectivities of subject focus, class size, stages of program, gender, charisma and the nature of formed student expectations. These matters have become of more material significance as quantitative student feedback has been elevated in institutional significance and therefore increasingly frame institutional (and arguably individual) perceptions of teaching effectiveness (or otherwise).

What was also apparent in the case studies was the confirmation of the contention that quantitative student evaluation tends to generate homogenised understandings of teaching and learning. Such understandings tend to defy the contemporary complexity of learning environments, students, stages of course development and realities of pedagogical innovation. The inherently reductive and ambiguous nature of averaged student ratings was broadly considered to defy the multiplicity of factors that intersect to form student learning outcomes.

Further, there can be little doubt that student evaluation is increasingly contested within the uncertain space between managerial, educational and marketing discourses in contemporary universities. In CHAT terms, this means that the conceptual tools that mediate the relationship between teachers and students (including student feedback) are now drawn from the conflicting activity systems of quality assurance, performance management and institutional marketing, rather than those offered by originating academic development discourses.

This contest means what regulates the use of student feedback is caught in the inherent uncertainties between the demands of these differing conceptual frameworks. This results in the communities that student evaluation responds to being more abstract and indeterminate in form, meaning responsibility for acting on its outcomes is similarly contested. This all suggests the need for a genuine debate in the sector as to the actual real utility of quantitative student feedback in the contemporary higher education institution. Although it may continue to fulfil (arguably in uneasy form) the extrinsic motives of assurance and marketing, does the increasingly complex environments of teaching and learning demand more sophisticated tools to inform professional judgment and shared dialogue around pedagogy?

Professionalism, Casualisation and Consumerism

Other important questions are also raised by the data presented in the case studies. The first is around the levels of professional autonomy afforded to the teaching academic in the contemporary higher education institution. The originating motives of student evaluation had a clear deference to both the professionalism and autonomy of teachers. This was not necessarily a simple construction in itself.

As noted earlier, student surveys evolved in their recent history as a result of several important pressures. The first of these was the rising student unrest in the late 1960s and early 1970s, which coincided with other mass social democratic movements of the period. This brought attention to variable teaching quality in universities, a matter that had been all but ignored until this time. In addition, around the same period, rising student enrolments created new and challenging pressures around student retention, particularly as drop out rates began to climb.

As student evaluation was introduced as a diagnostic means to both identify and importantly assist individual academics to improve their teaching approaches, its seminal form was orientated toward enhancing teacher professionalism through targeted pedagogical interventions and situated academic development initiatives. As it was further institutionalised, student evaluation became a means of also demonstrating teaching professionalism for the purposes of broad improvement of teaching or specifically for appointment and promotion.

However, as the strategic agenda of higher education institutions have shifted, so student evaluation has progressively intruded further into the notion the academic teacher as a (trusted) autonomous professional. At one level, given the reality that that most academics are not trained as teachers, it is perhaps easy to accept the contention that simplistic evaluative measures may be appropriate in regulating pedagogical approaches. Yet this would be to disregard the fact that teachers in higher education are entrusted with important professional responsibilities to plan, teach and assess a broad range of student learning each semester. This implies that teachers need to be both skilled and respected as professional educators, and equally that they are responsible for engaging professionally in teaching and learning activity.

The issue of the adequacy of teacher education is a separate matter, but one that is deserving of much greater attention than it is receiving in most universities. This itself reflects the relatively lesser parity of esteem of teaching (compared to that accorded to research) that often leads to overly instrumental understandings of pedagogy being held by university managers. It also no doubt reflects the increasing precarious and itinerant nature of academic teaching profession, which has seriously eroded the pedagogical capabilities of institutions.

The rise of quality assurance motives for student evaluation—which has tended to render the student voice as simultaneously a reductive and powerful force—has tended to further reinforced the drive toward de-professionalising higher education teaching. This has had the effect of diminishing the complexity of context and pedagogy, with teaching effectiveness being narrowly framed within a sense of consumption rather than learning efficacy. This has had the effect of oversimplifying the nature of teaching (and particularly teaching deficits) and the related framing of pedagogical assessments as something largely for student rating scales, rather than one for professional deliberation. It is particularly in this process that the higher education teaching has progressively become de-professionalised and subject to the inherent vagaries of student opinion.

Unsurprisingly, the implications of this de-professionalising—as well demonstrated in the case study sites—is most acutely felt by sessional, short-term and casually engaged teachers. Such teachers are normally engaged semester-to-semester and tend to be most often disconnected from the daily life of the faculty. As a result, in reality these teachers are most simply—and most frequently—judged by their student evaluation outcomes, which become in essence a performance appraisal as to whether they are re-engaged in the future. This motive has only been amplified with the rising pressures of the quality assurance discourses described earlier as the stakes for 'good' outcomes from student rating rise ever higher.

As the research presented here reveals, this reality is well understood by these teachers laboring under the considerable weight of transient employment, and they are more than conscious of the need to maintain elevated levels of student satisfaction. Unlike other permanently engaged academics, these teachers often cannot retail historical teaching achievements or research contributions. They are often not well known—or even unknown—in the faculty. Consequently their semester student ratings become inherently definitive of academic capability. These teachers are therefore under the greatest pressure to find strategies to maintain student ratings at the highest possible levels.

Given the precariously employed teacher is an increasingly familiar fixture of contemporary higher education, this is an issue that has significantly implications for teacher professionalism. If the growing number of non-tenured teachers believe that quantitative student evaluation is a critical ingredient to a successful transition to ongoing employment, there is real and understandable risk that appeasing student opinion (in order to achieve positive ratings) may undermine sound pedagogical decision-making, innovation or assessment standards. This must raise serious questions about the effect of casualisation of academic teaching on the quality of student learning, as this forced utilitarian motive around the needs for positive student evaluation to maintain employment must have implications for adopted pedagogies.

Further, as this research starkly demonstrated, the issue for all teachers (be they tenured or otherwise) remains the often-confounding reality of what a particular rating may mean or not mean in regard to pedagogical or other practices. The predominance of metrics around student feedback—especially when used in comparator forms—has created a difficult environment in which to assess relevance or otherwise of statistical assertions (be they either positive or negative). In an environment where teachers are increasingly held to account for these outcomes, so they are also more frequently called on to explain in particular about what *they* plan to do as a pedagogical response to (comparatively) negative student ratings. Again the professional ability of an academic teacher to weigh up such data against contextual factors—such as class composition, content complexity or pedagogical innovation—is sidelined in the broader pursuit of product consistency. Similarly we see a retreat in levels of institutional responsibility for outcomes. Hence, issues like poor availability for preparation time, over-enrolments, inadequate teaching facilities or technologies and rigid assessment requirements tend to remain in the shadows.

This burden of responsiveness to metrics also has the clear potential to also undermine the decision-making of academics when it comes to using various challenging, confronting or disruptive pedagogies that may result in less favourable student feedback. The rise of the 'student-as consumer' with the steep increases to the private costs of higher education have intensified this effect, with arguably a great transactional sense of education overtaking more liberal notions of learning acquisition. As was noted earlier, this is the crux of the one of the core dilemmas around contemporary student feedback: does the university give the student what they want—as opposed to what they may need. Unmistakably university marketing is strongly pushing the former, whereas the notion of teaching professionalism would tend to harbour aspirations for the latter.

The evidence emerging from the case study data reported in this book (as well as elsewhere) raises one further essential question about professionalism. As the use of quantitative student data moves beyond the institution itself and into the public domain, the pressures are growing ever greater and the stakes ever higher for prospective student recruitment (and perhaps even levels of future funding). In the United Kingdom, we have seen this most starkly on display, where institutions ability to increase tuition fees being directly tied to levels of student satisfaction (as expressed in the *National Student Survey*).

This exposure will only intensify the institutional weigh given to student feedback data, inciting even further strengthened quality assurance strategies that target negative or 'below average' student feedback. Whilst it is certainly important that higher education institutions are properly accountable for their use of public and private resources, the real danger in this development is that forces outside the university itself begin to exert direct pressure on teaching practices and institutions scramble to find whatever has been successful elsewhere in improving levels of student satisfaction (regardless of its actual pedagogical effectiveness).

This loss of institutional autonomy has potentially profound long-term implications for local teaching practices. Instead of institutions using their own internal governance mechanisms and educational sources of advice, the risk is that wisdom is simply adopted from outside based on these levels of student satisfaction elsewhere. This has the potential to increasingly homogenise approaches to teaching and learning, encouraging the adoption of fads or other unproven approaches in the pursuit of ever higher levels of student satisfaction.

Given these range of realities, it is reasonable to suggest that the conventional quantitative student evaluation in the contemporary higher education is now terminally conflicted. As it has become progressively torn between a range of differing (and not necessarily compatible) educational and managerial imperatives, the fissures in the originating model of student evaluation have grown ever more profound. Into the future, it is apparent from this and other research on higher education institutions that we are likely to see the pressures on student evaluation grow as a means of:

- addressing rising demands for quality assurance of teaching practices to meet the relentless data demands of the education market (particularly for the formation of such things as university league tables and commercial guides for students)
- informing individual and collective academic performance management, as higher education management increasingly mimics the human resource management strategies characteristic of business sector
- fuelling institutional marketing in an increasingly competitive higher education environment, with escalating competitive pressures between institutions pressuring marketers to find all possible positive angles on teaching performance (and to demand improvement where this isn't apparent).

Evidence suggests that in the face of these heightening demands, the use of student evaluation to improve the quality of teaching will continue to fade under the powerful weight of these pressures. This is most poignantly reflected in the receding relationship between academic development units and student feedback, and conversely the strengthening of the link with central statistical or quality assurance frameworks in institutions. There is little to suggest this tendency is likely to be reversed—indeed the opposite is more likely.

As the experiences detailed in this book have also affirmed, this fissure between the student voice and academic development imperatives has resulted in the diagnostic and developmental dimensions of student evaluation evaporating in practice as pressures have grown for specified quantitative achievements that demonstrate base-level quality and/or individual teaching capability.

Moreover, as the responsibility for student feedback is being gradually privatised, academics are increasingly required to variously explain perceived 'deficit' outcomes, plan hasty remedial responses or rejoice in positive student feedback outcomes. This has created the ever-more familar imperatives for compulsion to participate, the making public of 'individual' data, related comparative assessments of individual and collective performance and the elevating of student feedback data as a proxy measure of teaching performativity. As the teachers participating in this research reflected, this has meant student evaluation is both broadly welcomed by most as a potentially valuable insight into the student voice, but equally unwelcome as a potentially reductive and unreasonable individual performance measure. This research lucidly demonstrates the implications of this: student feedback was equally an opportunity as it was a threat, as potentially developmental as it was individually derailing.

Finally—aside from this stark looming reality—there is also the fundamental epistemological question posed as a foundation for this book. That is, how effectively has quantitative student evaluation actually ever been—given its fragile subjectivities and inherently reductive form—as a legitimate arbiter of teaching quality or in actually driving successful pedagogical improvement? The evidence from situated practice presented here would suggest that its effect as a method of teaching improvement has not only been overstated, but it also may have actually worked to undermine academic judgment, teaching autonomy and, most seriously, teaching quality and educational standards in higher education.

Developmental Potential of Student Evaluation

As the research presented in this book demonstrates, there is considerable potential evident in the elevated use of learning-focused, qualitative student feedback, as well as in more collaborative forms of professional dialogue in which such data can be productively considered for its developmental potential. This offers the prospect of better informing and encouraging improved collective pedagogical reflection, providing a more powerful catalyst for thoughtful and sustainable educational development of programs. As the nature of higher education teaching becomes more complex and demanding, such a model offers a more sophisticated means of engaging with student learning than that offered by the reductive force of metrics. The case study research presented here well demonstrated the rising challenges of effectively distilling meaningful student feedback as it has become more contested and volatile activity in the contemporary institution. As the function of student feedback as a pedagogical tool for academic development has receded, so the competing dimensions of its use in quality assurance and performance management have been increasingly foregrounded and normalised in the life of the academy.

Yet, as the data presented here equally reaffirmed, student feedback remains a valuable catalyst to drive pedagogical and academic development. The cases illustrated the significant improvements in the levels of professional dialogue amongst teaching academics that can be generated when more qualitative and developed forms of student opinion are introduced into collective deliberations about pedagogical practices. This dialogue can also demonstrable generate substantial development and innovation, which subsequently improves the quality and effectiveness of student learning. The results of this approach generated several relatively high-level outcomes around improved student engagement, educational design and program epistemologies.

This research further confirmed the usefulness of foregrounding disturbances, tensions and contradictions generated by student feedback. This conceptual framing approach had the broad effect over time of elevating student feedback outcomes from the discourses of defence and remediation, to those of critical engagement and future development. It rendered the qualitative data and complex and contradictory, not necessarily definitive and unequivocal.

Inevitably, the scale and impact of such development was strongly framed by a series of factors: program history and culture, the level of academic engagement, forms of employment and the resource limitations inherent in the contemporary university. Nevertheless, sufficient evidence emerged from these case studies to suggest that heightened collective engagement with qualitative student opinion has a valuable potential for pedagogical and academic development. It demonstrated a potential to deepen and broaden dialogue around pedagogy, assessment and academic development needs.

Conversely, this work has also demonstrated some significant impediments that must be weighed against these affordances. Firstly, the strong mediating effect of conventional quantitative methods of assessing student opinion cannot be underestimated. Evidence presented from teaching academics demonstrated the prevailing hegemony of quantitative student evaluation at the personal, local, institutional and sectoral levels, a power that is strengthening as performance metrics become normalised.

This meant throughout the case studies that educational leaders—and not infrequently, participants more generally—were looking over their shoulders to assess how that which was being done in the action research would be seen, interpreted and regarded. However, they all shared one core concern: how could the program (and their contributing efforts) be justified in the absence of metrics? In one of the programs, this was even stronger where division existed about the value of recent changes, leading to calls for parallel orthodox evaluation measures to ensure 'proper' student evaluation.

Secondly, the resources required to build and sustain the alternative model were considerable. It was resource intensive and required the systematic collection, coding and reporting student feedback data, as well as facilitated discussions around these outcomes—and the identification of viable development alternatives. This level of resource commitment is a significant imposition on ever-tightening faculty budgets. The difficulties in sustaining this model toward the end of the research (and beyond it) were partly reflective of this dilemma. This must be considered in contrast to the clear attraction of maintaining orthodox forms of student feedback, with rating scales and automated processes producing simple reports that are readily generated with the push of a button.

Thirdly, there is considerable difficulty in sustaining levels of academic capability and enthusiasm for the levels of engagement required to genuinely build ongoing professional dialogue generated by the student voice. Aside from the reported reluctance of academics to engage in collective forms of reflective dialogue during semesters as the action research wore on, more participants found reasons to not (or partially) engage. The apparent reasons for this varied, from legitimate overwork, to a belief that adequate progress was being made in their absence, to implicit or explicit hostility to the approach.

As reported, there is also little doubt the complexity of the evaluative cycle also provided a considerable early barrier to engaged participation. These factors, combined with ongoing anxieties about the programs in a market-exposed area of the faculty, tended to allow those in more powerful positions to progressively dominate the outcomes. This effectively lessened the levels of collective dialogue and shared outcomes. Perhaps in resource poor and high-pressured teaching environments such an evolution is inevitable, and this of itself does not necessarily diminish the value of innovative use of student feedback. However, it did undoubtedly serve to lessen the extent of expansive learning of the group by reducing the levels of collective analysis and identification of measures to address collective tensions identified in teaching activity in the programs.

Finally, what also emerges from the research reported in this book as the important potential of boundary crossing that emerged as a result of higher-level engagement with student feedback. The stimulus of the CHAT-informed, action research model—however imperfect—did encourage many academics to engage much more directly with activities with which they normally held a more abstract relationship. The case study research demonstrated the potential pedagogical development that comes in dissolving boundaries with the professional context of disciplines. Although here the implications were specifically related to specific discipline-based education, the elevated use of student feedback and collective dialogue (especially drawing on those also working in practice contexts) clearly provides a tangible means of re-envisioning understandings and representations of professional domains of practice.

In addition, the *expansive learning evaluation cycle* produced a deeper engagement with questions of educational design, particularly in online environments. From initial levels of latent hostility or indifference, over the life of semesters participants rapidly developed an understanding and appreciation of the challenges of this challenging domain of educational design work. This came with the need to critically debate with designers those issues raised by students and the reasons why or why not design innovations should occur. This required some level of familiarity with the (erstwhile unfamiliar) discourses of educational design methods, complexity of online simulations and imperfect communication tools. Rather than simply being able to delegate, the model forced some real engagement and discrimination around potential options use of resources and longer-term ambitions. Over the life of the case studies, this made expectations more realistic and outcomes more tangible.

Similarly, the cycle provided a strong imperative for the development of situated forms of academic development. Although several participants had undertaken formal academic development programs, the majority of participants had not. The issues generated by elevated student feedback tended to also produce defined areas where collective academic development would be of immediate benefit.

The catalyst provided by a heightened form of feedback created a natural dialogue about local academic development needs and how these might be effectively addressed, producing a third boundary crossing. This resulted in a series of local academic development initiatives, which although not all successful, were useful as they were authentic to the context of teaching, accessible and generally relevant directly to course improvement. Arguably, the relevance of this form of situated academic development was a factor in the development trajectory in evidence in both programs considered in this research.

The experiences of this research suggest a potential way of rethinking the familiar forms of student feedback. Given the conflicted nature of quantitative forms of student feedback—and its gradual assimilation into the more brutalising discourses of quality assurance and performance management—it is timely to consider how student evaluation may function once again as a generator of professional knowledge to inform the design and improvement of pedagogical practice.

As this research has suggested, this reformation needs to be grounded in the fundamental reconsideration of the means by which student data is obtained and formed. It means abandoning reductive metrics as a legitimate method for determining teaching quality (as opposed to quality assurance) and embracing a more open and qualitative channel for students to input into the professional teaching dialogues of faculties. It is also important that the habitual reliance on raw forms of student data is also reconsidered. As with any form of data, its meaning rests with its patterns and themes, and it is important that the negativity that is inevitably occurring in much student feedback is reasonably framed within its broader context of meaning.

It also requires other ways of considering this data, inspired by more collective forms of professional dialogue that more effectively recognises that curriculum, educational design and pedagogy transcend single subjects. As difficult as it is in the increasingly fragmented employment realities of the modern higher education institution, it should also acknowledge that collaborative deliberation is most likely to produce thoughtful, supported and sustainable change across teaching programs.

As the teaching improvement motive recedes under the weight of more powerful imperative and teaching itself becomes an ever more complex activity, a new model of student evaluation centred on the needs of informing pedagogical practice has become more urgent. Therefore, the alternative formation that centres on the rich potentiality of the student voice as a generator of professional knowledge, a formation which draws more directly and expansively on what students are actually experts on—their own learning—would seem to be an overdue and largely unaddressed need.

Given quantitative models of student evaluation may not be necessarily persuasive or productive in generating and sustaining change in higher education environments as is often assumed, it is timely to consider alternative conceptions. The important limitations of orthodox forms of quantitative student evaluation identified in detail in this book were not mounted as an argument against the value of student evaluation in higher education environments. It is a significant contributor to pedagogical understanding and therefore cannot be considered is dispensable.

Toward a New Student Learning Evaluation Model

As the research presented here has demonstrated, a student evaluation model based on a broadened qualitative paradigm has the clear potential to respond more effectively to the increasingly complex, demanding and diversifying pedagogical contexts now emerging in contemporary higher education environments.

This alternative construction may also offer a more viable means of engaging in professional academic discourses, rather than in the more conventional reductive debates around rating metrics and their (primarily statistical) meanings. This also has the potential to enhance the productive mediating influence of academic development initiatives, that all to often operate at the fringes of contemporary student evaluation models.

There is no doubt that changing pedagogies in higher education are increasingly focused on student learning. This change is fundamentally challenging conventional models of evaluative practice centred on transmissive notions and particularly those reliant on quantitative evaluation approaches primarily grounded in the students casting their judgment on the quality of curriculum, teaching and assessment strategies. Considerable evidence has also been presented as to the desirability of broadening approaches to student evaluation, primarily by drawing on a more diverse range of data—not only from students, but also teachers themselves, their peers and from experiences of research-led practice. In addition, the evidence from research presented here suggests demonstrable pedagogical improvement is possible where student feedback is refocused on where their greatest expertise to comment and reflect rests: on their own learning experiences.

By encouraging students to focus in a qualitative form on what has afforded and what has hindered and their learning, evaluation data becomes a solid foundation for stimulating professional dialogue. By presenting this data in a thematic form and in the context of options for pedagogical improvement and priorities for academic development, student evaluation can become a generator of more productive and sustainable change in practices and teaching capabilities. By transforming the construction of student evaluation from individual-deficit discourses, into one centred on collective and collaborative professional dialogue, the student voice can become a valued (rather than derided) input into academic thinking.

As Guba and Lincoln (1989) have argued in proposing what they describe as a *fourth generation evaluation* model, increasingly complex environments demand a move beyond simplistic measurement, descriptive and judgmental orientations to a paradigm centred on evaluation as negotiation. This paradigm casts evaluation as less a scientific or technical process, and more one that is necessarily social, political and value-orientated. This is built on the contention that contemporary evaluation needs to be understood as 'sense-making' and hence a co-construction between evaluators and evaluands (Guba and Lincoln 1989).

This perspective understands evaluative practice as an essentially sociocultural activity in its design and intent. This means it encounters the environments of social meaning, of power and of mediation, and is shaped as well as shaping by the context in which it developed.

Finally, it asserts contemporary evaluation needs to embody a bias for negotiated action, which explicitly engages participants in evaluation and in related responses. In the case of student evaluation, this implies involving teachers, students and faculty in defining possible forms of pedagogical improvement. This necessarily encourages all participants in the evaluation process to be mutually engaged in defining paths forward and similarly identifying tensions, conflicts and impediments to such progress.

Table 9.1 Considering characteristics of orthodox and prospective *learning evaluation model*

Orientation	Orthodox evaluation model	Learning evaluation model
Form of data	Primarily quantitative	Primarily qualitative
Data sources	Student opinion	Broad range of intelligence
Method	Deficit-incidental	Developmental-continuous
Primary level	Atomised-subject level	Integrated-programme level
Focus	Teachers and curriculum	Student learning outcomes
Teacher role	Largely peripheral as receiver	Essential as co-constructor
Use	Remedial action	Program and academic development
Visibility	Individualised, but comparatively assessed with the whole	Shared and transparent within program
Motive	Individual legitimacy	Enhancing student learning
Dynamic	Accumulated and compared	Enacted and re-evaluated
Evaluation function	Abstracted and objective	Embedded and inter-subjective

This epistemology would seem to present an essential underpinning for an alternative conception of student evaluation for higher education settings. An epistemology that draws at qualitative depth on student's perceptions of learning affordances and hindrances has the potential to create a powerful and productive dialectical interplay with professional judgment. This interplay is critical in that it is ultimately orientated toward more sophisticated developmental actions that are more urgent in ever more complex and challenging environments of higher education learning.

As Table 9.1 illustrates, such an alternative conception of student evaluation would represent a fundamentally different approach to current orthodox forms. Central to this is a broadened form of data, a developmental rather than deficit conception of pedagogy and a bias towards development and sustainability (as opposed to accountability and abstraction).

As the comparison mounted in this table reflects, this more expansive approach to student evaluation does not effectively provide the kinds of comparable individual metric-based data favoured in the contemporary discourses of quality assurance and performance management. Hence, it necessarily does not represent an extension—but instead as an alternative—to conventional quantitative form of assessment.

The *Learning Evaluation* Cycle

The research reported in this book was based on an evaluative model framed by a complex CHAT-based, action research cycle (the *expansive learning evaluation cycle* as represented in Fig. 4.1). This cycle was a designed as an attempt to more effectively harness the developmental potential of the student voice. It also sought

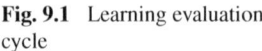

Fig. 9.1 Learning evaluation cycle

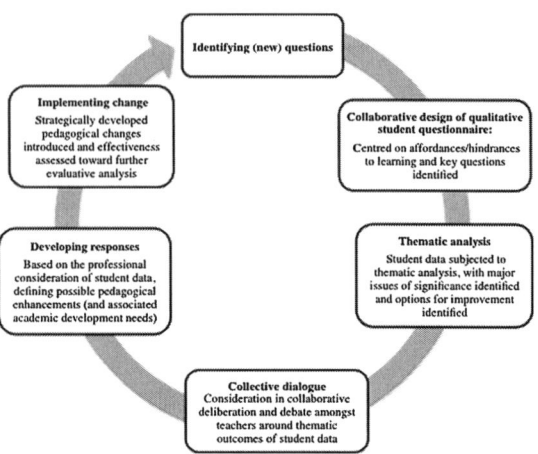

to encourage higher levels of academic collaboration, collective dialogue on teaching practices and pedagogical improvement, as well as enhance situated forms of learning amongst teachers in higher education settings. Although the cycle proved to broadly effective in achieving these ambitious objectives, its complexity and resource demands undermined its sustainability as a viable alternative student evaluation model.

Based on this experience, in tandem with my own understanding of student evaluation in environments of higher education, have led me to consider further what form a feasible alternative student evaluation model would take. This has produced a revised model I cast as a *learning evaluation cycle*. This is outlined in Fig. 9.1.

This model offers a simpler and more sustainable means of capturing and disseminating student experiences of their learning. As such, it continues to offer a CHAT-informed, action research model with which to spark productive academic dialogue through the contextual deliberation and debate of qualitative student data, performing as a stimulus for the improvement of shared pedagogical practices.

Unlike the cycle piloted within the case studies, it reduces the layers of consideration (so as to produce less ritualistic engagement) and the levels of external labour required to sustain the cycle. Though it remains desirable that academic development resources support the cycle, programs themselves equally can sustain its more modest demands for analysis and provocation. The model is grounded in a series of important principles related to the epistemological foundations on which it is designed. These principles include:

(a) *Focus on a conception of student learning as the defined object of a broader and more meaningful form of student evaluation*

The raw student voice is increasingly privileged in current models of quantitative student evaluation, with this data forming critical intelligence from their market perspective as 'consumers' of educational products. They are asked to cast ever more significant judgments using inherently subjective interpretations on the quality of teachers, teaching, curriculum and assessment.

The *learning evaluation cycle* moves the evaluative focus from these types of judgments to student learning outcomes. In doing so, it seeks student input from students on their real area of expertise: what has facilitated and impeded their own learning. Hence, the evaluative cycle seeks to reclaim the legitimate right of teaching academics to be subject to appropriate professional regard. As the data presented earlier in this book attested, current conventional approaches to student evaluation tend to afford what students may personally want over that which they may actually need (which may not always be popular).

Similarly, the cycle seeks to draw more broadly by consciously introducing the potentially rich array of other sources of intelligence on student learning that are rarely considered in orthodox quantitative forms of student evaluation. Here such things as teacher experiences and interpretations, the mediating forces of collaborative professional dialogue, recognition of pedagogical intentionality and evidence-based deliberation around levels of levels of student engagement.

(b) *Student evaluation is based on ongoing professional collaboration, reflection and construction of shared meaning at a program level*

Reflecting its broad socio-cultural foundations, the *learning evaluation cycle* recognises that higher education is enacted in a contested and fundamentally social environment which is strongly mediated by historical approaches and its primary artefacts (most notably curriculum, learning materials and assessment). It also acknowledges that student evaluation must link to the 'particular physical, psychological, social and cultural contexts within which (it is) formed and to which (it) refers.' (Guba and Lincoln 1989, p. 8).

In situated practice, this means creating structured opportunities for facilitated professional dialogue both preceding and at the conclusion of programs to allow for the construction of a collaborative and reflective approach to evaluating student learning. This defies the conventional notion of 'after the event' responses to student feedback, as it engenders a culture of ongoing responsiveness—one grounded in rich data, collaborative dialogue and pedagogical analysis—in program decision-making.

Moreover, students engage in a program of study rather than engage with singular, atomised subjects. This level of analysis therefore affords a more credible level of activity to reflect upon for students casting evaluative judgments about their learning. Here the notion of program remains something that is naturally occurring in form rather than an imposed pre-conceived construction. It is an important feature of the cycle that the level of collaboration is organic, reflecting the logical patterns of student engagement in their learning.

(c) *Use of formal and informal qualitative data to inform professional debates around specific actions and program development to enhance student learning.*

Student evaluation in higher education is necessarily a complex activity and hence needs to adopt an expansive orientation that productively draws on a diverse range of qualitative data. This cycle embodies this notion, recognising that such data will be generated from multiple sources. Some will be collected formally—such as from student feedback questionnaires—whilst other data will emerge informally as formal data is further considered. Informal sources perform a critical role in this cycle, with data produced through academic dialogue and reflection, as well as such things as ongoing peer interaction, assessments of student engagement and alternative pedagogical approaches identified elsewhere.

As such, evaluative data at the heart of this cycle is both social and transparent in form. This is not designed to preclude teachers from seeking personal insights via more conventional forms of evaluation, only that data in this broader evaluation are necessarily open to inter-subjectivities borne of collective reflection on broader realities exposed around the nature of student learning. The explicit focus of this cycle is on dialogue-based, social learning with an explicit orientation toward developmental motives to enhance student learning.

(d) *Designed reflexively to engage with the broad history, evolution, culture and pedagogical aspirations of the program itself*

Essential to conflating evaluation and action is the need to embed the specific design of the learning evaluation cycle in the unique character of programs. Programs develop over time, accumulating defined ways of working, signature pedagogies and critical artefacts. Student evaluation with a developmental motive needs to take account of these influential historical foundations, not least of all because of fragile academic tolerance for ungrounded change in an environment of resource decline.

Similarly, programs evolve through various stages from initiation, consolidation and review. This also provides an important context for evaluative discourses. Finally, student evaluation also needs to take account of the strategic aspirations that underpin programs: that is, what is it aiming to educationally achieve (both in the short and longer terms)?

All of these elements are fundamentally important as a frame for the design and dialogic form of the *learning evaluation cycle.* These engender in its method a more sophisticated scaffold for the specific design of the evaluation, the issues it interrogates and the development options it considers feasible. Hence, this cycle is centred on the intent of organic and emergent forms of evaluative design, with this form of analysis directly assimilating into the day-to-day life of the program (rather than adopt generic or abstracted form).

(e) *Melding student evaluation and academic development, maximising the possibilities of relevant, timely and situated academic development support*

The role and function of student evaluation in *learning evaluation cycle* is not abstracted or objectified, but integrated and connected with program development. Equally, its design encourages the ongoing identification of academic development needs identified as useful to enhance program development. This is facilitated by the collaborative formation of professional dialogue, which creates the imperative

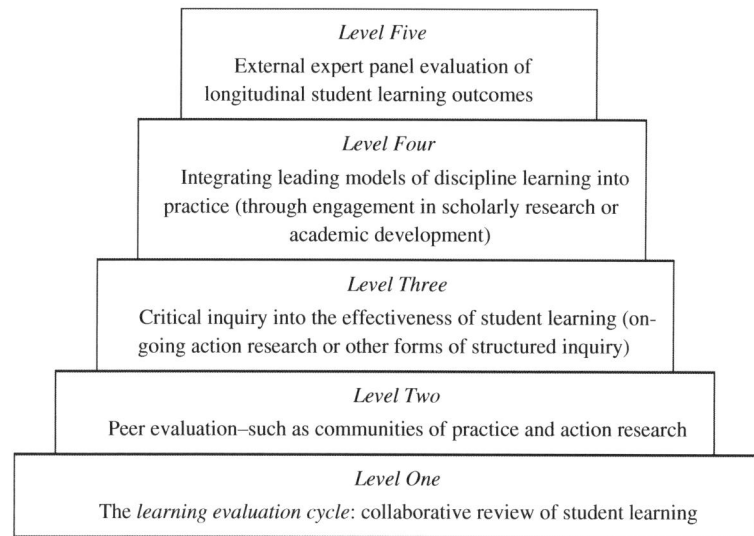

Level Five
External expert panel evaluation of
longitudinal student learning outcomes

Level Four
Integrating leading models of discipline learning into
practice (through engagement in scholarly research or
academic development)

Level Three
Critical inquiry into the effectiveness of student learning (ongoing action research or other forms of structured inquiry)

Level Two
Peer evaluation–such as communities of practice and action research

Level One
The *learning evaluation cycle*: collaborative review of student learning

Fig. 9.2 A possible incremental framework of evaluating the quality of higher education learning

to reflexively respond to evaluative assessments which identify enhancing teacher capability as necessary to achieve agreed pedagogical objectives.

This approach also has the potential to incite more situated and relevant forms of academic development. The case study outcomes demonstrated the considerable and reflexive developmental value of situating academic development, rather than having it abstracted from local academic practice. Although this more situated role for academic development is more complex and resource intensive, it potentially allows more potent and authentic engagement with teaching academics around shared rather than dyadic meanings (i.e. 'discipline' versus education).

Finally, although the focus in this proposed model is specifically on the challenges of transforming student evaluation, it needs to be considered within its broader context: as an important (though not exclusive) means of improving student learning. Student evaluation practices—whatever form they adopt in practice—necessarily co-exist with other potential forms of intelligence on the quality of pedagogical practices.

As Fig. 9.2 suggests, other forms of evaluation of pedagogies are critical to ensure that there is a breadth and depth to understandings, as well as to avoid the risks of myopic judgments on effectiveness. As this incremental framework outlined suggests, the learning evaluation model provides an important foundation to this process, however it is not enough of itself. It forms an essential—but not exclusive element—of this broader form of interpretive analysis.

Conclusion

This book was intended to offer an ambitious attempt to reconsider the foundational assumptions of student evaluation and its contemporary contested function in higher education.

Unlike the vast majority of studies in this area, which focus on questionnaire design or its assimilation of its outcomes into practice, it set out to understand the foundational paradigms of student feedback within the social forces that historically shaped its form, its function and its contemporary state. It also sought to explore the potential of student feedback to develop and improve academic teaching practice.

What emerged from this analysis was an account of quantitative student evaluation being adopted in many sites of higher education from an earlier history in the United States, under the imperative of rising concerns around teaching quality with the growth of universities in the 1980s. Later drives for efficiency and accountability introduced quality assurance and performance management dimensions, transforming student evaluation from an academic development fringe dweller to a more prominent institutional tool.

In the contemporary institution, student evaluation occupies a contested and even paradoxical state—caught between the positive imperatives of improvement, the largely benign discourses of quality assurance and the more treacherous climbs of performance management. It is unlikely that any of these imperatives will disappear. Indeed, data presented in the case studies presented in this book would suggest these multiple imperatives would only heighten as social expectations of higher education intensify further in a knowledge-based economy, where pressures on resources grow ever greater and students are further reformed into consumers.

What the situated research presented here suggests is that it is no longer realistic to rely on orthodox quantitative student evaluation for the divergent demands of quality assurance, performance management and pedagogical improvement. These are increasingly three quite distinct and increasingly contradictory imperatives, with the first two of these now largely overwhelming the third. Therefore, more complex curricula and teaching environments in higher education demand a more sophisticated method of articulating, analysing and acting on the student voice than can be offered by increasingly by a model centred on the (often predatory) use of student ratings and institutional rankings.

This is the key thesis that underpinned this book and its attempt to reconceptualise a more expansive form of evaluation centred more directly on student learning. It was founded on the belief that more complex learning environments demand more complex forms of evaluation than that offered by orthodox student ratings based evaluation. Although this orthodox form of evaluation enjoys a high level of institutional acceptance as a reductive quality assurance mechanism, its demonstrable impact on pedagogical practice and its credibility more generally as influential on academic thinking is not well justified.

More complex learning environments are demanding much more of teaching academics, melding the emergent demands of more heterogeneous student demands, multiple sites and environments of learning, the integration of learning technologies and the elevating expectations of research and service obligations. It is difficult to see how a series of student generated ratings of teachers and courses is contributing to this eclectic mission. Indeed, it seems it may instead by only making it more complex by forcing teachers to restrain pedagogical change, appeal to student sentiment or most disastrously, reduce standards.

The time has now arrived to re-consider evaluative orthodoxies in higher education. To respond to the complex ecology of higher education, academics necessarily have to become much more autonomous and engaged learning professionals, who are able to self-monitor, reflect, collaborate on current and improved practice and be subject to peer-level review and scrutiny (Eraut 1994; Walker 2001).

The initial evidence of the *expansive learning evaluation cycle* presented here suggests that this type of approach offers a viable potential alternative to the orthodox form, one that would contribute to this developing the professional identity and pedagogical insights of teaching academics. However, further research needs to be undertaken to judge its ability to transform conventional evaluation assumptions in the collective academic mind and sustain significant and ongoing change in individual and collective pedagogical practices that are increasingly demanded in the new complex environments of higher education.

Therefore, the challenge is for higher education institutions committed to quality learning to consider moving beyond well-trodden conventional approaches to student feedback and to investigate deeper and more qualitative engagement. Such an engagement offers the real potential to generate more substantial professional dialogue centred on improvement and innovation, rather than one increasingly operating within the discourses of deficit and defence. Alternative approaches to student evaluation (such as that advocated in this book) may again allow the substance of student feedback to be re-orientated back toward its seminal objective of improving the quality of teaching and student learning. Otherwise, all the evidence suggests that student evaluation is doomed to become an ever more unwelcomed metric of quality assurance and performance management in the future higher education institution.

Appendix

Appendix 1: Identified critical tensions of contemporary student evaluation

Identified tensions	Broad thematic categories identified	Questions emerging relating to student feedback identified
Ambiguous or precarious position of the academic teacher as simultaneously discipline expert and expert educator	(a) Academic as needing to simultaneously possess expert professional currency and advanced pedagogical capabilities (including now multi-modal design-teaching skills) (b) Growing institutional expectations of being accomplished researcher and service role (c) Ongoing resource decline and changing models of pedagogy requires new forms of engagement of teaching staff	• What is the right balance between the discipline and educational sense of 'effective' teaching (and how do students/university administrators understand this) • Need to understand student learning of discipline knowledge and practice (as opposed to just what a teacher does in facilitating this) • What do the evolving use of online/simulated pedagogies mean: need for better sense of what are effective forms of higher education for students • Imperative to add to scholarly knowledge of discipline-based education, as unique and under-explored: student feedback a highly useful qualitative data source for developing this further. • Can the student voice be used as a learning process that acts as situated academic development, particularly given the limitations that many academics face in undertaking structured academic development programs?

(continued)

© Springer International Publishing Switzerland 2016
S. Darwin, *Student Evaluation in Higher Education*,
DOI 10.1007/978-3-319-41893-3

Identified tensions	Broad thematic categories identified	Questions emerging relating to student feedback identified
Differing expectations between the desired and possible outcomes of student learning	(a) Pressure for graduates with highly defined and assessed knowledge capability, versus demonstrable need for the capacity for ongoing learning in transforming field of professional practice (b) Differing levels of teaching capability/availability and inevitable resource limitations constrain pedagogical range (c) Powerful work of external scrutiny and assessment in framing curriculum approaches	• Need for clarity in the design and effect of assessment on meeting these dual imperatives, as well as how assessment can be better developed to enhance student learning (rather than 'test' knowledge acquisition) • How can student feedback assist in understanding if students are being adequately introduced/ exposed to emerging trends in discipline areas, whilst also being able to complete assessment requirements? • How do we build a stronger collective teaching capability and what is the role of student feedback in shaping this? • Is it necessary to re-negotiate expectations with administrators/ regulators over expected graduate capabilities: strengthening curriculum relationships between learning and work (and not just toward work)?
Complex-heterogeneous expectations of graduate learning outcomes	(a) Increasing heterogeneous capabilities/learning experiences in student entry level (b) More complex social, legislative and technological expectations for graduates (c) Greater demands for professional accountability	• Is the curriculum meeting diverse entry-level capabilities/experiences of students? • How do we evaluate the effectiveness of these more complex and necessary strategies for student learning? • What are the implications for students working more independently online and in small groups, rather than in conventional classroom learning environments? • Does this mirror the likely future practice and do students understand this as the driver? • Can professional relevance of assessment be enhanced using student feedback?

(continued)

Identified tensions	Broad thematic categories identified	Questions emerging relating to student feedback identified
Growing uncertainty around the rights and responsibilities of academics, students and institutions	(a) Recasting of student-as-consumer (especially in fee paying postgraduate higher education) (b) Greater consequent institutional pressure to meet student expectations and thereby maintain/expand enrolment numbers (c) Expanded technology reach: blurring of the teaching role	• How do we manage the core tension between pragmatic desire of students to complete and the need to ensure high quality learning outcomes? • Can more in-depth forms of student feedback (i.e. qualitative data) actually improve our ability to attract and retain students over time (or just better expose inherent pedagogical flaws/limitations)? • Can higher education institutions regard this form of qualitative evaluation as legitimate for assurance/performance management processes? • How do we evaluate effective online teaching (as opposed to conventional forms of teaching) and what can student feedback provide to inform this assessment? • How can we determine the effectiveness of online tools/simulations/communication and how they relate to teaching and learning effectiveness?
Heightening demands for accountability in academic practices	(a) Privileging of metrics (i.e. assessment outcomes/student opinion data) to assess teaching quality (b) Potential disincentive for innovative-disruptive change as perceived threat to academic standards	• How can we evaluate credibly without the use of quantitative data, given this is accepted (both institutionally and sector-wide) as the most reliable form of student evaluation? • How can we avoid individual-deficit orientated use of student feedback, and conversely what is relevance to subjects/teachers so problems can be addressed? • What is the balance in using elevated student feedback with own professional judgment (and how to these perspectives, which are often at odds, intersect)? • How can pedagogical innovation be encouraged and nurtured (as change can be difficult and not without problems for students)? How are the consequences of changed practices understood, rather than as a representation of personal or collective failure?

Appendix 2: Issues, tensions and potential options identified in evaluation process

Identified Issues (derived from teacher/student data)	Primary Tensions (identified by the researcher)	Potential Course Development Options (debated in post-program workshop)
Considerable student frustration around the dissonance between learning experiences and summative exam-based assessment: how can forms of assessment (and the exams specifically) more reliably and validly assess the knowledge, skills and capabilities that are taught in the program and required for practice?	Breadth of student engagement in learning design/ explicit practice focus *versus* professional accreditation demands/ assessment reliability-validity across cohorts	*General Assessment:* Increased number of practice-based assessment activities, assessment progressively timed during subjects, assessment of contributions to discussion or client management, increased use of 'informal' or formative assessment. *Exams:* More scaffolding around likely questions, issuing of non-assessable practice exams, access to previous exams, generation of a more positive climate around the exam context, design of student intercommunication online space around assessment to facilitate peer support
Significant student work-load in teaching periods inhibiting required levels of preparation and engage-ment: how can the limited teaching periods be further enhanced to allow students to sense they are suffi-ciently prepared for assess-ment and later workplace practice?	Intensive-blended teaching model assumes strong learner self direction and engagement *versus* Students part time combining demand-ing work and study, often adopting a necessarily prag-matic approach	Earlier release of learning materials/ activities to allow early start, inclusion of podcasts on key issues that can be downloaded to portable media devices for more flexible engagement, content review to ensure alignment of learning materials/activities with both needs of practice and assessment, reshaping student expectations of commitment in blended learning program, introduc-tion of re-occurring cases throughout subjects to increase research efficiency, teacher professional development to further improve the effectiveness of teaching, communication and assess-ment practices
Student disorientation in navigating online program site and methods of using the site effectively: how can the online learning technologies used in the subjects be more effec-tively harnessed to enhance the student learning experience?	Imperative to create a rich and engag-ing online site that allows the use of multiple technolo-gies and high levels of self-direction *versus* Limited student exposure to both the online learning platform and use of Web 2.0 technolo-gies, low tolerance for ambiguity-disorientation	Creation of an online 'road map' for students that includes key guides on technologies and the expectations in subjects of their use, some improved consistency across the subjects around expectations of students online and these communicated consistently, creation of frequently asked questions site for students online, simplification of the strategies for use of online blog tool, establishing email alerts to students of additions and changes across subjects, further professional development on the effective pedagogical use of learning technologies

(continued)

Identified Issues (derived from teacher/student data)	Primary Tensions (identified by the researcher)	Potential Course Development Options (debated in post-program workshop)
Student concern about inequitable workload and different levels of pre-existing expertise being offered in collaborative work: how can we create a greater sense of a community of practice between students within the subjects as a means of allowing greater self direction, more equitable online participation and peer support?	The rich affordances of online technologies to allow ongoing peer collaboration/sharing of perceptions across differing domains of practice *versus* The individualistic nature of online engagement and subsequent assessment, the personal connection with local professional contexts and related expectations	Establish special interest spaces online for students with different needs (i.e. para-professionals, students currently in professional environments, overseas/remote students etc.), introduce/increase assessment around online contributions, create scaffolding resources online for students who sense a deficit in particular aspects of their knowledge or skills, more systematic introduction of online environment in face-to-face intensives, additional professional development for program teachers in facilitating and sustaining online engagement
Are there strategies to engender clearer student expectations (and related teacher-student protocols) and greater levels of flexibility whilst ensuring students retain a sense of direction in their engagement: how do we increase student certainty and satisfaction around the program?	Imperative to improve student sense of navigating the program, enhance the utility/scaffolding of its flexible dimensions/transparency of assessment *versus* Limitations in teacher capabilities (physical/technical), maintenance of pedagogical paradigm of self-direction and restrictive accreditation standards that curtail levels of possible transparency	Development of a more defined framework of expectations for students in orientation, introduction of an online road map, establishing reasonable response times for student enquiries and assessment across the program, introduction of more standards forms of feedbacks via program wide templates, move toward assessment rubrics for assessment, strategies to increase transparency in assessment, open access to learning resources, enhanced scaffolding where students need further support, more flexible learning resources via web based technologies, advocacy of changes around exam-based assessment

References

Adams, M. J. D., & Umbach, P. D. (2012). Nonresponse and online student evaluations of teaching: Understanding the influence of salience, fatigue, and academic environments. *Research in Higher Education, 53*(5), 576–591. doi:10.1007/s11162-011-9240-5

Aleamoni, L. M. (1999). Student rating myths versus research facts from 1924 to 1998. *Journal of Personnel Evaluation in Education, 13*(2), 153–166. doi:10.1023/a:1008168421283

Anderson, G. (2006). Assuring quality/resisting quality assurance: Academics' responses to 'quality' in some Australian universities. *Quality in Higher Education, 12*(2), 161–173. doi:10.1080/13538320600916767

Arreola, R. (2000). *Developing a comprehensive faculty evaluation system: A handbook for college faculty and administrators in designing and operating a comprehensive faculty evaluation system* (2nd ed.). Boulton, MA: Anker Publishing.

Arthur, L. (2009). From performativity to professionalism: Lecturers' responses to student feedback. *Teaching in Higher Education, 14*(4), 441–454.

AVCC. (1981). *Academic staff development: Report of the AVCC working party.* Canberra: Australian Vice-Chancellors' Committee.

Avery, R. J., Bryant, W. K., Mathios, A., Kang, H., & Bell, D. (2006). Electronic course evaluations: Does an online delivery system influence student evaluations? *The Journal of Economic Education, 37*(1), 21–37. doi:10.3200/JECE.37.1.21-37

Ballantyne, R., Borthwick, J., & Packer, J. (2000). Beyond student evaluation of teaching: Identifying and addressing academic staff development needs. *Assessment & Evaluation in Higher Education, 25*(3), 221–236. doi:10.1080/713611430

Barrie, S., Ginns, P., & Prosser, M. (2005). Early outcomes and impact of an institutionally aligned, student focussed learning perspective on teaching quality assurance. *Assessment and Evaluation in Higher Education, 30*(6), 641–656.

Barrie, S., Ginns, P., & Symons, R. (2008). *Student surveys on teaching and learning.* Final Report. Sydney: The Carrick Institute for Learning and Teaching in Higher Education.

Benton, S. L., & Cashin, W. (2014). Student ratings of instruction in college and university courses. In M. B. Paulsen (Ed.), *Higher education: Handbook of theory and research* (Vol. 29, pp. 279–326). Dordrecht, The Netherlands: Springer.

Berk, R. A. (2006). *Thirteen strategies to measure college teaching.* Sterling VA: Stylus.

Biggs, J., & Collis, K. (1982). *Evaluating the quality of learning: The SOLO taxonomy.* New York: Academic Press.

Biggs, J., & Tang, C. (2007). *Teaching for quality learning at university* (3rd ed.). Berkshire: Open University Press.

Blackmore, J. (2009). Academic pedagogies, quality logics and performative universities: Evaluating teaching and what students want. *Studies in Higher Education, 34*(8), 857–872. doi:10.1080/03075070902898664

© Springer International Publishing Switzerland 2016   181
S. Darwin, *Student Evaluation in Higher Education*,
DOI 10.1007/978-3-319-41893-3

Bowden, J., & Marton, F. (1998). *The university of learning: Beyond quality and competence in higher education*. London: Kogan Page.

Brookfield, S. (1995). *Becoming a critically reflective teacher*. San Francisco: Jossey-Bass.

Bryant, P. T. (1967). By their fruits ye shall know them. *Journal of Higher Edcuation, 38*, 326–330.

Carr, W., & Kemmis, S. (1986). *Becoming critical: Education, knowledge and action research*. Geelong: Deakin University.

Cashin, W. (1988). *Student ratings of teaching: A summary of the research*. IDEA Paper No.20. Manhattan: Center for Faculty Development, Kansas State University.

Centra, J. A. (1993). *Reflective faculty evaluation: Enhancing teaching and determining faculty effectiveness*. San Francisco: Jossey-Bass.

Chalmers, D. (2007). *A review of Australian and international quality systems and indicators of learning and teaching*. Retrieved from Strawberry Hills: The Carrick Institute for Learning and Teaching in Higher Education. http://www.olt.gov.au/system/files/resources/T%26L_ Quality_Systems_and_Indicators.pdf

Chan, C. K. Y., Luk, L. Y. Y., & Zeng, M. (2014). Teachers' perceptions of student evaluations of teaching. *Educational Research and Evaluation, 20*(4), 275–289. doi:10.1080/13803611.2014. 932698

Chisholm, M. G. (1977). Student evaluation: The red herring of the decade. *Journal of Chemical Education, 54*(1), 22–23.

Cole, M. (1996). *Cultural psychology: A once and future dicipline*. Cambridge: Harvard University Press.

Cole, R. E. (1991). Participant observer research: An activist role. In W. F. Whyte (Ed.), *Participatory action research* (pp. 159–168). Newbury Park: Sage.

Coledrake, P., & Stedman, L. (1998). *On the brink: Australian universities confronting their future*. St Lucia: University of Queensland Press.

Cresswell, J. W. (2005). *Educational research: Planning, conducting and evaluating quantitative and qualitative research*. Upper Saddle River: Pearson Merill Prentice Hall.

Daniels, H. (2008). *Vygotsky and research*. Oxon: Routledge.

Davies, M., Hirschberg, J., Lye, J., & Johnston, C. (2009). A systematic analysis of quality of teaching surveys. *Assessment & Evaluation in Higher Education, 35*(1), 83–96. doi:10.1080/ 02602930802565362

Dommeyer, C., Baum, P., Hanna, R., & Chapman, K. (2004). Gathering faculty teaching evaluations by in-class and online surveys: Their effects on response rates and evaluations. *Assessment and Evaluation in Higher Education, 29*(5), 611–623.

Dressel, P. L. (1961). The essential nature of evaluation. In D. A. Associates (Ed.), *Evaluation in higher education*. Boston: Houghton Mifflin Co.

Dressel, P. L. (1976). *Handbook of academic evaluation*. San Francisco: Jossey-Bass.

Edstrom, K. (2008). Doing course evaluation as if learning matters most. *Higher Education Research and Development, 27*(2), 95–106.

Engeström, Y. (1987). *Learning by expanding: An activity theoretical approach to development research*. Helsinki: Orienta-Konsultit.

Engeström, Y. (1999). Activity theory and individual and social transformation. In Y. Engeström & R. Miettinen (Eds.), *Perspectives on activity theory* (pp. 19–39). Cambridge: Cambridge University Press.

Engeström, Y. (2000). From individual action to collective activity and back: Development work research as an interventionist methodology. In P. Luff, J. Hindmarsh, & C. Heath (Eds.), *Workplace studies*. Cambridge: Cambridge University Press.

Engeström, Y. (2001). Expansive learning at work: Toward an activity theoretical reconceptualization. *Journal of Education and Work, 14*(1).

Engeström, Y. (2007). Enriching the theory of expansive learning: Lessons from journeys toward coconfiguration. *Mind, Culture, and Activity, 14*(1–2), 23–39. doi:10.1080/10749030701307689

Engeström, Y. (2007). From communities of practice to mycorrhizae. In J. Hughes, N. Jewson, & L. Unwin (Eds.), *Communities of practice: Critical perspectives*. London: Routledge.

Engeström, Y., & Miettinen, R. (1999). Introduction. In Y. Engestrom, R. Miettinen, & R.-L. Punamaki (Eds.), *Perspectives on activity theory*. Cambridge: Cambridge University Press.

Eraut, M. (1994). *Developing professional knowledge and competence* London: Falmer Press.

Flood Page, C. (1974). *Student evaluation of teaching: The American experience*. London: Society for Resarch Into Higher Education.

Furedi, F. (2006). *Where have the intellectuals gone? Confronting 21st century philistinism* (2nd ed.). London: Continuum.

Gibbs, G. (n.d.). *On student evaluation of teaching*. Oxford Learning Institute, University of Oxford. Retrieved from https://isis.ku.dk/kurser/blob.aspx?feltid=157745.

Glense, C. (2006). *Becoming qualitative researchers: An introduction* (3rd ed.). New York: Pearson Education.

Gravestock, P., & Gregor-Greenleaf, E. (2008). *Student course evaluations: Research, models and trends*. Toronto: Higher Education Quality Council of Ontario.

Griffin, P., Coates, H., McInnes, C., & James, R. (2003). The development of an extended course experience questionnaire. *Quality in Higher Education, 9*(3), 259–266.

Guba, E. G., & Lincoln, Y. S. (1989). *Fourth generation evaluation*. Newbury Park: SAGE Publications.

Harvey, L. (2003). Student Feedback [1]. *Quality in Higher Education, 9*(1), 3–20.

Huxham, M., Layboorn, P., Cairncross, S., Gray, M., Brown, N., Goldfinch, J., et al. (2008). Collecting student feedback: A comparsion of questionnaire and other methods. *Assessment and evaluation in higher education, 12*(1).

Johnson, R. (1982). *Academic development units in Australian universities and Colleges of Advanced Education*. Canberra: Commonwealth Tertiary Education Commission/Australian Government Publishing Service.

Johnson, R. (2000). The authority of the student evaluation questionnaire. *Teaching in Higher Education, 5*(4), 419–434.

Jonassen, D., & Rohrer-Murphy, L. (1999). Activity theory as a framework for designing constructivist learning environments. *Educational Technology: Research and Development, 47*(1), 61–79.

Kember, D., & Leung, D. (2008). Establishing the validity and reliability of course evaluation questionnaires. *Assessment and Evaluation in Higher Education, 33*(4), 341–353.

Kember, D., Leung, Y. P., & Kwan, K. P. (2002). Does the use of student feedback questionnaires improve the overall quality of teaching? *Assessment and Evaluation in Higher Education, 27*(5), 411–425.

Knapper, C. (2001). Broadening our Approach to Teaching Evaluation. *New directions for teaching and learning: Fresh approaches to the evaluation of teaching, 88*.

Knapper, C., & Alan Wright, A. (2001). Using portfolios to document good teaching: Premises, purposes, practices. In C. Knapper & P. Cranton (Eds.), *Fresh approaches to the evaluation of teaching* (Vol. 88, pp. 19–30). New York: John Wiley & Sons.

Kulik, J. (2001). Student ratings: Validity, utility and controversy. *New directions for institutional research, 109*.

Langemeyer, I., & Nissen, M. (2006). Activity theory. In B. Somekh & C. Lewin (Eds.), *Research methods in social sciences*. London: Sage.

Laurillard, D. (2002). *Rething university teaching: A conversationa framework for the effective use of learning technologies*. London: Routledge Falmer.

Leont'ev, A. N. (1978). *Activity, consciousness and personality*. Englewood Cliffs: Prentice-Hall.

Luria, A. R. (1976). *Cognitive development: Its cultural and social foundations*. Cambridge: Harvard University Press.

Marginson, S. (1997). *Educating Australia: Government, economy and citizen since 1960*. Cambridge: Cambridge University Press.

Marginson, S. (2009). University rankings, government and social order: Managing the field of higher education according to the logic of performative present-as-future. In M. Simons, M. Olssen, & M. Peters (Eds.), *Re-reading education polocies: Studying the policy agenda of the 21st century*. Rotterdam: Sense Publishers.

Marsh, H. W. (1982). Validity of students' evaluations of college teaching: A multitrait-multi-method analysis. *Journal of Education Psychology, 74*, 264–279.

Marsh, H. W. (1987). Students' evaluations of university teaching: research findings, methodological issues and directions for future research. *International Journal of Educational Research, 11*, 253–388.

Marsh, H. W. (2007). Students' evaluations of university teaching: dimensionality, reliability, validity, potential biases and usefulness. In R. P. Perry & J. C. Smart (Eds.), *The scholarship of teaching and learning in higher education: An evidence-based perspective* (pp. 319–383). Dordrecht, The Netherlands: Springer.

Marsh, H. W., & Roche, L. A. (1994). *The use of student evaluations of university teaching to improve teaching effectiveness.* Canberra ACT: Department of Employment, Education and Training.

Marshall, C., & Rossman, C. B. (1999). *Designing qualitiatve research* (3rd ed.). Thousand Oaks: Sage.

Martens, E. (1999). *Mis/match of aims, concepts and structures in the student evaluation of teaching schemes: Are good intentions enough?* Paper presented at the Higher Education Research and Development Society of Australasia Annual Conference, Melbourne. http://www.herdsa.org.au/branches/vic/Cornerstones/authorframeset.html

Martin, L. H. (1964). *Tertiary education in Australia : Report of the committee on the future of tertiary education in Australia to the Australian universities commission.* Canberra: Australian Government Printer.

McKeachie, W. J. (1957). Student ratings of faculty: A research review. *Improving College and University Teaching, 5*, 4–8.

McKeachie, W. J., Lin, Y.-G., & Mann, W. (1971). Student ratings of teacher effectiveness: Validity studies. *American Educational Research Journal, 8*(3), 435–445. doi:10.2307/1161930

Miller, A. H. (1988). Student assessment of teaching in higher education. *Higher Education, 17*(1), 3–15. doi:10.2307/3446996

Moore, S., & Koul, N. (2005). Students evaluating teachers: Exploring the importance of faculty reaction to feedback on teaching. *Teaching in Higher Education, 10*(1), 57–73.

Moses, I. (1986). Self and student evaluation of academic staff. *Assessment & Evaluation in Higher Education, 11*(1), 76–86. doi:10.1080/0260293860110107

Noffke, S., & Somekh, B. (2006). Action research. In B. Somekh & C. Lewin (Eds.), *Research methods in the social sciences.* London: SAGE publications.

Norton, L. S. (2009). *Action research in teaching and learning: A practical guide to conducting pedagogical research in universities.* London: Routledge.

Nulty, D. (2008). The adequacy of response rates to online and paper surveys: What can be done? *Assessment and Evaluation in Higher Education, 33*(3), 301–314.

Postholm, M. B. (2009). Research and development work: Developing teachers as researchers or just teachers? *Educational Action Research, 17*(4), 551–565. doi:10.1080/09650790903309425

Powney, J., & Hall, S. (1998). *Closing the loop: The impact of student feedback on students' subsequent learning.* University of Glasgow: The Scottish Council for Research in Education.

Prosser, M., & Trigwell, K. (1999). *Understanding learning and teaching: The experience in higher education.* Buckingham: Open University Press.

Ramsden, P. (1991). A performance indicator of teaching quality in higher education: The course experience questionnaire. *Studies in Higher Education, 16*(2), 129–150.

Ramsden, P. (1992). *Learning to teach in higher education.* London: Routledge.

Remmers, H. H. (1927). The purdue rating scale for instructors. *Educational Administration and Supervision, 6*, 399–406.

Richardson, J. T. E. (2005). Instruments for obtaining student feedback: A review of the literature. *Assessment and Evaluation in Higher Education, 30*(4), 387–415.

Rogoff, B. (1995). Observing sociocultural activity on three planes: Participatory appropriation, guided participation and apprenticeship. In J. V. Wertsch, P. Del Rio, & A. Alvarez (Eds.), *Sociocultural studies of the mind.* Cambridge: Cambridge University Press.

Sannino, A., Daniels, H., & Gutierrez, K. (2009). Activity theory between historical engagement and future-making practice. In A. Sannino, H. Daniels, & K. Gutierrez (Eds.), *Learning and expanding with acitvity theory* (pp. 1–18). Cambridge: Cambridge University Press.

Schmelkin, L. P., Spencer, K. J., & Gellman, E. (1997). Faculty perspectives on course and teacher evaluations. *Research in Higher Education, 38*(5), 575–590.

Schram, T. H. (2003). *Coceptualizing qualitative inquiry: Mindwork for fieldwork in education and the social sciences.* Upper Saddle River: Merrill Prentice Hall.

Schuck, S., Gordon, S., & Buchanan, J. (2008). What are we missing here? Problematising wisdoms on teaching quality and professionalism in higher education. *Teaching in Higher Education, 13*(5), 537–547.

Smith, C. (2008). Building effectiveness in teaching through targetted evaluation and response: Connecting evaluation to teaching improvement in higher education. *Assessment and Evaluation in Higher Education, 33*(5), 517–533.

Smith, I. D. (1980). Student assessment of tertiary teachers. *Vestes, 1980*, 27–32.

Spencer, K., & Pedhazur Schmelkin, L. (2002). Student perspectives on teaching and evaluation. *Assessment and Evaluation in Higher Education, 27*(5), 397–409.

Stacey, R. (2000). *Strategic management and organisational dynamics* (3rd ed.). Essex: Pearson Education.

Stark, S., & Torrance, H. (2006). Case study. In B. Somekh & C. Lewin (Eds.), *Research methods in the social sciences.* London: SAGE Publications.

Stein, S. J., Spiller, D., Terry, S., Harris, T., Deaker, L., & Kennedy, J. (2012). *Unlocking the impact of tertiary teachers' perceptions of students evaluations of teaching.* Wellington: Ako Aotearoa National Centre for Tertiary Teaching Excellence.

Stetsnko, A. (2005). Activity as object-related: Resolving the dichotomy of individual and collective planes of activity. *Mind, Culture and Activity, 12*(1), 70–88.

Surgenor, P. W. G. (2013). Obstacles and opportunities: Addressing the growing pains of summative student evaluation of teaching. *Assessment & Evaluation in Higher Education, 38*(3), 363–376. doi:10.1080/02602938.2011.635247

Toohey, S. (1999). *Designing courses for higher education.* Buckingham: Open University Press.

Tucker, B., Jones, S., & Straker, L. (2008). Online student evaluation improves course experience questionnaire results in physiotherapy program. *Higher Education Research and Development, 27*(3), 281–296.

Vygotsky, L. S. (1978). *Mind in society: The development of higher psychological processes.* Cambridge: Harvard University Press.

Wachtel, H. K. (1998). Student evaluation of college teaching effectiveness: A brief review. *Assessment & Evaluation in Higher Education, 23*(2), 191–212. doi:10.1080/0260293980230207

Walker, M. (2001). Mapping our higher education project. In M. Walker (Ed.), *Reconstructing professionalism in university teaching.* Buckingham: SHRE/Open University Press.

Watson, S. (2003). Closing the feedback loop: Ensuring effective action from student feedback. *Tertiary Education and Management, 9*(2), 145–157.

Wells, G., & Claxton, G. (2002). Introduction. In G. Wells & G. Claxton (Eds.), *Learning for life in the 21st century.* Oxford: Blackwell.

Wertsch, J. V. (1985). *Vygotsky and the social formation of mind.* Cambridge MA: Harvard University Press.

Willits, F., & Brennan, M. (2015). Another look at college student's ratings of course quality: Data from Penn state student surveys in three settings. *Assessment & Evaluation in Higher Education*, 1–20. doi:10.1080/02602938.2015.1120858

Yamagata-Lynch, L. C. (2010). *Activity systems analysis methods: Understanding complex learning environments.* New York: Springer.

Yamagata-Lynch, L. C., & Smaldino, S. (2007). Using activity theory to evaluate and improve K-12 school and university partnerships. *Evaluation and Program Planning, 30*(4), 364–380. doi:10.1016/j.evalprogplan.2007.08.003

Yin, R. K. (1994). *Case study research: Design and methods.* Thousand Oaks: SAGE publications.

Zabaleta, F. (2007). The use and misuse of student evaluations of teaching. *Teaching in Higher Education, 12*(1), 55–76.

Printed in Great Britain
by Amazon